ISBN 978-1-333-16185-9
PIBN 10630908

Forgotten Books is a registered trademark of FB &c Ltd.
Copyright © 2015 FB &c Ltd.
FB &c Ltd, Dalton House, 60 Windsor Avenue, London, SW19 2RR.
Company number 08720141. Registered in England and Wales.

For support please visit www.forgottenbooks.com

1 MONTH OF
FREE
READING

at

www.ForgottenBooks.com

By purchasing this book you are eligible for one month membership to ForgottenBooks.com, giving you unlimited access to our entire collection of over 700,000 titles via our web site and mobile apps.

To claim your free month visit:

www.forgottenbooks.com/free630908

English
Français
Deutsche
Italiano
Español
Português

www.forgottenbooks.com

Mythology Photography **Fiction**
Fishing Christianity **Art** Cooking
Essays Buddhism Freemasonry
Medicine **Biology** Music **Ancient
Egypt** Evolution Carpentry Physics
Dance Geology **Mathematics** Fitness
Shakespeare **Folklore** Yoga Marketing
Confidence Immortality Biographies
Poetry **Psychology** Witchcraft
Electronics Chemistry History **Law**
Accounting **Philosophy** Anthropology
Alchemy Drama Quantum Mechanics
Atheism Sexual Health **Ancient History**
Entrepreneurship Languages Sport
Paleontology Needlework Islam
Metaphysics Investment Archaeology
Parenting Statistics Criminology
Motivational

THE WORKS OF ARISTOTLE TRANSLATED INTO ENGLISH—

De Cælo; De Generatione et Corruptione. By J. L. Stocks and H. H. Joachim. New York: Oxford University Press. $3.35.

Even good Latinists do not hesitate to keep on their shelves the translation of St. Thomas, which the English Dominicans are now issuing to the great comfort of those to whom Latin is not a second tongue. And the far smaller body of philosophers whose Greek is fluent, will not grudge their less favored and much more numerous brethren a really good translation of the works of Aristotle, on which depend the whole of Scholastic Philosophy. Nor will they despise a translation with really adequate notes, such as this carries, of two treatises containing such fundamental portions of Aristotle's philosophy.

The second is, perhaps, the more interesting to us today, for it deals with "the coming-to-be and the passing-away," and thus attacks problems, such as that of "becoming," full of actuality, in spite of our changed ideas to as to the "elements," and in spite of the centuries which have rolled away since the author of these works discussed the utterances of Empedokles, Anaxagoras, and Leukippos. We welcome this translation, and hope it may be followed by other volumes until we have a really complete and scholarly edition of the Stagirite in English.

DE CAELO

BY

J. L. STOCKS, M.A., D.S.O.

FELLOW AND TUTOR OF ST. JOHN'S COLLEGE, OXFORD

OXFORD
AT THE CLARENDON PRESS
1922

Oxford University Press

London   Edinburgh   Glasgow   Copenhagen

New York   Toronto   Melbourne   Cape Town

Bombay   Calcutta   Madras   Shanghai

Humphrey Milford Publisher to the UNIVERSITY

PREFACE

THIS translation was begun many years ago in co-operation with Mr. H. B. Wallis of the Board of Education. Unfortunately he was obliged to turn to other work, but his original draft formed the basis of nearly half my version of the book.

Rather full textual notes are given throughout, the text of Prantl being taken as basis. (A complete table of the passages dealt with will be found in the Index, *s.v.* Text.) For this purpose I have collated the Vienna MS., J, from a photograph, and the reading of this MS. is noted in each case, either explicitly or by implication.

Mr. Ross's generous conception of an editor's responsibilities has been of the greatest service. He has saved me from many mistakes and has made many useful suggestions for the improvement of the translation. A few of his suggestions will be found recorded in the foot-notes as his; but for the most part he is merged in his translator.

J. L. S.

31st March, 1922.

CONTENTS

BOOK I. OF THE HEAVENLY BODIES

BOOK II. OF THE HEAVENLY BODIES (*continued*)

B
417
.A 5

BOOK III. OF THE SUBLUNARY BODIES

BOOK IV. OF THE SUBLUNARY BODIES (*continued*)

DE CAELO

BOOK I

1 THE science which has to do with nature clearly concerns **268ª**
itself for the most part with bodies and magnitudes and
their properties and movements, but also with the principles
of this sort of substance, as many as they may be. For of
things constituted by nature some are bodies and magni- 5
tudes, some possess body and magnitude,[1] and some are
principles of things which possess these.[2] Now a continuum
is that which is divisible into parts always capable of subdivision, and a body is that which is every way divisible.
A magnitude if divisible one way is a line, if two ways
a surface, and if three a body. Beyond these there is no
other magnitude, because the three dimensions are all that 10
there are, and that which is divisible in three directions is
divisible in all. For, as the Pythagoreans say, the world
and all that is in it is determined by the number three,
since beginning and middle and end give the number
of an 'all', and the number they give is the triad. And
so, having taken these three[3] from nature as (so to speak)
laws of it, we make further use of the number three in the 15
worship of the Gods.[4] Further, we use the terms in
practice in this way. Of two things, or men, we say 'both',
but not 'all': three is the first number to which the term
'all' has been appropriated.[5] And in this, as we have said,
we do but follow the lead which nature gives. Therefore, 20
since 'every' and 'all' and 'complete' do not differ from
one another in respect of form, but only, if at all,[6] in their

---

[1] i. e. animate things, such as plants and animals.

[2] e. g. matter and form, movement, or, in the case of living things,
soul.

[3] Viz. beginning, middle, and end.

[4] Oaths, for instance, usually appeal to three Gods, as in the
Homeric appeal to Zeus, Athene, and Apollo (Prantl).

[5] Reading εἰλήφαμεν with E and Prantl. The other MSS. have
φαμέν (FLM) or κατάφαμεν (HJ).

[6] Reading εἴπερ ἄρα with FHMJ.

matter and in that to which they are applied, body alone
among magnitudes can be complete. For it alone is determined by the three dimensions, that is, is an 'all'.[1]
But if it is divisible in three dimensions it is every way
25 divisible, while the other magnitudes are divisible in one
dimension or in two alone : for the divisibility and continuity
of magnitudes depend upon the number of the dimensions,
one sort being continuous in one direction, another in two,
another in all. All magnitudes, then, which are divisible
are also continuous. Whether we can also say that what-
30 ever is continuous is divisible does not yet, on our present
grounds, appear. One thing, however, is clear. We cannot
268^b pass beyond body to a further kind, as we passed from
length to surface, and from surface to body. For if we
could, it would cease to be true that body is complete
magnitude. We could pass beyond it only in virtue of
a defect in it; and that which is complete cannot be
5 defective, since it has being in every respect.[2] Now bodies
which are classed as parts of the whole[3] are each complete
according to our formula, since each possesses every dimension. But each is determined relatively to that part which
is next to it by contact, for which reason each of them
is in a sense many bodies. But the whole of which they are
parts must necessarily be complete, and thus, in accordance
10 with the meaning of the word, have being, not in some
respects only, but in every respect.[4]

The question as to the nature of the whole, whether it is 2
infinite in size or limited in its total mass, is a matter for

---

[1] Body alone is so determined, and only what is so determined is
a totality (an 'all'). Put a comma, instead of a full stop, after τρισίν.
The words τοῦτο δ' ἐστὶ πᾶν are difficult to interpret. Prantl makes
τοῦτο predicate, and translates as though we had τὸ πᾶν instead of πᾶν.
Simplicius gives no help.

[2] To be incomplete or defective is to lack being in some respect.

[3] i.e. the elements.

[4] The 'parts' or elements are bodies, and therefore complete in the
sense just given to the word. They are, however, only parts, and as
such limited in their being by the juxtaposition of other parts. This
suggests a development of the notion of completeness which will make
the term 'complete' applicable only to the unrestricted being of the
whole.

subsequent inquiry.[1]   We will now speak of those parts of
the whole which are specifically distinct.[2]   Let us take
this as our starting-point.   All natural bodies and magni- 15
tudes we hold to be, as such, capable of locomotion; for
nature, we say, is their principle of movement.[3]   But all
movement that is in place, all locomotion, as we term it,
is either straight or circular or a combination of these two,
which are the only simple movements.   And the reason of
this is that these two, the straight and the circular line, are 20
the only simple magnitudes.   Now revolution about the
centre is circular motion, while the upward and downward
movements are in a straight line, 'upward' meaning
motion away from the centre, and 'downward' motion
towards it.   All simple motion, then, must be motion
either away from or towards or about the centre.   This
seems to be in exact accord with what we said above:[4] 25
as body found its completion in three dimensions, so its
movement completes itself in three forms.

Bodies are either simple or compounded of such; and by
simple bodies I mean those which possess a principle of
movement in their own nature, such as fire and earth with
their kinds, and whatever is akin to them.[5]   Necessarily,
then, movements also will be either simple or in some sort 30
compound—simple in the case of the simple bodies, com- 269^a
pound in that of the composite—and in the latter case the
motion will be that of the simple body which prevails in the
composition.   Supposing, then, that there is such a thing as
simple movement, and that circular movement is an instance
of it, and that both movement of a simple body is simple and

---

[1] See c. vii.
[2] i. e. the elements, which represent the ultimate distinctions of kind
among bodies.
[3] Cf. *Phys.* 192^b 20.
[4] Reading ἠκολουθηκέναι κατὰ λόγον with all MSS. except E.
[5] Τὰ τούτων εἴδη ('with their kinds') can hardly mean *kinds of* fire
and earth (e. g. sandy and stony earth, flame and glowing coal), as
Simplicius supposes, for there is no variety of movement corresponding
to this variety of kind.   Rather, as Alexander supposes, the phrase is
a generalizing formula (ἀντὶ τοῦ καθόλου πᾶν πῦρ . . . καὶ καθόλου πᾶσαν
γῆν): fire and its kind, earth and its kind, and other species of the
same genus (viz. air and water, and the 'fifth body' of which the stars
are made).

simple movement is of a simple body (for if it is movement
5 of a compound it will be in virtue of a prevailing simple
element), then there must necessarily be some simple body
which revolves naturally and in virtue of its own nature[1]
with a circular movement. By constraint, of course, it may
be brought to move with the motion of something else
different from itself, but it cannot so move naturally, since
there is one sort of movement natural to each of the simple
bodies. Again, if the unnatural movement is the contrary
10 of the natural and a thing can have no more than one contrary, it will follow that circular movement, being a simple
motion, must be unnatural, if it is not natural, to the body
moved. If then (1) the body, whose movement is circular,
is fire or some other element, its natural motion must be the
contrary of the circular motion. But a single thing has
a single contrary; and upward and downward motion are
15 the contraries of one another.[2] If, on the other hand,
(2) the body moving with this circular motion which is
unnatural to it is something different from the elements,
there will be some other motion which is natural to it.
But this cannot be. For if the natural motion is upward,
it will be fire or air, and if downward, water or earth.
Further, this circular motion is necessarily primary. For the
20 perfect is naturally prior to the imperfect, and the circle is
a perfect thing. This cannot be said of any straight line:
—not of an infinite line; for, if it were perfect, it would
have a limit and an end: nor of any finite line; for in
every case there is something beyond it,[3] since any finite
line can be extended. And so, since the prior movement
25 belongs to the body which is naturally prior, and circular
movement is prior to straight, and movement in a straight
line belongs to simple bodies—fire moving straight upward
and earthy bodies straight downward towards the centre—
since this is so, it follows that circular movement also must

---

[1] Reading ἑαυτοῦ with all MSS. except E.
[2] Therefore neither of these can be *also* the contrary of circular
motion. Thus there is *no* simple motion opposed as contrary to the
circular.
[3] Reading πασῶν γάρ ἐστί τι ἐκτός (ἐστί is omitted by E alone).

be the movement of some simple body.[1] For the movement of composite bodies is, as we said, determined by that simple body which preponderates in the composition. 30 These premises clearly give the conclusion that there is in nature some bodily substance other than the formations we know, prior to them all and more divine than they. But it may also be proved as follows. We may take it that all movement is either natural or unnatural, and that the movement which is unnatural to one body is natural to another—as, for instance, is the case with the upward and downward movements, which are natural and unnatural to 35 fire and earth respectively. It necessarily follows that 269^b circular movement, being unnatural to these bodies, is the natural movement of some other. Further, if, on the one hand, circular movement is *natural* to something, it must surely be some simple and primary body which is ordained to move with a natural circular motion, as fire is ordained 5 to fly up and earth down. If, on the other hand, the movement of the rotating bodies about the centre is *unnatural*, it would be remarkable and indeed quite inconceivable that this movement alone should be continuous and eternal, being nevertheless contrary to nature. At any rate the evidence of all other cases goes to show that it is the unnatural which quickest passes away. And so, if, as 10 some say, the body so moved is fire, this movement is just as unnatural to it as downward movement; for any one can see that fire moves in a straight line away from the centre. On all these grounds, therefore, we may infer with confidence that there is something beyond the bodies that are 15 about us on this earth, different and separate from them; and that the superior glory of its nature is proportionate to its distance from this world of ours.[2]

---

[1] From his premises Aristotle is here entitled to conclude, not merely that circular movement is the movement of a simple body, but also that it is the movement of a simple body prior to the other simple bodies. Prantl therefore inserts προτέρου after τινός and appeals to Simplicius's paraphrase for corroboration. Simplicius, however, not only does not corroborate the conjecture but actually points out that this part of the conclusion is suppressed (ὅπερ ὡς σαφὲς παρῆκε). The insertion of προτέρου does not really make the argument any clearer.

[2] Cf. Plato, *Phaedo*, III B.

In consequence of what has been said, in part by way of 3
assumption and in part by way of proof, it is clear that not
20 every body either possesses lightness or heaviness. As
a preliminary we must explain in what sense we are using
the words 'heavy' and 'light', sufficiently, at least, for our
present purpose:[1] we can examine the terms more closely
later, when we come to consider their essential nature.[2] Let
us then apply the term 'heavy' to that which naturally
moves towards the centre, and 'light' to that which moves
naturally away from the centre. The heaviest thing will be
25 that which sinks to the bottom of all things that move
downward, and the lightest that which rises to the surface
of everything that moves upward. Now, necessarily,[3] everything which moves either up or down possesses lightness or
heaviness or both—but not both relatively to the same
thing: for things are heavy and light relatively to one
another; air, for instance, is light relatively to water, and
30 water light relatively to earth. The body, then, which
moves in a circle cannot possibly possess either heaviness
or lightness. For neither naturally nor unnaturally can it
move either towards or away from the centre. Movement
in a straight line certainly does not belong to it *naturally*,
since one sort of movement is, as we saw, appropriate to
each simple body, and so we should be compelled to identify
35 it with one of the bodies which move in this way. Suppose,
then, that the movement is *unnatural*. In that case, if it is
270^a the downward movement which is unnatural, the upward
movement will be natural; and if it is the upward which is
unnatural, the downward will be natural. For we decided
that of contrary movements, if the one is unnatural to anything, the other will be natural to it. But since the natural
movement of the whole and of its part—of earth, for in-
5 stance, as a whole and of a small clod—have one and the
same direction, it results, in the first place, that this body
can possess no lightness or heaviness at all (for that would
mean that it could move by its own nature either from or

---

[1] Reading ἱκανῶς ὡς πρός (ὡς is omitted by E alone).
[2] Below, Bk. IV, cc. i–iv.
[3] Reading ἀνάγκη δή (δέ is in F alone).

towards the centre, which, as we know, is impossible); and, secondly, that it cannot possibly move in the way of locomotion by being forced violently aside in an upward or downward direction. For neither naturally nor un- 10 naturally can it move with any other motion but its own, either itself or any part of it, since the reasoning which applies to the whole applies also to the part.

It is equally reasonable to assume that this body will be ungenerated and indestructible and exempt from increase and alteration, since everything that comes to be comes into being from its contrary and in some substrate, and passes 15 away likewise in a substrate by the action of the contrary into the contrary, as we explained in our opening discussions.[1] Now the motions of contraries are contrary. If then this body can have no contrary, because there can be no contrary motion to the circular, nature seems justly to have 20 exempted from contraries the body which was to be ungenerated and indestructible. For it is in contraries that generation and decay subsist. Again, that which is subject to increase increases upon contact with a kindred body, which is resolved into its matter.[2] But there is nothing out 25 of which this body can have been generated.[3] And if it is exempt from increase and diminution,[4] the same reasoning leads us to suppose that it is also unalterable. For alteration is movement in respect of quality; and qualitative states and dispositions, such as health and disease, do not come into being without changes of properties. But all natural bodies which change their properties we see to be 30 subject without exception to increase and diminution. This is the case, for instance, with the bodies of animals and

---

[1] *Phys.* I. vii–ix. For the phrase, cf. 311ᵃ 12.

[2] Omitting καὶ τὸ φθῖνον φθίνει (l. 23). These words are omitted by three representative MSS. (EFJ), are not referred to by Simplicius or Themistius, and are an awkward intrusion in the sentence since what follows applies only to increase. For the doctrine, cf. *De Gen. et Corr.* I. v.

[3] Increase is effected by generation of one kindred body out of another. This body has no contrary out of which it can be generated. Therefore it cannot increase.

[4] Reading ἄφθιτον with H (so Prantl). All other MSS. have ἄφθαρτον; but the rare ἄφθιτον would be easily altered to the commoner word. Simplicius has ἄφθαρτον, but explains that φθίσις is a kind of φθορά and so ἄφθαρτον may be used for ἄφθιτον.

their parts and with vegetable bodies, and similarly also
with those of the elements. And so, if the body which
moves with a circular motion cannot admit of increase
35 or diminution, it is reasonable to suppose that it is also
unalterable.

270ᵇ   The reasons why the primary body is eternal and not subject to increase or diminution, but unaging and unalterable
and unmodified, will be clear from what has been said to any
one who believes in our assumptions. Our theory seems to
5 confirm experience and to be confirmed by it   For all men
have some conception of the nature of the gods, and all who
believe in the existence of gods at all, whether barbarian or
Greek, agree in allotting the highest place to the deity,
surely because they suppose that immortal is linked with
immortal and regard any other supposition as inconceivable.
10 If then there is, as there certainly is, anything divine, what
we have just said about the primary bodily substance was
well said. The mere evidence of the senses is enough to
convince us of this, at least with human certainty. For in
the whole range of time past, so far as our inherited records
15 reach,[1] no change appears to have taken place either in the
whole scheme of the outermost heaven or in any of its
proper parts. The common name, too, which has been
handed down from our distant ancestors even to our own
day, seems to show that they conceived of it in the fashion
which we have been expressing. The same ideas, one must
20 believe, recur in men's minds not once or twice but again
and again. And so, implying that the primary body is
something else beyond earth, fire, air, and water, they gave
the highest place a name of its own, *aither*, derived from the
fact that it ' runs always'[2] for an eternity of time. Anaxa-
25 goras, however, scandalously misuses this name, taking
aither as equivalent to fire.[3]

It is also clear from what has been said why the number

---

[1] Simplicius says he 'has been told' that there are written astronomical records (ἀστρῴας τηρήσεις ἀναγράπτους) in Egypt for the past
630,000 years and in Babylon for the past 1,440,000 years.
[2] i.e. αἰθήρ from ἀεὶ θεῖν. The derivation was suggested by Plato
(*Cratylus*, 410 B).
[3] i.e. deriving αἰθήρ from αἴθειν. Cf. Bk. III, 302ᵇ 4.

of what we call simple bodies cannot be greater than it is.
The motion of a simple body must itself be simple, and we
assert that there are only these two simple motions, the
circular and the straight, the latter being subdivided into 30
motion away from and motion towards the centre.

4   That there is no other form of motion opposed as
contrary to the circular may be proved in various ways.
In the first place, there is an obvious tendency to oppose
the straight line to the circular.   For concave and convex 35
are not only regarded as opposed to one another, but they 271^a
are also coupled together and treated as a unity in opposition to the straight.   And so, if there is a contrary
to circular motion, motion in a straight line must be recognized as having the best claim to that name.   But the
two forms of rectilinear motion are opposed to one another
by reason of their places; for up and down is a difference 5
and a contrary opposition in place.[1]   Secondly, it may be
thought that the same reasoning which holds good of the
rectilinear path applies also to the circular, movement from
A to *B* being opposed as contrary to movement from *B* to
A. But what is meant is still rectilinear motion. For that is
limited to a single path, while the circular paths which pass 10
through the same two points are infinite in number.[2]   Even
if we are confined to the single semicircle and the opposition
is between movement from *C* to *D* and from *D* to *C* along
that semicircle, the case is no better.   For the motion is the
same as that along the diameter, since we invariably regard
the distance between two points as the length of the straight
line which joins them.[3]   It is no more satisfactory to construct a circle and treat motion along one semicircle as 15
contrary to motion along the other.   For example, taking

[1] The point of this elliptical argument seems to be that, while the
generally admitted case of contrary opposition (viz. that of upward
and downward motion) rests on a contrary opposition of places (viz.
above and below), no such ground can be suggested for the opposition
of circular to rectilinear motion.

[2] Fig. I.   [3] Fig. II.

a complete circle, motion from E to F on the semicircle G may be opposed to motion from F to E on the semicircle H.[1] But even supposing these are contraries, it in no way follows that the reverse motions on the complete cir-
20 cumference are contraries. Nor again can motion along the circle from A to B be regarded as the contrary of motion from A to C:[1] for the motion goes from the same point towards the same point, and contrary motion was distinguished as motion from a contrary to its contrary.[2] And even if the motion round a circle is the contrary of the reverse motion, one of the two would be ineffective: for both move to the same point, because[3] that which moves
25 in a circle, at whatever point it begins, must necessarily pass through all the contrary places alike. (By contrarieties of place I mean up and down, back and front, and right and left; and the contrary oppositions of movements are determined by those of places.) One of the motions, then, would be ineffective, for if the two motions were of equal strength,[4] there would be no movement either way, and if
30 one of the two were preponderant, the other would be inoperative. So that if both bodies were there, one of them, inasmuch as it would not be moving with its own movement, would be useless, in the sense in which a shoe is useless when it is not worn. But God and nature create nothing that has not its use.[5]

---

[1] Fig. III.

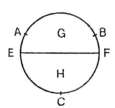

[2] *Phys.* V. v, 229ᵇ21.
[3] Reading ὅτι for the ἔτι of our MSS. after Simplicius, who had both readings before him.
[4] Prantl's alteration of γάρ into ἄρ' is not needed. The γάρ refers back to the remark 'one of the two would be ineffective'. That remark is therefore repeated in the text.
[5] The bearing of this argument is clear if it is remembered that the assertion of the existence of a certain movement necessarily involves for Aristotle the assertion of the existence of a body which naturally exhibits the movement. Similarly the assertion that a movement is inoperative involves the assertion that a body is inoperative.

5   This being clear, we must go on to consider the questions 271^b
which remain. First, is there an infinite body, as the
majority of the ancient philosophers thought, or is this an
impossibility? The decision of this question, either way, is
not unimportant, but rather all-important, to our search for 5
the truth.¹ It is this problem which has practically always
been the source of the differences of those who have written
about nature as a whole. So it has been and so it must
be; since the least initial deviation from the truth is
multiplied later a thousandfold.² Admit, for instance, the 10
existence of a minimum magnitude, and you will find that
the minimum which you have introduced, small as it is, causes
the greatest truths of mathematics to totter. The reason
is that a principle is great rather in power than in extent;
hence that which was small at the start turns out a giant at
the end. Now the conception of the infinite possesses this
power of principles, and indeed in the sphere of quantity
possesses it in a higher degree than any other conception; so 15
that it is in no way absurd or unreasonable that the assumption that an infinite body exists should be of peculiar
moment to our inquiry. The infinite, then, we must now
discuss, opening the whole matter from the beginning.

Every body is necessarily to be classed either as simple
or as composite;³ the infinite body, therefore, will be either
simple or composite. But it is clear, further, that if the simple 20
bodies are finite, the composite must also be finite, since
that which is composed of bodies finite both in number and
in magnitude is itself finite in respect of number and
magnitude: its quantity is in fact the same as that of the
bodies which compose it. What remains for us to consider,
then, is whether any of the simple bodies can be infinite in
magnitude, or whether this is impossible. Let us try the 25
primary body first, and then go on to consider the others.

The body which moves in a circle must necessarily be
finite in every respect, for the following reasons. (1) If the
body so moving is infinite, the radii drawn from the centre

¹ Reading τὴν περὶ τῆς with FHMJ. The phrase recurs in this form
in *Met.* 993ᵃ 30.
² After Plato, *Cratylus*, 436 D.
³ The ἔσται of all other MSS. is preferable to E's εἶναι.

30 will be infinite.[1]   But the space between infinite radii is
infinite : and by the space between the radii I mean the
area outside which no magnitude which is in contact with
the two lines can be conceived as falling.[2]   This, I say, will
be infinite : first, because in the case of finite radii it is always
272ᵃ finite ; and secondly,[3] because in it one can always go on to
a width greater than any given width ; thus the reasoning
which forces us to believe in infinite number, because there is
no maximum, applies also to the space between the radii.
Now the infinite cannot be traversed, and if the body is
infinite the interval between the radii is necessarily infinite :
5 circular motion therefore is an impossibility.   Yet our eyes
tell us that the heavens revolve in a circle, and by argument
also we have determined that there is something to which
circular movement belongs.

(2) Again, if from a finite time a finite time be subtracted,
what remains must be finite and have a beginning.   And if
10 the time of a journey has a beginning, there must be
a beginning also of the movement, and consequently also
of the distance traversed.   This applies universally.   Take
a line, ACE, infinite in one direction, E, and another line,
BB, infinite in both directions.[4]   Let ACE describe a circle,

---

[1] 'The centre', when not in any way qualified, means the centre
of the earth, which is taken by Aristotle to be also the centre of all the
revolutions of the heavenly bodies.   He cannot here mean the centre
of the supposed infinite body, since to that no shape has yet been given.

[2] The last phrase (οὗ μηδέν ἐστιν ἔξω λαβεῖν) seems to have been mis-
understood by Prantl.   A comparison of this passage with others in
which what is practically the same phrase occurs (esp. *Met.* 1021ᵇ 12,
1055ᵃ 12) shows (*a*) that οὗ is governed by ἔξω ('outside which'), and
(*b*) that the phrase is roughly equivalent to τέλειον.   The point here
is that by διάστημα he means, not a straight line spanning the interval
between the radii, but the whole area enclosed between the two radii
and the portion of the circumference which connects their extremities.
In l. 30 read, after διάστημα, δέ rather than γάρ, which is in E alone.

[3] Reading ἔτι with the MSS.; Prantl's ἐπεί seems to have nothing
to recommend it.   It will then be necessary to put a full-stop after
διαστήματος in l. 3.   This sentence gives, of course, a second reason
for taking the διάστημα to be infinite.

[4] FIG. IV.

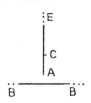

revolving upon C as centre. In its movement it will cut 15
BB continuously for a certain time. This will be a finite
time, since the total time is finite in which the heavens
complete their circular orbit, and consequently the time
subtracted from it, during which the one line in its motion
cuts the other, is also finite. Therefore there will be
a point at which ACE began for the first time to cut BB.
This, however, is impossible.[1] The infinite, then, cannot
revolve in a circle ; nor could the world, if it were infinite.[2] 20

(3) That the infinite cannot move may also be shown as
follows. Let A be a finite line moving past the finite line,
B. Of necessity A will pass clear of B and B of A at the
same moment; for each overlaps the other to precisely the 25
same extent. Now if the two were both moving, and
moving in contrary directions, they would pass clear of one
another more rapidly; if one were still and the other
moving past it, less rapidly ; provided that the speed of the
latter were the same in both cases. This, however, is clear :
that it is impossible to traverse an infinite line in a finite
time. Infinite time, then, would be required. (This we 30
demonstrated above in the discussion of movement.[3]) And

---

[1] In this argument the ascertained fact that the revolution of the
heavens occupies a limited time is used to prove the finitude of its
path and consequently also of the body itself. *BB* represents an
infinite line drawn within the infinite body and therefore 'traversed' by
that body in its revolution. But there can be no point at which the
contact of *ACE* with *BB* either begins or ends, while there is a time
within which the revolution is completed. Therefore the revolving
body is not infinite.—Possibly the centre of the movement of *ACE*
should be *A* (as in F and Simpl.) rather than *C*.

[2] Movement of the 'world' (κόσμος) is here used for movement of
the 'heaven' (οὐρανός). Either κόσμος stands for the heavenly body,
as in *Nic. Eth.* 1141^b 1, or the movement and the infinity are treated
for the moment as attributes of the whole.

[3] Aristotle refers to the *Physics*, here and elsewhere, as continuous
with the *De Caelo*. Different parts of the *Physics* are referred to by
different names. Simplicius (p. 226, 19) observes that *Phys.* I–IV are
cited as 'the discussion of principles' (περὶ ἀρχῶν) and *Phys.* V–VIII
as 'the discussion of movement' (περὶ κινήσεως). In *Phys.* VIII,
257^a 34, Aristotle refers back to an earlier passage as occurring ἐν τοῖς
καθόλου τοῖς περὶ φύσεως; and Simplicius, commenting on this (*Comm.
in Phys.* p. 1233, 30), 'infers' that *Phys.* I–V are the περὶ φύσεως and
Phys. VI–VIII the περὶ κινήσεως. But his inference is false. The
reference is not, as he thought, to V. iv. The principle had been
asserted earlier, viz. in III. i. The 'general considerations concerning
nature' may therefore be identified with the 'discussion of principles',
and the *Physics* may be divided in the middle, i.e. at the end of
Book IV.—The reference in this passage is to *Phys.* VI. vii.

it makes no difference whether a finite is passing by an
272ᵇ infinite or an infinite by a finite. For when A is passing B,
then B overlaps[1] A, and it makes no difference whether B
is moved or unmoved, except that, if both move, they pass
clear of one another more quickly. It is, however, quite
possible that a moving line should in certain cases pass one
which is stationary quicker than it passes one moving in an
5 opposite direction. One has only to imagine the movement
to be slow where both move and much faster where one is
stationary. To suppose one line stationary, then, makes no
difficulty for our argument, since it is quite possible for A to
pass B at a slower rate when both are moving than when only
10 one is. If, therefore, the time which the finite moving line
takes to pass the other is infinite, then necessarily the time
occupied by the motion of the infinite past the finite is also
infinite. For the infinite to move at all is thus absolutely
impossible; since the very smallest movement conceivable
must take an infinity of time. Moreover the heavens
certainly revolve, and they complete their circular orbit in
15 a finite time; so that they pass round the whole extent of
any line within their orbit, such as the finite line AB. The
revolving body, therefore, cannot be infinite.

(4) Again, as a line which has a limit cannot be infinite,
or, if it is infinite, is so only in length,[2] so a surface cannot

---

[1] Reading κἀκείνη παραλλάττει ἐκείνην with FHMJ. The alternative
to παραλλάττει, παρ', rests upon the sole authority of E : for L has
παραλλάττῃ. Παρ' is intolerable, since it must stand for φέρεται παρά
and thus attributes movement to B, of which in the same sentence it is
said that it may be unmoved.
[2] The reading is doubtful. It is difficult to attach any other sense
to the possession of πέρας ('limit') than a denial of infinity; in which
case ἀλλ' εἴπερ, ἐπὶ μῆκος means 'or if a finite line is infinite, it is so in
length'. The antecedent thus appears to contradict both itself and
the consequent. Simplicius preserves a variant for ἐπὶ μῆκος, ἐπὶ
θάτερα. ('A finite line can only be infinite, if at all, in one direction'.)
—Perhaps, however, the text is correct. The sentence may be para-
phrased as follows. A limited line cannot be infinite: lines, in fact,
can only be infinite, if at all, in that respect in which they are unlimited : but there is nothing in the nature of 'line' to determine the
length of any given line: consequently, it is only in respect to length
that infinity is ever ascribed to lines. (Mr. Ross suggests that ᾗ should
be read instead of ἧς in l. 17. 'A line cannot be infinite in that respect
in which it is a limit.' The line is the limit of the plane, i. e. a limit
in respect of breadth. Similarly the plane is the limit in respect of
depth. This correction has support from the translation of Argyropylus
('ex ea parte qua finis est'), and is probably right.)

be infinite in that respect in which it has a limit; or, indeed, if it is completely determinate, in any respect whatever. Whether it be a square or a circle or a sphere, it cannot be 20 infinite, any more than a foot-rule can. There is then no such thing as an infinite sphere or square or circle, and where there is no circle there can be no circular movement, and similarly where there is no infinite at all there can be no infinite movement; and from this it follows that, an infinite circle being itself an impossibility, there can be no circular motion of an infinite body.

(5) Again, take a centre C, an infinite line, AB, another 25 infinite line at right angles to it, E, and a moving radius, CD.[1] CD will never cease contact with E, but the position will always be something like CE, CD cutting E at F.[2] The infinite line, therefore, refuses to complete the circle.[3]

(6) Again, if the heaven is infinite and moves in a circle, 30 we shall have to admit that in a finite time it has traversed the infinite. For suppose the fixed heaven infinite, and that which moves within it equal to it. It results that when the infinite body has completed its revolution, it has traversed an infinite equal to itself in a finite time. But **273^a** that we know to be impossible.

(7) It can also be shown, conversely, that if the time of revolution is finite, the area traversed must also be finite;

---

[1] Also, of course, infinite.

[2] FIG. V.

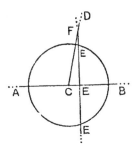

[3] The 'infinite line' is the infinite radius CD, which is unable to complete the circle owing to its inability to extricate its outer extremity from that of the other infinite, E. The MSS. vary between κύκλωι (EL), κύκλω (M), and κύκλον (HFJ: the last, however, has ωι *suprascriptum*). In FMJ περίεισι follows instead of preceding κύκλον (κύκλω M). Perhaps κύκλον περίεισιν should be read with FJ, though either reading will give the sense required.

but the area traversed was equal to itself; therefore, it is itself finite.[1]

5 We have now shown that the body which moves in a circle is not endless or infinite, but has its limit.

Further, neither that which moves towards nor that **6** which moves away from the centre can be infinite. For the upward and downward motions are contraries and are therefore motions towards contrary places. But if one of a pair 10 of contraries is determinate, the other must be determinate also. Now the centre is determined; for, from whatever point the body which sinks to the bottom starts its downward motion, it cannot go farther than the centre. The centre, therefore, being determinate, the upper place must also be determinate. But if these two places are determined 15 and finite, the corresponding bodies must also be finite. Further, if up and down are determinate, the intermediate place is also necessarily determinate. For, if it is indeterminate, the movement within it will be infinite[2]; and that we have already shown to be an impossibility.[3] The middle region then is determinate, and consequently any body which either is in it, or might be in it, is determinate. 20 But the bodies which move up and down may be in it, since the one moves naturally away from the centre and the other towards it.

From this alone it is clear that an infinite body is an impossibility; but there is a further point. If there is no such thing as infinite weight, then it follows that none of these bodies can be infinite. For the supposed infinite 25 body would have to be infinite in weight. (The same argument applies to lightness: for as the one supposition involves 'infinite weight, so the infinity of the body which rises to the surface involves infinite lightness.) This is

---

[1] The preceding six arguments start from the hypothesis of an infinite body and show the difficulties involved in the consequent assumption of an infinite path and in the infinite time needed for its completion. The converse argument starts from known finite time of revolution and argues from that to the finitude of the path traversed and of the body which traverses it.

[2] Reading εἴη ἡ κίνησις with FHMJ Simpl.

[3] *Phys.* VIII. viii.

proved as follows. Assume the weight to be finite, and take an infinite body, AB, of the weight C. Subtract from the infinite body a finite mass, BD, the weight of which 30 shall be E. E then is less than C, since it is the weight of a lesser mass.[1] Suppose then that the smaller goes into the greater a certain number of times, and take BF bearing **273ᵇ** the same proportion to BD which the greater weight bears to the smaller. For you may subtract as much as you please from an infinite. If now the masses are proportionate to the weights, and the lesser weight is that of the lesser mass, the greater must be that of the greater. The 5 weights, therefore, of the finite and of the infinite body are equal. Again, if the weight of a greater body is greater than that of a less, the weight of GB will be greater than that of FB;[1] and thus the weight of the finite body is greater than that of the infinite. And, further, the weight of unequal masses will be the same, since the infinite and the finite cannot be equal. It does not matter whether the 10 weights are commensurable or not. If (a) they are *incommensurable* the same reasoning holds. For instance, suppose E multiplied by three is rather more than C: the weight of three masses of the full size of BD will be greater than C. We thus arrive at the same impossibility as 15 before. Again (b) we may assume weights which are *commensurate*; for it makes no difference whether we begin with the weight or with the mass. For example, assume the weight E to be commensurate with C, and take from the infinite mass a part BD of weight E. Then let a mass BF be taken having the same proportion to BD which the 20 two weights have to one another. (For the mass being infinite you may subtract from it as much as you please.) These assumed bodies will be commensurate in mass and in weight alike. Nor again does it make any difference to our demonstration whether the total mass has its weight equally or unequally distributed. For it must always be possible to take from the infinite mass a body of equal 25

[1] FIG. VI.

C

weight to *BD* by diminishing or increasing the size of the section to the necessary extent.[1]

From what we have said, then, it is clear that the weight of the infinite body cannot be finite. It must then be infinite. We have therefore only to show this to be impossible in order to prove an infinite body impossible. But 30 the impossibility of infinite weight can be shown in the following way. A given weight moves a given distance in a given time; a weight which is as great and more moves the same distance in a less time, the times being in inverse 274^a proportion to the weights. For instance, if one weight is twice another, it will take half as long over a given movement. Further, a finite weight traverses any finite distance in a finite time. It necessarily follows from this that infinite weight, if there is such a thing, being, on the one 5 hand, as great and more than as great as the finite,[2] will move accordingly, but being, on the other hand, compelled to move in a time inversely proportionate to its greatness, cannot move at all.[3] The time should be less in proportion as the weight is greater. But there is no proportion between the infinite and the finite: proportion can only hold between a less and a greater *finite* time. And though you may say that the time of the movement can be continually 10 diminished, yet there is no minimum.[4] Nor, if there were,

---

[1] Delete comma after ΒΔ.

[2] There can be no doubt that the comma should follow, not precede, καὶ ἔτι (l. 5). The phrase τοσόνδε ὅσον τὸ πεπερασμένον καὶ ἔτι is parallel to the τοσοῦτον καὶ ἔτι of 273^b 31. Bonitz (*Ind.* 291^a 7) takes καὶ ἔτι in this way, but appears to interpret the phrase as indicating the distance moved, which is impossible.—For the use of καὶ ἔτι cf. *Met.* 1021^a 6.

[3] Because, as explained in the following sentences, there is no time for it to move in. The argument is: the infinite may (μέν) be regarded loosely as something exceedingly great, in which case it follows simply that it moves exceedingly fast: so far there is no difficulty: but (δέ) as soon as you begin to specify *how* great it is and *how* fast it moves the difficulties become insuperable.

[4] ἀλλ᾽ ἀεὶ ἐν ἐλάττονι is probably an opponent's objection. It is an application of the argument mentioned in 272^a 1. We talk of number as infinite, A. says there, because there is no maximum. Similarly the advocate of infinite weight says, 'At any rate the weight can be increased and the time proportionately diminished *ad infinitum*'. But the motion of the infinite, to be conceivable, must according to Aristotle occupy *a time*; and any time, however small, will be a time in which the given movement could be effected by a finite body.

would it help us. For some finite body could have been found greater than the given finite in the same proportion which is supposed to hold between the infinite and the given finite;[1] so that an infinite and a finite weight must have traversed an equal distance in equal time. But that is impossible. Again, whatever the time, so long as it is finite, in which the infinite performs the motion, a finite 15 weight must necessarily move a certain finite distance in that same time. Infinite weight is therefore impossible, and the same reasoning applies also to infinite lightness. Bodies then of infinite weight and of infinite lightness are equally impossible.

That there is no infinite body may be shown, as we have shown it, by a detailed consideration of the various cases. 20 But it may also be shown universally, not only by such reasoning as we advanced in our discussion of principles[2] (though in that passage we have already determined universally the sense in which the existence of an infinite is to be asserted or denied), but also suitably to our present purpose in the following way. That will lead us to a further question. Even if the total mass is not infinite, it may 25 yet be great enough to admit a plurality of universes. The question might possibly be raised whether there is any obstacle to our believing that there are other universes composed on the pattern of our own, more than one, though stopping short of infinity. First, however, let us treat of the infinite universally.

---

[1] What difficulty there is in this sentence is due to the elliptical expression and to the tacit inference from a proportion between the times to a proportion between the bodies. What is known is the ratio between the imaginary minimum time assigned to the infinite body and some other finite time. A. speaks of this known ratio as a ratio between the infinite body and another body. The argument is: take any other finite body (ἕτερον): its ratio to the infinite may be determined by their respective times: but another finite body (ἄλλο τι πεπερασμένον) could be found in the same ratio (on the basis of a comparison of times) to the first. Thus a finite body will cover the same distance as the infinite body in the same time, which is absurd.— The comma after λόγῳ in l. 11 should be deleted. μεῖζον belongs to the predicate both of the relative clause and of the main sentence. Neither Simplicius nor Alexander (as reported by Simplicius) seems to have interpreted the words quite correctly.

[2] *Phys.* III. iv–viii (see n. on 272ᵃ 30). Read εἰρημένους with FM.

30   Every body must necessarily be either finite or infinite, **7** and if infinite, either of similar or of dissimilar parts. If its parts are *dissimilar*, they must represent either a finite or an infinite number of kinds. That the kinds cannot be *infinite* is evident, if our original presuppositions remain
274^b unchallenged. For the primary movements being finite in number, the kinds of simple body are necessarily also finite, since the movement of a simple body is simple, and the simple movements are finite, and every natural body must
5 always have its proper motion. Now if[1] the infinite body is to be composed of a *finite* number of kinds, then each of its parts must necessarily be infinite in quantity, that is to say, the water, fire, &c., which compose it. But this is impossible, because, as we have already shown, infinite weight and lightness do not exist. Moreover it would be necessary also that their places should be infinite in extent,
10 so that the movements too of all these bodies would be infinite. But this is not possible, if we are to hold to the truth of our original presuppositions and to the view that neither that which moves downward, nor, by the same reasoning, that which moves upward, can prolong its movement to infinity. For it is true in regard to quality, quantity, and place alike that any process of change is
15 impossible which can have no end. I mean that if it is impossible for a thing to have come to be white, or a cubit long, or in Egypt, it is also impossible for it to be in process of coming to be any of these. It is thus impossible for a thing to be moving to a place at which in its motion it can never by any possibility arrive. Again, suppose the body to exist in dispersion, it may be maintained none the less that the total of all these scattered particles, say, of fire, is
20 infinite.[2] But body we saw to be that which has extension every way. How can there be several dissimilar elements, each infinite? Each would have to be infinitely extended every way.

It is no more conceivable, again, that the infinite should exist as a whole of *similar* parts. For, in the first place,

---

[1] Reading εἴγε with FHMJ.
[2] 'As Anaxagoras seems to have supposed' (Simpl.).

there is no other ⟨straight⟩ movement beyond those mentioned : we must therefore give it one of them. And if so,
we shall have to admit either infinite weight or infinite 25
lightness. Nor, secondly, could the body whose movement
is circular be infinite, since it is impossible for the infinite
to move in a circle. This, indeed, would be as good as
saying that the heavens are infinite, which we have shown
to be impossible.

Moreover, in general, it is impossible that the infinite 30
should move at all. If it did, it would move either naturally or by constraint : and if by constraint, it possesses also
a natural motion, that is to say, there is another place,
infinite like itself, to which it will move. But that is
impossible.[1]

That in general it is impossible for the infinite to be acted
upon by the finite or to act upon it may be shown as
follows.

⟨1. *The infinite cannot be acted upon by the finite.*⟩ Let 275^{a}
A be an infinite, B a finite, C the time of a given movement
produced by one in the other. Suppose, then, that A was
heated, or impelled, or modified in any way, or caused to
undergo any sort of movement whatever, by B in the time
C. Let D be less than B ; and, assuming that a lesser
agent moves a lesser patient in an equal time, call the quan- 5
tity thus modified by D, E. Then, as D is to B, so is E
to some finite quantum. We assume that the alteration of
equal by equal takes equal time, and the alteration of less
by less or of greater by greater takes the same time, if the
quantity of the patient is such as to keep the proportion
which obtains between the agents, greater and less. If so, 10
no movement can be caused in the infinite[2] by any finite
agent in any time whatever. For a less agent will produce
that movement in a less patient in an equal time, and the
proportionate equivalent of that patient will be a finite

---

[1] Because an infinite place cannot exclude, or be 'other' than, any
finite place. This argument applies to natural as well as unnatural
movement : for a body moves naturally in the effort to reach its place.
—Read τόπος ἄλλος ἴσος with EL, confirmed by Simplicius (τόπος ἴσος
ἄλλος, 239, 24).

[2] Read κινηθήσεται with Simplicius and all MSS. except E.

quantity, since no proportion holds between finite and infinite.

⟨2. *The infinite cannot act upon the finite.*⟩ Nor, again, can
15 the infinite produce a movement in the finite in any time whatever. Let A be an infinite, B^1 a finite, C the time of action. In the time C, D will produce that motion in a patient less than B, say F. Then take E, bearing the same proportion to D as the whole BF bears to F. E will produce the motion in BF in the time C. Thus the finite and
20 the infinite effect the same alteration in equal times. But this is impossible; for the assumption is that the greater effects it in a shorter time. It will be the same with any time that can be taken, so that there will be no time in which the infinite can effect this movement. And, as to infinite time, in that nothing can move another or be moved by it. For such time has no limit, while the action and reaction have.

⟨3. *There is no interaction between infinites.*⟩ Nor can
25 infinite be acted upon in any way by infinite. Let A and B be infinites, CD being the time of the action of A upon B. Now the whole B was modified in a certain time, and the part of this infinite, E, cannot be so modified in the same time, since we assume that a less quantity makes the movement in a less time. Let E then, when acted upon by A,
30 complete the movement in the time D. Then, as D is to CD, so is E to some finite part of B. This part will necessarily be moved by A in the time CD. For we suppose that the same agent produces a given effect on a greater
275ᵇ and a smaller mass in longer and shorter times, the times and masses varying proportionately. There is thus no finite time in which infinites can move one another. Is their time then infinite? No, for infinite time has no end, but the movement communicated has.

5 If therefore every perceptible body possesses the power of acting or of being acted upon, or both of these, it is impossible that an infinite body should be perceptible. All bodies, however, that occupy place are perceptible. There is therefore no infinite body beyond the heaven. Nor again is there anything of limited extent beyond it. And so

---

¹ Called BF a few lines below.

beyond the heaven there is no body at all. For if you suppose it an object of intelligence, it will be in a place— 10 since place is what 'within' and 'beyond' denote—and therefore an object of perception. But nothing that is not in a place is perceptible.[1]

The question may also be examined in the light of more general considerations as follows. The infinite, considered as a whole of similar parts, cannot, on the one hand, move in a circle. For there is no centre of the infinite, and that which moves in a circle moves about the centre. Nor again 15 can the infinite move in a straight line. For there would have to be another place infinite like itself to be the goal of its natural movement and another, equally great, for the goal of its unnatural movement. Moreover, whether its rectilinear movement is natural or constrained, in either case the force which causes its motion will have to be 20 infinite. For infinite force is force of an infinite body, and of an infinite body the force is infinite. So the motive body also will be infinite. (The proof of this is given in our discussion of movement,[2] where it is shown that no finite thing possesses infinite power, and no infinite thing finite power.) If then that which moves naturally can also move unnaturally, there will be two infinites, one which causes, and 25 another which exhibits the latter motion. Again, what is it that moves the infinite? If it moves itself, it must be animate. But how can it possibly be conceived as an infinite animal? And if there is something else that moves it, there will be two infinites, that which moves and that which is moved, differing in their form and power.[3]

---

[1] These sentences are rather disjointed and read more like rough notes than a finished argument. The final remark seems inconsequent. We should expect: 'but what is not perceptible cannot occupy a place'; so that the hypothesis that the body beyond the heaven is νοητόν contradicts itself. The main point, however, is that all these connected attributes are inapplicable to an object of intelligence like the Platonic εἶδος.

[2] *Phys.* VIII. x.

[3] The last argument (from 'Again, what is it . . .') is not a mere repetition of the preceding. The preceding sentence shows that an infinite disturbing force is needed to account for any unnatural movement of an infinite body. Finally, it is suggested that even the natural or normal movement of such a body would presuppose an independent infinite force. Again, the foregoing argument applied only to rectilinear

30 If the whole is not continuous, but exists, as Democritus
and Leucippus think, in the form of parts separated by
void, there must necessarily be one movement of all the
multitude. They are distinguished, we are told, from one
276^a another by their figures; but their nature is one, like many
pieces of gold separated from one another. But each piece
must, as we assert, have the same motion. For a single
clod moves to the same place as the whole mass of earth,
and a spark to the same place as the whole mass of fire.
So that if it be weight that all possess, no body is, strictly
5 speaking, light; and if lightness[1] be universal, none is
heavy. Moreover, whatever possesses weight or lightness
will have its place either at one of the extremes or in the
middle region. But this is impossible while the world is
conceived as infinite. And, generally, that which has no
centre or extreme limit, no up or down, gives the bodies no
10 place for their motion; and without that movement is
impossible. A thing must move either naturally or unnaturally, and the two movements are determined by the
proper and alien places. Again, a place in which a thing
rests or to which it moves unnaturally, must be the natural
15 place for some other body, as experience shows. Necessarily, therefore, not everything possesses weight or lightness,
but some things do and some do not. From these arguments then it is clear that the body of the universe is not
infinite.

We must now proceed to explain why there cannot be **8**
more than one heaven—the further question mentioned
above.[2] For it may be thought that we have not proved
20 universally of bodies that none whatever can exist outside

movement, since unnatural circular movement has been shown to be
impossible: but the last argument would apply equally to circular
movement. The remark 'if it moves itself, it must be animate'
implies that it is incorrect to think of the natural movement of the
elements as self-movement. It is only movement uninfluenced by
any sublunary body. That self-movement is impossible Aristotle has
already shown in *Phys.* VII.
  [1] Prantl misprints εἰ for εἰ.
  [2] In l. 18 Prantl's λέγομεν seems to be a misprint for λέγωμεν.—
'Heaven' here stands of course for world (οὐρανός = κόσμος).—The
reference is to c. vi (274^a 24).

our universe, and that our argument applied only to those of indeterminate extent.

Now all things rest and move naturally and by constraint. A thing moves naturally to a place in which it rests without constraint, and rests naturally in a place to which it moves without constraint. On the other hand, 25 a thing moves by constraint to a place in which it rests by constraint, and rests by constraint in a place to which it moves by constraint. Further, if a given movement is due to constraint, its contrary is natural. If, then, it is by constraint that earth moves from a certain place to the centre here, its movement from here to there will be natural, and if earth from there rests here without constraint, its movement hither will be natural. And the natural movement 30 in each case is one.[1] Further, these worlds, being similar in nature to ours, must all be composed of the same bodies as it. Moreover each of the bodies, fire, I mean, and earth and their intermediates, must have the same power as in **276ᵇ** our world. For if these names are used equivocally, if the identity of name does not rest upon an identity of form in those elements and ours, then the whole to which they belong can only be called a world by equivocation. Clearly, then, one of the bodies will move naturally away from the 5 centre and another towards the centre, since fire must be identical with fire, earth with earth, and so on, as the fragments of each are identical in this world. That this must be the case is evident from the principles laid down m our discussion of the movements;[2] for these are limited in number, and the distinction of the elements depends upon the distinction of the movements. Therefore, since the 10 movements are the same, the elements must also be the same everywhere. The particles of earth, then, in another world move naturally also to our centre and its fire to our circumference. This, however, is impossible, since, if it were true, earth must, in its own world, move upwards, and 15 fire to the centre; in the same way the earth of our world

---

[1] Reading μία δ' ἤ with EF²M Alex. The γάρ of the other MSS. and Simpl. is misleading and suggests an argument where there is none. The principle is simply stated for future use.

[2] Above, cc. ii–iv.

must move naturally away from the centre when it moves towards the centre of another universe.[1] This follows from the supposed juxtaposition of the worlds. For either we must refuse to admit the identical nature of the simple 20 bodies in the various universes, or, admitting this, we must make the centre and the extremity one as suggested. This being so, it follows that there cannot be more worlds than one.[2]

To postulate a difference of nature in the simple bodies according as they are more or less distant from their proper places is unreasonable. For what difference can it make whether we say that a thing is this distance away or that? 25 One would have to suppose a difference proportionate to the distance and increasing with it, but the form is in fact the same. Moreover, the bodies must have some movement, since the fact that they move is quite evident.[3] Are we to say then that all their movements, even those which are mutually contrary, are due to constraint? No, for a body which has no natural movement at all cannot be moved by 30 constraint. If then the bodies have a natural movement,

---

[1] In l. 17 the comma which Prantl places after φύσιν should be placed instead after μέσον. It is needed in this place in order to show that the following clause (διὰ τὸ . . . ἀλλήλους) is explanatory of the ἀνάγκη of l. 14, not of φέρεσθαι in l. 16.

[2] If there is one centre and one extremity, there is only one heaven or world. (Read τούτου δ' ὄντος, ἀδύνατον κτλ. Prantl's ἀτόπου is found only in F and J, and in both it is preceded by τοῦ, which shows that it is an adscript intended to explain the meaning of τούτου.)—The argument of the chapter down to this point is a single *reductio ad absurdum*. Simplicius tries unsuccessfully to interpret it as a series of reductions. The remainder of the chapter reasserts the conclusion here drawn by closing up various pathways of escape. In truth there is only one way of escape, as Aristotle here says, viz. to deny the identity of the fire and earth in the other worlds with that in our own; but the contention takes a variety of forms—(1) 'distance makes a difference'; (2) 'they have no movement, or only move by constraint'; (3) 'the goal of their movement is only the same *in kind* as that of the corresponding elements here'. These suggestions are refuted in what follows.

[3] Throughout this paragraph when Aristotle speaks of 'the bodies' he is thinking of the fire, earth, &c., supposed to constitute another κόσμος. He is not proving over again the proposition that the four elements have each a natural motion, but considering what would be their motion in another world existing beside our own. The empirical evidence of movement here appealed to must be that of the fire and earth of this world; but a thing that did not move would not be a body at all.

the movement of the particular instances of each form must necessarily have for goal a place numerically one, i.e. a particular centre or a particular extremity. If it be suggested that the goal in each case is one in form but numerically more than one, on the analogy of particulars **277^a** which are many though each undifferentiated in form, we reply that the variety of goal cannot be limited to this portion or that but must extend to all alike.[1] For all are equally undifferentiated in form, but any one is different numerically from any other. What I mean is this: if the 5 portions in this world behave similarly both to one another and to those in another world, then the portion which is taken hence will not behave differently either from the portions in another world or from those in the same world, but similarly to them, since in form no portion differs from another. The result is that we must either abandon our present assumptions or assert that the centre and the 10 extremity are each numerically one. But this being so, the heaven, by the same evidence and the same necessary inferences, must be one only and no more.

A consideration of the other kinds of movement also makes it plain that there is some point to which earth and fire move naturally. For in general that which is moved changes from something into something, the starting- 15 point and the goal being different in form, and always it is a finite change.[2] For instance, to recover health is to change from disease to health, to increase is to change from smallness to greatness. Locomotion must be similar: for it also has its goal and starting-point—and therefore the starting-point and the goal of the natural movement must differ in form—just as the movement of coming to health does not take any direction which chance 20

---

[1] Read τῷ μὲν τῷ δ' οὔ with FLJ Simpl. The meaning is that since none but a 'numerical' difference can be postulated between the portions (e.g. of earth) in this world and those in another, and since a difference of goal can only be justified by a difference in the body, we should have to suppose a distinct goal for every single portion of earth; which is absurd.

[2] A full-stop, rather than a comma, is needed after μεταβολή in l. 16. Three principles are laid down and all are illustrated in the case of locomotion. But the instances of health and increase are used only to illustrate the first.

or the wishes of the mover may select.[1] Thus, too, fire and
earth move not to infinity but to opposite points ; and since
the opposition in place is between above and below, these
will be the limits of their movement.[2] (Even in circular
movement there is a sort of opposition between the ends of
the diameter, though the movement as a whole has no
25 contrary : so that here too the movement has in a sense an
opposed and finite goal.) There must therefore be some
end to locomotion : it cannot continue to infinity.

This conclusion that local movement is not continued to
infinity is corroborated by the fact that earth moves more
quickly the nearer it is to the centre, and fire the nearer it
30 is to the upper place. But if movement were infinite speed
would be infinite also ; and if speed then weight and lightness. For as superior speed in downward movement
implies superior weight, so infinite increase of weight necessitates infinite increase of speed.[3]

277ᵇ Further, it is not the action of another body that makes
one of these bodies move up and the other down ; nor is it
constraint, like the ʿextrusionʾ of some writers.[4] For in
that case the larger the mass of fire or earth the slower
would be the upward or downward movement ; but the fact

---

[1] ll. 18–19, the full-stop after ποῖ should be deleted, and the words
δεῖ ἄρα . . . φέρεσθαι should be marked as a parenthesis. Locomotion,
like healing, has a determinate direction, and that involves a difference
of form between its two terms.

[2] The remarks which follow concerning circular motion are a kind
of footnote and would be best marked as a parenthesis.

[3] In l. 29 it is tempting to read εἰ δ' εἰς ἄπειρον ἦν for εἰ δ' ἄπειρον ἦν,
but no evidence of such a reading survives. The sense of the paragraph is plain. We observe an increase of speed in a falling body as
it approaches the earth. The explanation, on our view, is the proximity
of the goal. But if there is no goal, the movement, and with it the
increase of speed, is capable of continuing to infinity. But infinite
speed means infinite weight, which has already (c. vi) been proved
impossible. The Greek of the last sentence is puzzling and may be
corrupt. Accepting the text of Bekker and Prantl, we must translate
as follows : ʿas that which by reason of speed is lower than another
body would be presumed speedy by reason of weight, so if there were
infinite increase of weight there would also be infinite increase of
speed.ʾ (The alteration of an accent is required : βάρει for βαρεῖ in
l. 32.) The sentence is clumsy, but it gives the required sense.
Simplicius seems to have interpreted the passage as above. In l. 31
ἑτέρου is found in F alone, all the other MSS. giving ἕτερον ; but
ἑτέρου must be right.

[4] The atomists, Leucippus and Democritus.

is the reverse: the greater the mass of fire or earth the quicker always is its movement towards its own place. 5 Again, the speed of the movement would not increase towards the end if it were due to constraint or extrusion; for a constrained movement always diminishes in speed as the source of constraint becomes more distant, and a body moves without constraint to the place whence it was moved by constraint.

A consideration of these points, then, gives adequate assurance of the truth of our contentions. The same could also be shown with the aid of the discussions which fall 10 under First Philosophy,[1] as well as from the nature of the circular movement, which must be eternal both here and in the other worlds. It is plain, too, from the following considerations that the universe must be one.

The bodily elements are three, and therefore the places of the elements will be three also; the place, first, of the body 15 which sinks to the bottom, namely the region about the centre; the place, secondly, of the revolving body, namely the outermost place, and thirdly, the intermediate place, belonging to the intermediate body. Here in this third place will be the body which rises to the surface; since, if not here, it will be elsewhere, and it cannot be elsewhere: for we have two bodies, one weightless, one endowed with weight, and below is the place of the body endowed with 20 weight, since the region about the centre has been given to the heavy body. And its position cannot be unnatural to it, for it would have to be natural to something else, and there is nothing else. It must then occupy the intermediate place. What distinctions there are within the intermediate itself we will explain later on.

We have now said enough to make plain the character and number of the bodily elements, the place of each, and further, in general, how many in number the various places are. 25

9　We must show not only that the heaven is one,[2] but also that more than one heaven is impossible, and, further,

---

[1] i.e. Metaphysics.　Cf. *Met.* Λ. 8.

[2] Prantl misprints εἰς for εἷς.　For οὐρανός read ὁ οὐρανός with M. J, like EHL, omits the word οὐρανός altogether.

that, as exempt from decay and generation, the heaven is eternal. We may begin by raising a difficulty. From 30 one point of view it might seem impossible that the heaven should be one and unique,[1] since in all formations and products whether of nature or of art we can distinguish the shape in itself and the shape in combination with matter. 278^a For instance the form of the sphere is one thing and the gold or bronze sphere another; the shape of the circle again is one thing, the bronze or wooden circle another. For when we state the essential nature of the sphere or circle we do not include in the formula gold or bronze, 5 because they do not belong to the essence, but if we are speaking of the copper or gold sphere we do include them. We still make the distinction even if we cannot conceive or apprehend any other example beside the particular thing. This may, of course, sometimes be the case: it might be, for instance, that only one circle could be found; yet none the less the difference will remain between the being of circle and of this particular circle, the one being form, the other form in matter, 10 i.e. a particular thing. Now since the universe is perceptible it must be regarded as a particular; for everything that is perceptible subsists, as we know, in matter. But if it is a particular, there will be a distinction between the being of 'this universe' and of 'universe' unqualified. There is a difference, then, between 'this universe' and simple 'universe'; the second is form and shape, the first 15 form in combination with matter; and any shape or form has, or may have, more than one particular instance.

On the supposition of Forms such as some assert, this must be the case, and equally on the view that no such entity has a separate existence. For in every case in which the essence is in matter it is a fact of observation that the particulars of like form are several or infinite in 20 number. Hence there either are, or may be, more heavens

---

[1] More correctly: that the heaven should be *necessarily* one and unique. The argument here set out only attempts to prove the possibility of more than one world, and Aristotle replies by proving the impossibility of more than one. Alexander (cited by Simpl.) points out this defect in the statement.

than one.[1] On these grounds, then, it might be inferred
either that there are or that there might be several heavens.
We must, however, return and ask how much of this argument is correct and how much not.

Now it is quite right to say that the formula of the
shape apart from the matter must be different from that
of the shape in the matter, and we may allow this to be 25
true. We are not, however, therefore compelled to assert
a plurality of worlds. Such a plurality is in fact impossible
if this world contains the entirety of matter, as in fact
it does. But perhaps our contention can be made clearer
in this way. Suppose 'aquilinity' to be curvature in the
nose or flesh, and flesh to be the matter of aquilinity. 30
Suppose, further, that all flesh came together into a single
whole of flesh endowed with this aquiline quality. Then
neither would there be, nor could there arise, any other
thing that was aquiline. Similarly, suppose flesh and bones
to be the matter of man, and suppose a man to be created
of all flesh and all bones in indissoluble union. The 35
possibility of another man would be removed. Whatever
case you took it would be the same. The general rule 278ᵇ
is this: a thing whose essence resides in a substratum
of matter can never come into being in the absence of
all matter.[2] Now the universe is certainly a particular
and a material thing: if however it is composed not of
a part but of the whole of matter, then though the being 5
of 'universe' and of 'this universe' are still distinct, yet
there is no other universe, and no possibility of others
being made, because all the matter is already included
in this. It remains, then, only to prove that it is composed
of all natural perceptible body.

First, however, we must explain what we mean by 'heaven' 10
and in how many senses we use the word, in order to make
clearer the object of our inquiry. (a) In one sense, then, we call

---

[1] The οἱ before οὐρανοί is attributed only to E, and to it 'dubio'
J has it. But the article does not seem to be required here. In
corresponding passages in this chapter it is omitted.

[2] Read τινὸς ὕλης. The omission of τινός in E must be a mere slip.
All the other MSS., as well as Simpl., have τινὸς ὕλης, and E is full of
small omissions.

'heaven' the substance of the extreme circumference of the whole, or that natural body whose place is at the extreme circumference. We recognize habitually a special right to 15 the name 'heaven' in the extremity or upper region, which we take to be the seat of all that is divine.[1] (*b*) In another sense, we use this name for the body continuous with the extreme circumference, which contains the moon, the sun, and some of the stars ; these we say are 'in the heaven'. (*c*) In yet another sense we give the name to all body 20 included within the extreme circumference, since we habitually call the whole or totality 'the heaven'. The word, then, is used in three senses.

Now the whole included within the extreme circumference must be composed of *all* physical and sensible body, because there neither is, nor can come into being, any body outside 25 the heaven. For if there is a natural body outside the extreme circumference it must be either a simple or a composite body, and its position must be either natural or unnatural. But it cannot be any of the simple bodies. For, first, it has been shown[2] that that which moves in a circle 30 cannot change its place. And, secondly, it cannot be that which moves from the centre or that which lies lowest. *Naturally* they could not be there, since their proper places are elsewhere ; and if these are there *unnaturally*, the exterior place will be natural to some other body, since a place which is unnatural to one body must be natural to another : but we saw that there is no other body besides 35 these.[3] Then it is not possible that any simple body should 279ᵃ be outside the heaven. But, if no simple body, neither can any mixed body be there : for the presence of the simple body is involved in the presence of the mixture. Further neither can any body come into that place : for it will do so either naturally or unnaturally, and will be either simple 5 or composite ; so that the same argument will apply, since it makes no difference whether the question is 'does *A*

---

[1] Place a full-stop after φαμεν. In the next line συνέχες should be συνεχές.

[2] Read τὸ μὲν γάρ. The μέν is wanted, and is omitted by E alone. The reference is to cc. ii and iii above.

[3] c. ii above.

exist?' or ' could A come to exist?'   From our arguments
then it is evident not only that there is not, but also that there
could never come to be, any bodily mass whatever outside
the circumference. The world as a whole, therefore, includes
all its appropriate matter, which is, as we saw, natural
perceptible body. So that neither are there now, nor have
there ever been, nor can there ever be formed more heavens 10
than one, but this heaven of ours is one and unique and
complete.

It is therefore evident that there is also no place or void
or time outside the heaven. For in every place body can
be present; and void is said to be that in which the presence
of body, though not actual, is possible; and time is the 15
number of movement. But in the absence of natural body
there is no movement, and outside the heaven, as we have
shown, body neither exists nor can come to exist. It is
clear then that there is neither place, nor void, nor time,
outside the heaven. Hence whatever is there, is of such
a nature as not to occupy any place, nor does time age it;
nor is there any change in any of the things which lie beyond 20
the outermost motion; they continue through their entire
duration unalterable and unmodified, living the best and
most self-sufficient of lives. As a matter of fact, this word
' duration' possessed a divine significance for the ancients,
for the fulfilment which includes the period of life of any
creature, outside of which no natural development can fall,
has been called its duration. On the same principle the 25
fulfilment of the whole heaven, the fulfilment which includes
all time and infinity, is ' duration'—a name based upon the
fact that it *is always*[1]—duration immortal and divine.
From it derive the being and life which other things,
some more or less articulately but others feebly, enjoy. 30
So, too, in its discussions concerning the divine, popular
philosophy[2] often propounds the view that whatever is

---

[1] i.e. αἰών is derived from ἀεὶ ὤν.

[2] Aristotle refers apparently under this name to elementary hand-
books of philosophy current among his audience. It is usual to
identify them with the ἐξωτερικοὶ λόγοι, as Simpl. does in his commentary on this passage. See Bonitz, *Ind. Ar.*, s. v. Ἀριστοτέλης,
105^a 27.

divine, whatever is primary and supreme, is necessarily unchangeable. This fact confirms what we have said. For there is nothing else stronger than it to move it—

35 since that would mean more divine—and it has no defect

279ᵇ and lacks none of its proper excellences. Its unceasing movement, then, is also reasonable, since everything ceases to move when it comes to its proper place, but the body whose path is the circle has one and the same place for starting-point and goal.

Having established these distinctions, we may now pro- 10
5 ceed to the question whether the heaven is ungenerated or generated, indestructible or destructible. Let us start with a review of the theories of other thinkers; for the proofs of a theory are difficulties for the contrary theory.[1] Besides, those who have first heard the pleas of our adversaries will be more likely to credit the assertions
10 which we are going to make. We shall be less open to the charge of procuring judgement by default. To give a satisfactory decision as to the truth it is necessary to be rather an arbitrator than a party to the dispute.

That the world was generated all are agreed, but, genera-tion over, some say that it is eternal, others say that it is destructible like any other natural formation.[2] Others
15 again, with Empedocles of Acragas and Heraclitus of Ephesus, believe that there is alternation in the destructive process, which takes now this direction, now that, and continues without end.[3]

---

[1] Prantl misprints τὺν ἐναντίων for τῶν ἐναντίων in l. 6.

[2] The former view, according to Alexander (*ap.* Simpl.), is that of Orpheus (i.e. of Orphic cosmogony), Hesiod, and Plato, while the latter is that of Democritus and his school.

[3] Cf. Burnet, E.G.P.³ p. 157 (§ 77). Heraclitus and Empedocles are agreed in believing in periodic changes in the constitution of our world as a whole. For both, the world exists, as it were, in a succession of lives (below, 280ᵃ 14); and the view is a kind of compromise between that which regards it as eternal and that which gives it a single life ended by annihilation. The phrase 'alternation in the destructive process' is somewhat inaccurate, since the alternation may be described as between generation and destruction (Empedocles' Love and Strife, Stoic διακόσμησις and ἐκπύρωσις). But it is intelligible. Aristotle is here classing the theory for convenience with those that hold to a destructible world, and the antithesis is between destruction ἁπλῶς and destruction with alternation. Later he explains that this

Now to assert that it was generated and yet is eternal is to assert the impossible; for we cannot reasonably attribute to anything any characteristics but those which observation detects in many or all instances. But in this case the facts 20 point the other way: generated things are seen always to be destroyed. Further, a thing whose present state had no beginning and which could not have been other than it was at any previous moment throughout its entire duration, cannot possibly be changed.[1] For there will have to be some cause of change, and if this had been present earlier it would have made possible another condition of that to which any other condition was impossible. Suppose that the world was formed 25 out of elements which were formerly otherwise conditioned than as they are now. Then (1) if their condition was always so and could not have been otherwise, the world could never have come into being.[2] And (2) if the world did come into being, then, clearly, their condition must have been capable of change and not eternal: after combination therefore they will be dispersed, just as in the past after dispersion they came into combination, and this process either has been, or could have been, indefinitely repeated. But if this is so, 30 the world cannot be indestructible, and it does not matter whether the change of condition has actually occurred or remains a possibility.

Some of those who hold that the world, though indestructible, was yet generated, try to support their case by a parallel which is illusory.[3] They say that in their statements about its generation they are doing what geometricians do when they construct their figures, not 35 implying that the universe really had a beginning, but

alternation is not φθορά at all. Burnet in his first edition proposed to excise φθειρόμενον, but the suggestion is now tacitly retracted. In his later editions Burnet wrongly states that what is here in question is the eternity of the first heaven. That has already been proved in c. iii, and the first heaven would not be referred to as ὁ κόσμος.

[1] A comma is required after αἰῶνα in l. 22, unless the comma after ἔχειν in the preceding line is deleted.

[2] The close coordination of εἰ μέν (in l. 25) with εἰ δέ (in l. 26) demands a comma, rather than a full-stop, after ἐγένετο.

[3] Simpl. refers the following argument to Xenocrates and the Platonists.

280^a for didactic reasons facilitating understanding by exhibiting
the object, like the figure, as in course of formation. The
two cases, as we said, are not parallel; for, in the construction of the figure, when the various steps are completed
the required figure forthwith results; but in these other
demonstrations what results is not that which was required.[1]
5 Indeed it cannot be so; for antecedent and consequent, as
assumed, are in contradiction. The ordered, it is said,[2]
arose out of the unordered; and the same thing cannot
be at the same time both ordered and unordered; there
must be a process and a lapse of time separating the two
10 states. In the figure, on the other hand, there is no
temporal separation.[3] It is clear then that the universe
cannot be at once eternal and generated.

To say that the universe alternately combines and dissolves
is no more paradoxical than to make it eternal but varying in shape. It is as if one were to think that there was now
15 destruction and now existence when from a child a man is
generated, and from a man a child. For it is clear that when
the elements come together the result is not a chance system
and combination, but the very same as before—especially
on the view of those who hold this theory, since they say
that the contrary is the cause of each state.[4] So that if
20 the totality of body, which is a continuum, is now in this
order or disposition and now in that, and if the combination
of the whole is a world or heaven, then it will not be the
world that comes into being and is destroyed, but only
its dispositions.

If the world is believed to be one, it is impossible to

---

[1] i.e. the geometricians can truly write Q. E. F. at the end of their
construction, but these cosmogonists cannot. The figure, or world,
constructed should be 'the same' (τὸ αὐτό) as that demanded in the
ὑπόθεσις.

[2] Cp. Plato, *Timaeus* 30 A.

[3] The construction of the cosmogonist cannot be a mere didactic
device like that of the geometrician; for the attributes successively
assumed in the construction of the world cannot exist simultaneously
as those assumed by the geometrician do.

[4] Here Aristotle clearly refers to Empedocles, rather than to
Heraclitus. The two causes of Empedocles are Love and Strife
(φιλία and νεῖκος), and since these are two it follows, Aristotle argues,
that the world would merely oscillate between two arrangements or
dispositions.

suppose that it should be, as a whole, first generated and then destroyed, never to reappear; since before it came into being there was always present the combination prior 25 to it, and that, we hold, could never change if it was never generated. If, on the other hand, the worlds are infinite in number the view is more plausible. But whether this is, or is not, impossible will be clear from what follows. For there are some who think it possible both for the ungenerated to be destroyed and for the generated to 30 persist undestroyed.[1] (This is held in the *Timaeus*,[2] where Plato says that the heaven, though it was generated, will none the less exist to eternity.) So far as the heaven is concerned we have answered this view with arguments appropriate to the nature of the heaven: on the general question we shall attain clearness when we examine the matter universally.[3]

11   We must first distinguish the senses in which we use the 280ᵇ words 'ungenerated' and 'generated', 'destructible' and 'indestructible'.[4]   These have many meanings, and though

---

[1] In l. 29 Prantl misprints κμί for καί.

[2] A colon instead of a full-stop is needed after Τιμαίῳ. The reference is to Plato, *Timaeus* 31. Plato is quoted as authority for the indestructible-generated not for the ungenerated-destructible, as the context shows.

[3] The general question is the mutual relations of the terms 'generated', 'ungenerated', 'destructible', 'indestructible', which have so far been considered only in their application to the heaven. The terms are discussed universally, i. e. apart from any special application, in cc. xi and xii. The combination attributed to Plato is refuted at the end of that discussion (283ᵃ 1 ff.). Simplicius found the argument of the last paragraph of this chapter (ll. 23 ff.) somewhat obscure. It deals, provisionally and subject to further investigation, with the view that the world is subject both to generation and to destruction in the sense in which the man Socrates is. Simpl. is probably right in supposing that under this head Aristotle is thinking of the atomists. Their infinite worlds were successive, if also co-existent. Aristotle here argues that if that out of which the world was formed had the capacity to give birth to a world, then that into which the world is destroyed will have the same capacity. Thus the theory of world-annihilation is dismissed as absurd, while the infinite succession of destructible worlds is left open. But the refutation even of the first of these views, and therefore *a fortiori* of the second, cannot be regarded as complete until the whole problem of generation and destruction has been examined.

[4] It is unfortunate that 'generated' and 'destructible' are not similar grammatical forms as the Greek γενητός and φθαρτός are. But from the analysis given by Aristotle it will be seen that in meaning the Greek verbal adjective tends to approximate to the past

it may make no difference to the argument, yet some confusion of mind must result from treating as uniform in its
5 use a word which has several distinct applications. The
character which is the ground of the predication will
always remain obscure.

The word 'ungenerated' then is used (*a*) in one sense
whenever something now is which formerly was not, no
process of becoming or change being involved. Such is the
case, according to some, with contact and motion, since
there is no process of coming to be in contact or in motion.
(*b*) It is used in another sense, when something which is
10 capable of coming to be, with or without process, does not
exist; such a thing is ungenerated in the sense that its
generation is not a fact but a possibility. (*c*) It is also
applied where there is general impossibility of any generation
such that the thing now is which then was not. And 'impossibility' has two uses: first, where it is untrue to say
that the thing can ever come into being, and secondly,
where it cannot do so easily, quickly, or well. In the
15 same way the word 'generated' is used, (*a*) first, where
what formerly was not afterwards is, whether a process of
becoming was or was not involved, so long as that which
then was not, now is; (*b*) secondly, of anything capable of
existing, 'capable' being defined with reference either to
truth or to facility; (*c*) thirdly, of anything to which the
passage from not being to being belongs,[1] whether already
actual, if its existence is due to a past process of becoming,
20 or not yet actual but only possible. The uses of the words
'destructible' and 'indestructible' are similar. 'Destructible' is applied (*a*) to that which formerly was and afterwards either is not or might not be, whether a period of
being destroyed and changed intervenes or not;[2] and (*b*)

participle, and therefore it is not worth while to insist on 'generable',
'ungenerable' for γενητός, ἀγένητος.

[1] For ἐὰν ᾖ γένεσις read ἐὰν ᾖ γένεσις. (M has ᾖ ἥ, but all other
MSS. have ἥ.) The correction was suggested by Hayduck (Greifswald Gymnasium Program, 1871, p. 11).

[2] The evidence afforded by Simpl. and the MSS., together with the
difficulty of establishing a precise correspondence between this definition of φθαρτόν and the parallel uses of 'ungenerated' (*b*) and
'generated' (*a*), might lead one to doubt the soundness of the text
at this point; but it is guaranteed by Aristotle's own citation at
281ᵇ 27.

sometimes we apply the word to that which a process of destruction may cause not to be; and also (c) in a third sense, to that which is easily destructible, to the 'easily- 25 destroyed', so to speak.[1] Of the indestructible the same account holds good. It is either (a) that which now is and now is not, without any process of destruction, like contact, which without being destroyed afterwards is not, though formerly it was; or (b) that which is but might not be, or which will at some time not be, though it now is.[2] For you exist now and so does the contact; yet both are destructible, 30 because a time will come when it will not be true of you that you exist, nor of these things that they are in contact. Thirdly (c) in its most proper use, it is that which is, but is incapable of any destruction such that the thing which now is later ceases to be or might cease to be; or again, that which has not yet been destroyed, but in the future may cease to be.[3] For indestructible is also used of that which **281**^a is destroyed with difficulty.[4]

---

[1] Aristotle carelessly omits to mention the other and more exact kind of possibility. Cf. 'ungenerated' (c) and 'generated' (b).

[2] The third ἤ (in l. 29) is not coordinate with the two which precede it (ll. 26, 28), and it would be well to mark this by putting a colon instead of a comma after εἰσίν in l. 28. Simplicius read ἢ καὶ οὐκ in l. 29, and the addition of καί would be an improvement.

[3] Omit the οὐκ inserted by Prantl before ἐνδεχόμενον. The ὂν δέ which Prantl's note attributes to Simplicius is found only in one inferior MS. and is not printed in Heiberg's text of the commentary. J also has no word between ἐφθαρμένον and ἐνδεχόμενον, nor had Alexander.

[4] Read λέγεται γάρ for λέγεται δέ, and place a colon instead of a full-stop before λέγεται. This alteration is conjectural, but it is preferable to Hayduck's excision of ἢ καὶ ... εἶναι (ll. 33, 34), and without some alteration the Greek will not give a satisfactory sense. The account given of 'indestructible' is closely parallel to that given of 'ungenerated' above. Sense (a) of 'indestructible' (ll. 26-28) turns on the absence of process, like sense (a) of 'ungenerated', even repeating the same instance, touch. In sense (b) (ll. 28-31) 'indestructible' covers all that has not been destroyed, as 'ungenerated' in sense (b) covers what has not yet come into being: as 'ungenerated' includes all possible existents which are now non-existent, so 'indestructible' includes all possible non-existents which are now existent. There remains the third and proper sense, viz. potentiality or possibility, subdivided in the case of 'ungenerated', according to an ambiguity in the word possible, into (i) strict and final impossibility (τῷ μὴ ἀληθὲς εἶναι εἰπεῖν), (ii) popular or 'practical' impossibility (τῷ μὴ ῥᾳδίως μηδὲ ταχὺ ἢ καλῶς). The third sense of 'indestructible' is introduced by τὸ δὲ μάλιστα κυρίως in l. 31, and its subdivision is effected by ἢ καί in l. 33. The words before ἢ καί assert the final

This being so, we must ask what we mean by 'possible'
and 'impossible'. For in its most proper use the predicate
'indestructible' is given because it is impossible that the
thing should be destroyed, i. e. exist at one time and not at
5 another. And 'ungenerated' also involves impossibility
when used for that which cannot be generated, in such
fashion that, while formerly it was not, later it is. An instance is a commensurable diagonal. Now when we speak
of a power[1] to move[2] or to lift weights, we refer always to
the maximum. We speak, for instance, of a power to lift
a hundred talents or walk a hundred stades—though
a power to effect the maximum is also a power to effect any
10 part of the maximum—since we feel obliged in defining the
power to give the limit or maximum. A thing, then, which
is capable of a certain amount as maximum must also be
capable of that which lies within it. If, for example, a man
can lift a hundred talents, he can also lift two, and if he can
walk a hundred stades, he can also walk two. But the
15 power is of the maximum, and a thing said, with reference
to its maximum,[3] to be incapable of so much is also incapable of any greater amount. It is, for instance, clear
that a person who cannot walk a thousand stades will also
be unable to walk a thousand and one. This point need
not trouble us, for we may take it as settled that what is, in
the strict sense, possible is determined by a limiting maxi-
20 mum. Now perhaps the objection might be raised that

removal of the possibility of non-existence, and the following clause
relaxes the requirement as popular use demands. Even if the possibility of destruction has not been finally removed, a thing may be
called 'indestructible' in this sense if it has not been destroyed.
'For (λέγεται γάρ) what is not easily destroyed is called indestructible.'
By calling this the proper sense, whether in its stricter or more
popular use, Aristotle must mean that the verbal adjective in -τος
should not in precise speech be allowed to approximate, as it often
does, to a past participle passive. (Simplicius's interpretation of this
passage is quite inadmissible, but he was confused by faulty MSS.)

[1] 'Power' (δύναμις) must be taken throughout as the noun corresponding to the adjective 'possible' (δυνατόν).

[2] The MSS. have κινηθῆναι στάδια ἑκατόν ('to move a hundred
stades'). The translation omits the reference to distance, which
seems clearly out of place. The words στάδια ἑκατόν, which occur
more than once in the context, probably got their place in this clause
through a copyist's mistake.

[3] Prantl misprints ὑπερβαλήν for ὑπερβολήν.

there is no necessity in this, since he who sees a stade need 25
not see the smaller measures contained in it, while, on the
contrary, he who can see a dot or hear a small sound will
perceive what is greater. This, however, does not touch
our argument. The maximum may be determined either
in the power or in its object.[1] The application of this is
plain. Superior sight is sight of the smaller body, but
superior speed is that of the greater body.

12 Having established these distinctions we can now proceed
to the sequel. If there are things capable both of being
and of not being, there must be some definite maximum
time of their being and not being ; a time, I mean, during 30
which continued existence is possible to them and a time
during which continued non-existence is possible. And
this is true in every category, whether the thing is, for example, 'man', or 'white', or 'three cubits long', or whatever
it may be. For if the time is not definite in quantity, but
longer than any that can be suggested and shorter than
none, then it will be possible for one and the same thing to 281^b
exist for infinite time and not to exist for another infinity.
This, however, is impossible.

Let us take our start from this point. The impossible
and the false have not the same significance. One use of
'impossible' and 'possible', and 'false' and 'true', is hypo- 5
thetical. It is impossible, for instance, on a certain
hypothesis that the triangle should have its angles equal to
two right angles, and on another the diagonal is commensurable. But there are also things possible and impossible,
false and true, absolutely. Now it is one thing to be absolutely false, and another thing to be absolutely impossible.
To say that you are standing when you are not standing is
to assert a falsehood, but not an impossibility. Similarly 10

---

[1] i. e. sometimes the maximum is an actual maximum (determined
'in the object', ἐπὶ τοῦ πράγματος), e. g. in the case of weight-lifting,
where the largest weight lifted serves to define the power; sometimes
it is an actual minimum, determined as maximum 'in the power' (ἐπὶ
τῆς δυνάμεως), e. g. in the case of vision, where the smallest object seen
serves to define the capacity. Cf. the distinction between the μέσον
τοῦ πράγματος (or κατὰ τὸ πρᾶγμα) and the μέσον πρὸς ἡμᾶς in *Eth. Nic.*
1106^a 26 ff.

to say that a man who is playing the harp, but not singing,
is singing, is to say what is false but not impossible. To
say, however, that you are at once standing and sitting, or
that the diagonal is commensurable, is to say what is not
only false but also impossible. Thus it is not the same
thing to make a false and to make an impossible hypothesis ;[1]
15 and from the impossible hypothesis impossible results follow.
A man has, it is true, the capacity at once of sitting and
of standing, because when he possesses the one he also
possesses the other ; but it does not follow that he can at
once sit and stand, only that at another time he can do the
other also. But[2] if a thing has for infinite time more than
one capacity, another time is impossible and the times must
20 coincide. Thus if anything which exists for infinite time is
destructible, it will have the capacity of not being. Now if
it exists for infinite time let this capacity be actualized ;[3]
and it will be in actuality at once existent and non-existent.
Thus a false conclusion would follow because a false assumption was made, but if what was assumed had not been
25 impossible its consequence would not have been impossible.[4]

Anything then which always exists is absolutely imperishable. It is also ungenerated, since if it was generated
it will have the power for some time of not being. For as
that which formerly was, but now is not, or is capable at
some future time of not being, is destructible, so that which
is capable of formerly not having been is generated.[5] But
in the case of that which always is, there is no time for such
30 a capacity of not being, whether the supposed time is finite

---

[1] Cf. *Anal. Prior.* 34^a 1 ff. for this distinction. There should be
a colon rather than a full-stop after ἀδύνατον. The production of like
consequences is of course not peculiar to the impossible hypothesis :
it applies equally to the false hypothesis. See *loc. cit.*

[2] Read εἰ δέ with FHMJ for εἰ δή. There is no semblance of
inference. Simplicius makes the connexion antithetical.

[3] For ἔσται read ἔστω with all MSS. (except E) and Simpl. The
μὴ εἶναι which follows δύναται in FHMJ must have been a copyist's
mistake.

[4] The assumption in this case was both false and impossible.

[5] The words are taken in their 'most proper' sense, as the qualification 'absolutely' in l. 25 suggests; viz. as conveying a strict and
demonstrable possibility or impossibility. See foregoing chapter.

or infinite; for its capacity of being must include the finite time since it covers infinite time.[1]

It is therefore impossible that one and the same thing should be capable of always existing and of always not-existing.[2] And 'not always existing', the contradictory, is also excluded. Thus it is impossible for a thing always to exist and yet to be destructible. Nor, similarly, can it be **282^a** generated. For of two attributes if B cannot be present without A, the impossibility of A proves the impossibility of B. What always is, then, since it is incapable of ever not being, cannot possibly be generated. But since the contradictory of ' that which is always capable of being' is 5 'that which is not always capable of being'; while 'that which is always capable of not being' is the contrary, whose contradictory in turn is 'that which is not always capable of not being', it is necessary that the contradictories of both terms should be predicable of one and the same thing, and thus that, intermediate between what always is and what always is not, there should be that to which being and not-being are both possible; for the contradictory of 10 each will at times be true of it unless it always exists. Hence that which not always is not will sometimes be and sometimes not be; and it is clear that this is true also of that which cannot always be but sometimes is and therefore sometimes is not.[3] One thing, then, will have the power of being and of not being, and will thus be intermediate between the other two.

Expressed universally our argument is as follows. Let there be two attributes, A and B, not capable of being 15 present in any one thing together, while either A or C and

---

[1] In l. 29 after μὴ εἶναι a full-stop is required instead of a comma. The construction of the following clauses is difficult. The translation given above proceeds on the hypothesis that no stop is required after ἀεὶ ὄν (l. 30) and that δυνατὸν ... ὥστε μὴ εἶναι is equivalent to δυνατὸν μὴ εἶναι. I cannot find another case of δυνατὸν ὥστε, but similar uses of ὥστε are fairly common in Aristotle (see Bonitz, *Ind. Ar.*, p. 873^a 20). οὔτ' ἄπειρον οὔτε πεπερασμένον (sc. χρόνον) is a loose epexegesis of οὐκ ἔστιν ἐν ᾧ χρόνῳ, and perhaps should be preceded by a comma.

[2] Καὶ ἀεὶ μὴ εἶναι is the reading of FJ Simpl. Since the omission of ἀεί in the other MSS. is easily accounted for, it seems best to accept this. (J at the first attempt omitted the καί.)

[3] After ποτε ὄν a comma, not a colon.

either B or D are capable of being present in everything. Then C and D must be predicated of everything of which neither A nor B is predicated. Let E lie between A and B; for that which is neither of two contraries is a mean between them. In E both C and D must be present, for 20 either A or C is present everywhere and therefore in E. Since then A is impossible, C must be present, and the same argument holds of D.[1]

Neither that which always is, therefore, nor that which always is not is either generated or destructible. And clearly whatever is generated or destructible is not eternal. If it were, it would be at once capable of always being and capable of 25 not always being, but it has already been shown[2] that this is impossible. Surely then whatever is ungenerated and in being must be eternal, and whatever is indestructible and in being must equally be so.[3] (I use the words 'ungenerated' and 'indestructible' in their proper sense, 'ungenerated' for that which now is and could not at any previous time have been truly said not to be; 'indestructible' for that which now is and cannot at any future time 30 be truly said not to be.[4]) If, again, the two terms are coincident,[5] if the ungenerated is indestructible, and the indestructible ungenerated, then each of them is coincident

---

[1] The four letters $ABCD$ are to be allotted as follows: A is 'that which is always capable of being' = 'what always is', B is its contrary, 'that which is always capable of not being' = 'what always is not', C is its contradictory, 'that which is not always capable of being', and D is the contradictory of B, 'that which is not always capable of not being'. C and D might also be described by the terms 'what not always is' and 'what not always is not' respectively.

[2] 281ᵇ 18 ff.

[3] The question-mark should come at the end of the line after ὂν δέ, preceded by a comma at εἶναι.

[4] i. e. each term has its third sense as defined in chapter xi (280ᵇ 11, 31).

[5] The term 'coincidence' is used in this passage to express the mutual involution (called by later writers ἀντακολουθία) of predicates. This mutual involution is here described by Aristotle in terms which mean that the two terms 'follow' or 'accompany' one another. But later on (e. g. in 282ᵇ 10, 27, 32) he frequently says simply that one predicate 'follows' another when he means that the two terms are mutually involved. To avoid confusion I have expressed the relation in terms of coincidence throughout.—The ἤ following the parenthesis introduces an alternative proof to the same effect as that which preceded the parenthesis.

with 'eternal'; anything ungenerated is eternal and anything 282^b indestructible is eternal.   This is clear too from the definition of the terms.   Whatever is destructible must be generated ; for it is either ungenerated or generated, but, if ungenerated, it is by hypothesis [1] indestructible.   Whatever, further, is generated must be destructible.   For it is either destructible or indestructible, but, if indestructible, it is by 5 hypothesis [1] ungenerated.

If, however, 'indestructible' and 'ungenerated' are not coincident, there is no necessity that either the ungenerated or the indestructible should be eternal.   But they must be coincident, for the following reasons.   The terms 'generated' and 'destructible' are coincident ; this is obvious from our former remarks, since between what always is and 10 what always is not there is an intermediate which is neither, and that intermediate is the generated and destructible. For whatever is either of these is capable both of being and of not being for a definite time : in either case, I mean, there is a certain period of time during which the thing is and another during which it is not.   Anything therefore which is generated or destructible must be intermediate. 15 Now let A be that which always is and B that which always is not, C the generated, and D the destructible. Then C must be intermediate between A and B.   For in their case there is no time in the direction of either limit,[2] in which either A is not or B is.   But for the generated

---

[1] 281^b 25 ff.   But Aristotle proceeds to give a proof of the mutual involution of these terms.   If the destructible is generated and the generated is destructible, it follows that the ungenerated is eternal and the indestructible is eternal, and this is the thesis set out for proof in 282^a 25.   But the proof here given of the antecedent depends on the assumption that 'ungenerated' and 'indestructible' are coincident, which assumption is now proved.   Aristotle's procedure, however, is needlessly complicated.   Having proved the coincidence of 'generated' and 'destructible' by assuming the coincidence of 'ungenerated' and 'indestructible', he now proves the coincidence of the latter by proving (on other lines) the coincidence of the former.

[2] i. e., in effect, 'neither in the past nor in the future'.   But time, of course, has no limit.   The notion of limit is transferred to the indestructible-ungenerated from the destructible-generated.   The being of the latter class is necessarily limited in both directions, by birth on one side and death on the other, and the same terms limit its notbeing.   These two limits of finite existence are used to describe the two directions of infinite existence.

20 there must be such a time either actually or potentially, though not for A and B in either way. C then will be, and also not be, for a limited length of time, and this is true also of D, the destructible. Therefore each is both generated and destructible. Therefore 'generated' and 'destructible' are coincident. Now let E stand for the ungenerated,
25 F for the generated, G for the indestructible, and H for the destructible. As for F and H, it has been shown that they are coincident. But when terms stand to one another as these do, F and H coincident, E and F never predicated of the same thing but one or other of everything, and G and
30 H likewise, then E and G must needs be coincident. For suppose that E is not coincident with G, then F will be, since either E or F is predicable of everything. But of that of which F is predicated H will be predicable also. H will
283^a then be coincident with G, but this we saw to be impossible. And the same argument shows that G is coincident with E.

Now the relation of the ungenerated (E) to the generated (F) is the same as that of the indestructible (G) to the destructible (H). To say then that there is no reason why anything should not be generated and yet indestructible or
5 ungenerated and yet destroyed, to imagine that in the one case generation and in the other case destruction occurs once for all, is to destroy part of the data.[1] For (1) everything is capable of acting or being acted upon, of being or not being, either for an infinite, or for a definitely limited space of time; and the infinite time is only a possible alternative because it is after a fashion defined, as a length of
10 time which cannot be exceeded. But infinity in one direction is neither infinite nor finite. (2) Further, why, after always existing, was the thing destroyed, why, after an infinity of not being, was it generated, at one moment rather than another? If every moment is alike and the moments are infinite in number, it is clear that a generated or destructible thing existed for an infinite time. It has

---

[1] Aristotle now proceeds to apply his results to the refutation of the view attributed in 280^a 30 to Plato's *Timaeus*. He there promised to give a clearer demonstration of its absurdity when the terms 'generated', 'ungenerated', &c. should be investigated on their own account and apart from the special case of the heaven.

therefore for an infinite time the capacity of not being
(since the capacity of being and the capacity of not being 15
will be present together),[1] if destructible, in the time before
destruction, if generated, in the time after generation. If
then we assume the two capacities to be actualized, opposites will be present together.[2] (3) Further, this second
capacity will be present like the first at every moment, so
that the thing will have for an infinite time the capacity
both of being and of not being; but this has been shown
to be impossible.[3] (4) Again, if the capacity is present prior 20
to the activity, it will be present for all time, even while the
thing was as yet ungenerated and non-existent, throughout
the infinite time in which it was capable of being generated.
At the time, then, when it was not, at that same time it had
the capacity of being, both of being then and of being there-
after, and therefore for an infinity of time.[4]

It is clear also on other grounds that it is impossible 25
that the destructible should not at some time be destroyed.
For otherwise it will always be at once destructible and in
actuality indestructible,[5] so that it will be at the same time

[1] The words ἅμα γὰρ . . . καὶ εἶναι are plainly parenthetical, since the
τὸ μέν, τὸ δέ which follow explain the clause which precedes them.
They should be enclosed in brackets and the colon after χρόνον deleted.

[2] Read ἃ δύναται. Prantl's note is incorrect. The facts are as
follows: ἃ δύναται FM Simpl., ἃ δύνανται EL, ἀδύνατα HJ. Bekker
prints the last, though attested by only one of his MSS.

[3] The third argument is distinct from the second in that the second
arrives at an *absurdum* by actualizing the capacity, while the third
points out that the co-presence of two such capacities has already
been admitted to be impossible. Cf. 282ᵃ 5, 'that which is always
capable of being' is the contrary of 'that which is always capable of
not being'. Alexander seems to have maintained that our third argument was not a distinct argument at all; but the short account of his
view given by Simpl. is not convincing.

[4] A colon is required after ὕστερον. Aristotle is proving that the
capacity was present for infinite time, which in argument (3) he
assumed as evident without proof.

[5] Prantl's note as to the reading in l. 26 is inaccurate. The words
καὶ ἄφθαρτον (not καὶ φθαρτόν) were lacking in the MSS. used both by
Alexander and by Simpl.; and they interpreted the sentence without
those words to mean—'it will be at once eternal and in actuality
destructible'; but 'in actuality destructible' means 'destroyed', and
therefore the assertion is not justified by the context. Alex., however, suggested the insertion of the words καὶ ἄφθαρτον, and Simpl.
says he 'has come across' a manuscript in which the words are found.
καὶ ἄφθαρτον seems to have been added to E upon revision, but all our
other MSS. have the words, and it is best to retain them in the text.

capable of always existing and of not always existing.
Thus the destructible is at some time actually destroyed.
The generable, similarly, has been generated, for it is capable
of having been generated and thus also of not always
existing.[1]

30   We may also see in the following way how impossible it
is either for a thing which is generated to be thenceforward
indestructible, or for a thing which is ungenerated and has
always hitherto existed to be destroyed. Nothing that is by
chance can be indestructible or ungenerated, since the pro-
283[b] ducts of chance and fortune are opposed to what is, or comes
to be, always or usually, while anything which exists for a
time infinite either absolutely or in one direction, is in existence either always or usually. That which is by chance, then,
is by nature such as to exist at one time and not at another.
But in things of that character the contradictory states
5 proceed from one and the same capacity, the matter of the
thing being the cause equally of its existence and of its non-
existence. Hence contradictories would be present together
in actuality.[2]

---

[1] The end of this paragraph from καὶ εἰ γενητόν seems to be a short
statement of the parallel argument with regard to generation. If this
is so we require a comma instead of a full-stop after φθαρτόν. τὸ
φθαρτόν can hardly be the subject of γέγονεν, as Prantl's stopping
suggests. The last words, καὶ μὴ ἀεὶ ἄρα εἶναι, are unsatisfactory,
since, though they draw a true consequence, it is one more directly
appropriate to φθορά than to γένεσις. It is tempting to read καὶ μὴ ἀεὶ
ἄρα μὴ εἶναι. We should then have the relevant consequence and
a more precise parallelism between the two arguments.—The point
of the paragraph as a whole is to remove the possibility of an escape,
by means of a doctrine of unrealized possibilities, from the conclusion
already drawn that what is generated is also destructible. (Simpl.
appositely quotes *Timaeus* 41 A, B, where the permanence of the world-
order depends on the will and promise of the Demiurge.) Aristotle
always maintains that an unrealized possibility in this sense is
inconceivable.

[2] For Prantl's καὶ ἅμα read ἅμα. The καί is omitted by FMJ Simpl.—
The notions of 'chance' (τὸ αὐτόματον) and 'fortune' (τύχη) are fully
discussed in *Phys.* II. iv–vi, the exclusion of the 'necessary' and the
'usual' (283[a] 32) being explained in II. v. It is there plainly implied
that chance had actually been suggested by earlier writers as the
generative cause of the world (196[a] 33, 198[a] 10). The reason why
they had recourse to this notion would be that chance means a cause
quite external to the nature of the thing considered; and thus the
chance generation or destruction of the world would not involve the
consequence that in general and as such the world was either generated
or destructible. Aristotle's reply to the suggestion is simply that
chance necessarily implies intermittent being, so that a chance-

Further, it cannot truly be said of a thing now that it exists last year, nor could it be said last year that it exists now.[1] It is therefore impossible for what once did not exist later to be eternal. For in its later state it will possess the capacity of not existing, only[2] not of not existing at a time when it exists—since then it exists in actuality—but of not existing last year or in the past. Now suppose it to be in actuality what it is capable of being. It will then be true to say now that it does not exist last year. But this is impossible. No capacity relates to being in the past, but always to being in the present or future. It is the same with the notion of an eternity of existence followed later by non-existence. In the later state the capacity will be present for that which is not there in actuality.[3] Actualize, then, the capacity. It will be true to say now that this exists last year or in the past generally.

Considerations also not general like these but proper to the subject show it to be impossible that what was formerly eternal should later be destroyed or that what formerly was not should later be eternal. Whatever is destructible or generated is always alterable. Now alteration is due to contraries, and the things which compose the natural body are the very same that destroy it.[4]

---

eternal is a contradiction in terms. ('Fortune' is a name for chance within the sphere of conduct; and anything which can be caused by chance could also, according to Aristotle, be caused either by intelligence, as in the case of conduct, or by nature, as here. See *Phys.* l. c.)

[1] For ἐστί, ἐστίν read ἔστι, ἔστιν.—The concluding argument is introduced very abruptly, by a formula which shows that in Aristotle's mind the suggestion here criticized is only another form of the appeal to chance just dealt with. The suggestion is that a capacity may be limited in respect of time of fulfilment. Aristotle refutes it by assuming that its authors admit (a) that the *possession* of the capacity is not limited in time, and (b) that any capacity may be actualized.

[2] Before πλήν a comma is required instead of Prantl's full-stop.

[3] οὖ must be taken to stand for ἐκείνου ὅ, as in Simpl.'s paraphrase.—The meaning is that after the thing has ceased to be it still retains its capacity of existing at any time previous to that event.

[4] A comma is required after ἐναντίοις and, for συνίσταται, συνίσταται.

BOOK II

283^b 26   THAT the heaven as a whole neither came into being 1
nor admits of destruction, as some assert, but is one and
eternal, with no end or beginning of its total duration, con-
30 taining and embracing in itself the infinity of time, we may
convince ourselves not only by the arguments already set
forth but also by a consideration of the views of those who
differ from us in providing for its generation. If our view
is a possible one, and the manner of generation which they
284^a assert is impossible, this fact will have great weight in convincing us of the immortality and eternity of the world.
Hence it is well to persuade oneself of the truth of the
ancient and truly traditional theories, that there is some
immortal and divine thing which possesses movement, but
5 movement such as has no limit and is rather itself the limit
of all other movement. A limit is a thing which contains;
and this motion[1], being perfect, contains those imperfect
motions which have a limit and a goal, having itself no
beginning or end, but unceasing through the infinity of
10 time, and of other movements, to some the cause of their
beginning, to others offering the goal. The ancients gave
to the Gods the heaven or upper place, as being alone immortal; and our present argument testifies that it is indestructible and ungenerated. Further, it is unaffected by
15 any mortal discomfort, and, in addition, effortless; for it
needs no constraining necessity to keep it to its path, and
prevent it from moving with some other movement more
natural to itself. Such a constrained movement would
necessarily involve effort—the more so, the more eternal it
were—and would be inconsistent with perfection. Hence
we must not believe the old tale which says that the world
20 needs some Atlas to keep it safe—a tale composed, it would
seem, by men who, like later thinkers, conceived of all the

---

[1] Omit ἡ κυκλοφορία. The words are found only in L, and though
harmless are quite superfluous. There is no reference to κυκλοφορία
in Simpl.'s paraphrase.

upper bodies as earthy and endowed with weight, and
therefore supported it in their fabulous way upon animate
necessity. We must no more believe that than follow Empedocles when he says that the world, by being whirled
round, received a movement quick enough to overpower its 25
own downward tendency, and thus has been kept from
destruction all this time. Nor, again, is it conceivable that
it should persist eternally by the necessitation of a soul.[1]
For a soul could not live in such conditions painlessly or
happily, since the movement involves constraint, being im- 30
posed on the first body, whose natural motion is different,
and imposed continuously.[2] It must therefore be uneasy
and devoid of all rational satisfaction ; for it could not even,
like the soul of mortal animals, take recreation in the bodily
relaxation of sleep. An Ixion's lot must needs possess it, 35
without end or respite. If then, as we said, the view already 284ᵇ
stated of the first motion is a possible one, it is not only
more appropriate so to conceive of its eternity, but also on
this hypothesis alone are we able to advance a theory consistent with popular divinations of the divine nature.[3] But 5
of this enough for the present.

2   Since there are some who say that there is a right and
a left in the heaven, with those who are known as Pythagoreans—to whom indeed the view really belongs—we must
consider whether, if we are to apply these principles to the
body of the universe, we should follow their statement of 10
the matter or find a better way. At the start we may say

[1] The cosmic motions must not be regarded as imposed upon the
body of the cosmos by a world-soul as the human soul imposes movement on the human body. Such a notion necessarily implies constraint
on the part of the body and effort on the part of the soul, and therefore the movement could not be eternal. Aristotle has in mind, no
doubt, the world-soul of the *Timaeus*.

[2] Read εἴπερ κινεῖ φέρεσθαι πεφυκότος . . . ἄλλως καὶ κινεῖ συνεχῶς,
with all MSS. except E. Simpl.'s paraphrase supports this reading.—
The remarks which follow as to the absence of ' rational satisfaction '
recall verbally Plato, *Timaeus* 36 E θείαν ἀρχὴν ἤρξατο [ἡ ψυχή—the
world-soul] ἀπαύστου καὶ ἔμφρονος βίου πρὸς τὸν σύμπαντα χρόνον.

[3] By ' divination ' (μαντεία) Aristotle means, not any religious practice
of prophecy or the like, but simply the inspired guesses of common
sense—τὴν κοινὴν ταύτην ἔννοιαν ἣν ἔχομεν περὶ τῆς ἀπονίας καὶ μακαριό-
τητος τοῦ θείου (Simpl.).

E 2

that, if right and left are applicable, there are prior principles which must first be applied. These principles have been analysed in the discussion of the movements of animals,[1] for the reason that they are proper to animal

15 nature. For in some animals we find all such distinctions of parts as this of right and left clearly present, and in others some; but in plants we find only above and below. Now if we are to apply to the heaven such a distinction of parts, we must expect, as we have said, to find in it also that

20 distinction which in animals is found first of them all. The distinctions are three,[2] namely, above and below, front and its opposite, right and left—all these three oppositions we expect to find in the perfect body—and each may be called a principle. Above is the principle of length, right

25 of breadth, front of depth. Or again we may connect them with the various movements, taking principle to mean that part, in a thing capable of movement, from which movement first begins. Growth starts from above, locomotion from the right, sense-movement from in front (for front is

30 simply the part to which the senses are directed). Hence we must not look for above and below, right and left, front and back, in every kind of body, but only in those which, being animate, have a principle of movement within themselves. For in no inanimate thing do we observe a part from which movement originates. Some do not move at

35 all, some move, but not indifferently in any direction; fire,

285[a] for example, only upward, and earth only to the centre. It is true that we speak of above and below, right and left, in these bodies relatively to ourselves. The reference may be to our own right hands, as with the diviner, or to some similarity to our own members, such as the parts of

5 a statue possess; or we may take the contrary spatial order, calling right that which is to our left, and left that which is to our right.[3] We observe, however, in the things

---

[1] *De Incessu Anim.*, cc. iv, v.
[2] Prantl misprints γάν for γάρ.
[3] Bekker and Prantl are probably right in regarding the words which follow δεξιόν (viz. καὶ . . . ἔμπροσθεν) as spurious, though they are found in all MSS. except E. There is no trace of them in Simpl. or Them.

themselves none of these distinctions; indeed if they are turned round we proceed to speak of the opposite parts as right and left, above and below, front and back. Hence it 10 is remarkable that the Pythagoreans should have spoken of these two principles, right and left, only, to the exclusion of the other four, which have as good a title as they. There is no less difference between above and below or front and back in animals generally than between right and left. 15 The difference is sometimes only one of function,[1] sometimes also one of shape; and while the distinction of above and below is characteristic of all animate things, whether plants or animals, that of right and left is not found in plants. Further, inasmuch as length is prior to breadth, if above is the principle of length, right of breadth, and if the 20 principle of that which is prior is itself prior, then above will be prior to right, or let us say, since 'prior' is ambiguous, prior in order of generation.[2] If, in addition, above is the region from which movement originates, right the region in which it starts, front the region to which it is directed, then on this ground too above has a certain original 25 character as compared with the other forms of position. On these two grounds, then, they may fairly be criticized, first, for omitting the more fundamental principles, and secondly, for thinking that the two they mentioned were attributable equally to everything.

Since we have already determined that functions of this kind belong to things which possess a principle of movement,[3] and that the heaven is animate and possesses a prin- 30 ciple of movement,[4] clearly the heaven must also exhibit

---

[1] The right and left hands, for instance, differ in function but not in shape. It is implied that the difference of function underlies all the oppositions and determines the differences of shape where these occur. The differences of function are summarized above, 284ᵇ25–30.

[2] For the four main kinds of 'priority', see *Cat.* ch. xii (14ᵃ26 ff.). Additional distinctions are made in *Met.* Δ, ch. xi.

[3] i. e. to animals. This is laid down at the beginning of the present chapter, 283ᵇ13, where reference is made to the *De Incessu Animalium.* Cf. also *Phys.* VIII. 4, 254ᵇ7.

[4] Bk. I, 279ᵃ28, where it is stated to be the source of all life and movement. The term 'animate' (ἔμψυχος) has not hitherto been applied to it. The notion that the stars are 'inanimate' is rejected below, 292ᵃ20.

above and below, right and left. We need not be troubled
by the question, arising from the spherical shape of the
world, how there can be a distinction of right and left
285ᵇ within it, all parts being alike and all for ever in motion.
We must think of the world as of something in which right
differs from left in shape as well as in other respects, which
subsequently is included in a sphere. The difference of
function will persist, but will appear not to by reason
5 of the regularity of shape. In the same fashion must
we conceive of the beginning of its movement. For even
if it never began to move, yet it must possess a principle from which it would have begun to move if it had
begun, and from which it would begin again if it came to
a stand. Now by its length I mean the interval between
10 its poles, one pole being above and the other below; for
two hemispheres are specially distinguished from all others
by the immobility of the poles.[1] Further, by 'transverse'
in the universe we commonly mean, not above and below,
but a direction crossing the line of the poles, which, by
implication, is length: for transverse motion is motion
15 crossing motion up and down. Of the poles, that which we
see above us is the lower region, and that which we do not
see is the upper. For right in anything is, as we say, the
region in which locomotion originates, and the rotation of
the heaven originates in the region from which the stars
rise. So this will be the right, and the region where they
20 set the left. If then they begin from the right and move
round to the right, the upper must be the unseen pole. For
if it is the pole we see, the movement will be leftward,
which we deny to be the fact. Clearly then the invisible
pole is above. And those who live in the other hemisphere
25 are above and to the right, while we are below and to the
left. This is just the opposite of the view of the Pythagoreans, who make us above and on the right side and those
in the other hemisphere below and on the left side; the fact

---

[1] The unmoving poles mark out one among the infinite possible
bisections of the sphere as natural and intelligible. We thus arrive,
as explained in what follows, at an 'upper' and a 'lower' hemisphere.

being the exact opposite.[1] Relatively, however, to the
secondary revolution, I mean that of the planets, we are
above and on the right and they are below and on the left. 30
For the principle of their movement has the reverse position, since the movement itself is the contrary of the other:
hence it follows that we are at its beginning and they at its
end. Here we may end our discussion of the distinctions **286ᵃ**
of parts created by the three dimensions and of the consequent differences of position.

3 Since circular motion is not the contrary of the reverse
circular motion, we must consider why there is more than
one motion, though we have to pursue our inquiries at 5
a distance—a distance created not so much by our spatial
position as by the fact that our senses enable us to perceive
very few of the attributes of the heavenly bodies. But let

---

[1] Heath (*Aristarchus*, pp. 231–2) summarizes the argument as
follows: '"Right" is the place from which motion in space starts;
and the motion of the heaven starts from the side where the stars rise,
i.e. the east; therefore the east is "right" and the west "left". If
now (1) you suppose yourself to be lying along the world's axis with
your head towards the *north* pole, your feet towards the *south* pole,
and your right hand towards the east, then clearly the apparent motion
of the stars from east to west is over your *back* from your right side
towards your left; this motion, Aristotle maintains, cannot be called
motion "to the right", and therefore our hypothesis does not fit the
assumption from which we start, namely that the daily rotation "begins
from the right and is carried round towards the right (ἐπὶ τὰ δεξιά)".
We must therefore alter the hypothesis and suppose (2) that you are
lying with your head towards the *south* pole and your feet towards the
north pole. If then your right hand is to the east, the daily motion
begins at your right hand and proceeds over the front of your body
from your right hand to your left.' Heath points out that to us this
still gives a wrong result: the motion across your front will still be
from right to left; but he accepts Simpl.'s explanation that movement
to the front is regarded as rightward and motion to the back as leftward—ἡ γὰρ ἐπὶ δεξιὰ πάντως εἰς τὸ ἔμπροσθέν ἐστι. If this is true,
Heath's account is satisfactory. It is curious that the notion of rightward movement also gives trouble in the cosmology of Plato. Heath
has an entirely different solution of that difficulty, in which the
ordinary sense of 'to the right' is preserved (pp. 160–3). In view of
the solution of the present passage quoted above, perhaps there is
something after all to be said for the assertion of Proclus (*In Timaeum*
220 E), quoted by Heath only to be dismissed, that ἐπὶ δεξιά does not
mean εἰς τὸ δεξιόν but is confined to circular motion and means 'the
direction of a movement imparted by the right hand' (ἐφ᾽ ἃ τὸ δεξιὸν
κινεῖ). The discrimination of right and left in circular motions is
peculiarly difficult and ambiguous, as every child knows; and some
such use of ἐπὶ δεξιά may have been the Greek solution of the termino-
logical problem.

not that deter us. The reason must be sought in the
following facts. Everything which has a function exists
for its function. The activity of God is immortality, i. e.
10 eternal life.[1] Therefore the movement of that which is
divine must be eternal. But such is the heaven, viz.
a divine body, and for that reason to it is given the circular
body whose nature it is to move always in a circle.[2] Why,
then, is not the whole body of the heaven of the same
character as that part? Because there must be something
at rest at the centre of the revolving body; and of that
15 body no part can be at rest, either elsewhere or at the
centre. It could do so only if the body's natural movement
were towards the centre. But the circular movement is
natural, since otherwise it could not be eternal: for
nothing unnatural is eternal.[3] The unnatural is subsequent to the natural, being a derangement of the natural
20 which occurs in the course of its generation.[4] Earth then
has to exist; for it is earth which is at rest at the centre.
(At present we may take this for granted: it shall be explained later.[5]) But if earth must exist, so must fire. For,
if one of a pair of contraries naturally exists, the other, if
it is really contrary, exists also naturally. In some form it
25 must be present, since the matter of contraries is the same.
Also, the positive is prior to its privation (warm, for instance, to cold), and rest and heaviness stand for the priva-

[1] The argument is clear. ' God ' or ' divine ' means ' eternal '. All
body has motion. Therefore the notion of a divine body necessarily
involves the notion of an eternal movement.—Simpl. says wrongly that
θεός here stands for θεῖον σῶμα.

[2] The nature of the circular motion, and the reasons why it alone is
compatible with immutability and the other divine attributes, have
been explained in Bk. I, chaps. iii and iv.—The adjective ' circular '
(ἐγκύκλιος) here and in several other passages of this book is transferred from the motion to the body endowed with it.

[3] The body which is at the centre cannot be of the same nature, and
endowed with the same motion, as that which is at the extremity; for
the actual position and movement of one or the other would in that
case be unnatural. There must therefore be a body whose natural
position is at the centre and whose natural movement is towards the
centre.

[4] All change involves ' derangement ' (ἔκστασις), *Phys.* 222ᵇ 16:
cf. *Phys.* 241ᵇ 2. ἔκστασις is opposed to τελείωσις ('fulfilment', or
movement of a thing towards its ideal nature), *Phys.* 246ᵃ 17, ᵇ 2,
247ᵃ 3.

[5] See ch. xiv.

tion of lightness and movement. But further, if fire and earth exist, the intermediate bodies[1] must exist also : for each element stands in a contrary relation to every other. 30 (This, again, we will here take for granted and try later to explain.[2]) With these four elements generation clearly is involved, since none of them can be eternal : for contraries interact with one another and destroy one another. Further, it is inconceivable that a movable body should be eternal, if its movement cannot be regarded as naturally eternal : 35 and these bodies we know to possess movement.[3] Thus we **286ᵇ** see that generation is necessarily involved. But if so, there must be at least one other circular motion : for a single movement of the whole heaven would necessitate an identical relation of the elements of bodies to one another.[4] This matter 5 also shall be cleared up in what follows : but for the present so much is clear, that the reason why there is more than one circular body is the necessity of generation, which follows on the presence of fire, which, with that of the other bodies, follows on that of earth ; and earth is required because eternal movement in one body necessitates eternal rest in another.

4   The shape of the heaven is of necessity spherical ; for 10 that is the shape most appropriate to its substance and also by nature primary.

---

[1] viz. air and water.

[2] See *De Gen. et Corr.* II. iii, iv.

[3] Retaining the MSS. reading, which is confirmed by Simpl. and Them., τούτων δ' ἐστι κίνησις. If these words are taken to mean ταῦτα δ' ἐστι κινητά, the argument, though summarily stated, is complete and Prantl's conjecture is unnecessary. If it is granted that the sublunary elements move, generation is admitted, unless it can be shown that their movement is such as to be naturally eternal. But it has already been shown (*Phys.* 261ᵃ 31 ff.) that the rectilinear movements must be intermittent.

[4] A. is proving the necessity of the secondary revolution, i. e. that of the planets. 'If', he argues, 'there were only the movement of the fixed stars, and sun and moon were set in it and carried along with it, the varieties of summer and winter and the other seasons would disappear and the daily interchange would not follow its accustomed course. For if the sun were set in Cancer, we should have perpetual summer, and if it were set in Capricorn, perpetual winter : there would be no generation or destruction, not even the varied phases of the moon' (Simpl.). The further discussion promised here is to be found in *De Gen. et Corr.* II. x.

First, let us consider generally which shape is primary
among planes and solids alike. Every plane figure must
15 be either rectilinear or curvilinear. Now the rectilinear is
bounded by more than one line, the curvilinear by one only.
But since in any kind the one is naturally prior to the
many and the simple to the complex, the circle will be the
first of plane figures. Again, if by complete, as previously
20 defined,[1] we mean a thing outside which no part of itself
can be found, and if addition is always possible to the
straight line but never to the circular, clearly the line which
embraces the circle is complete. If then the complete is
prior to the incomplete, it follows on this ground also that
the circle is primary among figures. And the sphere holds
the same position among solids. For it alone is embraced
25 by a single surface, while rectilinear solids have several.
The sphere is among solids what the circle is among plane
figures. Further, those who divide bodies into planes and
generate them out of planes[2] seem to bear witness to the
truth of this. Alone[3] among solids they leave the sphere
30 undivided, as not possessing more than one surface: for the
division into surfaces is not just dividing a whole by cutting
it into its parts, but division of another fashion into parts
different in form.[4] It is clear, then, that the sphere is first
of solid figures.

If, again, one orders figures according to their numbers,
35 it is most natural to arrange them in this way. The circle
287[a] corresponds to the number one, the triangle, being the sum
of two right angles, to the number two. But if one is
assigned to the triangle, the circle will not be a figure
at all.

---

[1] *Phys.* III. 207[a] 8. For the terms of the definition cf. *sup.* 271[b] 31.
This notion of 'perfect' (or 'complete') is presupposed in the opening
chapter of this treatise.—In l. 19 read τῶν αὐτοῦ: the τῶν is omitted
only in E and F.

[2] Cf. *Phys.* VI. 1 and *inf.* Bk. III, ch. i for further criticisms of
these theories. The theory criticized is that expressed by Timaeus
the Pythagorean in Plato's dialogue of that name. (So Simpl. on
298[b] 33.)

[3] Prantl's μόνη is a misprint for μόνην.

[4] Both sphere and circle can of course be divided into parts, but
they cannot be geometrically analysed into constituents not themselves
spherical or circular. The geometrical analysis requires that the
constituent or 'part' shall be different in form from the whole.

Now the first figure belongs to the first body, and the first body is that at the farthest circumference. It follows that the body which revolves with a circular movement must be spherical. The same then will be true of the body 5 continuous with it: for that which is continuous with the spherical is spherical. The same again holds of the bodies between these and the centre. Bodies which are bounded by the spherical and in contact with it must be, as wholes, spherical; and the bodies below the sphere of the planets are contiguous with the sphere above them. The sphere then will be spherical throughout ; for every body within it 10 is contiguous and continuous with spheres.

Again, since the whole revolves, palpably and by assumption, in a circle, and since it has been shown that outside the farthest circumference there is neither void nor place, from these grounds also it will follow necessarily that the heaven is spherical. For if it is to be rectilinear in shape, it will follow that there is place and body and void 15 without it. For a rectilinear figure as it revolves never continues in the same room, but where formerly was body, is now none, and where now is none, body will be in a moment because of the projection at the corners. Similarly, if the world had some other figure with unequal 20 radii, if, for instance, it were lentiform, or oviform, in every case we should have to admit space and void outside the moving body, because the whole body would not always occupy the same room.[1]

Again, if the motion of the heaven is the measure of all movements whatever in virtue of being alone continuous and regular and eternal, and if, in each kind, the measure is 25 the minimum, and the minimum movement is the swiftest, then, clearly, the movement of the heaven must be the swiftest of all movements. Now of lines which return upon themselves[2] the line which bounds the circle is the shortest;

---

[1] This depends, as Simpl. observes, after Alexander, on the position of the axis of revolution. In the case of a perfect sphere alone the position of the axis is immaterial.

[2] Reading ἀφ' ἑαυτοῦ ἐφ' ἑαυτό, with Simpl. and the consensus of the MSS. The τοῦ and τό in Prantl's text are conjectural insertions. J has ἀφ' αὑτοῦ ἐφ' αὑτό.

and that movement is the swiftest which follows the shortest line.[1] Therefore, if the heaven moves in a circle
30 and moves more swiftly than anything else, it must necessarily be spherical.

Corroborative evidence may be drawn from the bodies whose position is about the centre. If earth is enclosed by water, water by air, air by fire, and these similarly by the upper bodies—which while not continuous are yet contiguous
287ᵇ with them [2]—and if the surface of water is spherical, and that which is continuous with or embraces the spherical must itself be spherical, then on these grounds also it is clear that the heavens are spherical. But the surface of water
5 is seen to be spherical if we take as our starting-point the fact that water naturally tends to collect in a hollow place— 'hollow' meaning 'nearer the centre'. Draw from the centre the lines AB, AC, and let their extremities be joined by the straight line BC. The line AD, drawn to the base of the triangle, will be shorter than either of the radii.[3]
10 Therefore the place in which it terminates will be a hollow place. The water then will collect there until equality is established, that is until the line AE is equal to the two radii. Thus water forces its way to the ends of the radii, and there only will it rest: but the line which connects the extremities of the radii is circular: therefore the surface of the water BEC is spherical.

15 It is plain from the foregoing that the universe is spherical. It is plain, further, that it is turned (so to speak) with a finish which no manufactured thing nor anything

---

[1] This is true if equality of effort (ἀπὸ τῆς αὐτῆς δυνάμεως Simpl.) is postulated. In a word, the underlying notion is rather the comparative *economy* than the comparative *swiftness* of movements.—For the origin of this argument Simpl. refers to *Tim.* 33 B.

[2] 'Continuous', 'contiguous', and the related terms are defined in *Phys.* V. iii. If these bodies were continuous with the heavenly body they would have to move with the same motion as it.

[3]

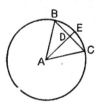

else within the range of our observation can even approach. For the matter of which these are composed does not admit of anything like the same regularity and finish as the substance of the enveloping body ; since with each step 20 away from earth the matter manifestly becomes finer in the same proportion as water is finer than earth.

5 Now there are two ways of moving along a circle, from *A* to *B* or from *A* to *C*,[1] and we have already explained[2] that these movements are not contrary to one another. But nothing which concerns the eternal can be a matter of 25 chance or spontaneity, and the heaven and its circular motion are eternal. We must therefore ask why this motion takes one direction and not the other. Either this is itself an ultimate fact or there is an ultimate fact behind it. It may seem evidence of excessive folly or excessive zeal to try to provide an explanation of some things, or of every- 30 thing, admitting no exception. The criticism, however, is not always just : one should first consider what reason there is for speaking, and also what kind of certainty is looked for, whether human merely or of a more cogent kind.[3] When any one shall succeed in finding proofs of greater precision, **288**^a gratitude will be due to him for the discovery, but at present we must be content with a probable solution.[4] If nature always follows the best course possible, and, just as upward movement is the superior form of rectilinear move-ment, since the upper region is more divine than the lower, 5 so forward movement is superior to backward, then front and back exhibits, like right and left, as we said before[5] and

If *A* is the 'right from which movement starts, why should the movement be towards *B* rather than towards *C*? Probably, answers Aristotle, because movement towards *B* is 'forward' and movement towards *C* 'backward' motion.

[2] I. iv.

[3] Bekker and Prantl prefer L's καρτερικώτερον to the καρτερώτερον of all other MSS. It is difficult to imagine why. There is good Platonic parallel for the use of καρτερός in this connexion (*Phaedo* 77 A, *Theaet.* 169 B).

[4] A similar caution is repeated at the beginning of ch. xii, 291^b 25. For this use of φαινόμενον cf. Bonitz, *Ind. Ar.* 809^a 24.

[5] Reading, with Prantl, ἔχει δὴ εἴπερ, and accepting his punctuation.

as the difficulty just stated itself suggests, the distinction of prior and posterior, which provides a reason and so solves our difficulty. Supposing that nature is ordered in the
10 best way possible, this may stand as the reason of the fact mentioned. For it is best to move with a movement simple and unceasing, and, further, in the superior of two possible directions.

We have next to show that the movement of the heaven **6**
15 is regular and not irregular. This applies only to the first heaven and the first movement; for the lower spheres exhibit a composition of several movements into one. If the movement is uneven, clearly there will be acceleration, maximum speed, and retardation, since these appear in all
20 irregular motions. The maximum may occur either at the starting-point or at the goal or between the two; and we expect natural motion to reach its maximum at the goal, unnatural motion at the starting-point, and missiles midway between the two.[1] But circular movement, having no be-

The passage as punctuated by Bekker is untranslatable. The apodosis undoubtedly begins at the word ἔχει. EL give ἔχει δὲ εἴπερ, the remaining MSS. ἔχει εἴπερ.—The existence of a 'front' and 'back' in the world was asserted in ch. ii. The priority of 'up', 'right', and 'front' over 'down', 'left', and 'back' is assumed in the same chapter, 284ᵇ 24.—The gist of the present rather involved and hesitating statement is that the only way to account for the direction of the heavenly movements is by means of these oppositions and the priority commonly attributed in each to one term over the other.

[1] It appears from *Meteorologica* I. iv, 341ᵇ—342ª that meteors and shooting stars come under the notion of 'missiles' or 'things thrown'. Their motion is compared to that of the stone of a fruit when it is made to fly through the air by being squeezed out from between the fingers. Ordinary throwing, e.g. of a stone or javelin, would of course also be included.—Simpl. and, by his report, Alexander are much puzzled by the statement in the text. Simpl. makes the wild suggestion that A. here regards animal movements as 'missile' motion, in that they are neither upward nor downward but horizontal. Alex. suggests that 'missile' movements may be said to have their maximum between goal and starting-point, because every earthly body has its goal either up or down, and the whole of the 'missile' movement, from beginning to end, takes place in the middle region. Alex. is probably right. It is to be remembered that all movement is either natural or unnatural, and that 'missile' movement can only be distinguished in principle as a mixture of the two; further that the body thrown must be composed of one or more of the four elementary bodies. 'Throwing' is thought of as a forced horizontal motion put upon one of these bodies, each of which has a 'goal', down (or up), and a 'starting-point', up (or down). In such a motion the maximum

ginning or limit or middle in the direct sense of the words,
has neither whence nor whither nor middle: for in time it
is eternal, and in length it returns upon itself without a 25
break. If then its movement has no maximum, it can
have no irregularity, since irregularity is produced by retardation and acceleration. Further, since everything that
is moved is moved by something, the cause of the irregularity of movement must lie either in the mover or in the
moved or in both. For if the mover moved not always 30
with the same force, or if the moved were altered and did
not remain the same, or if both were to change, the result
might well be an irregular movement in the moved. But
none of these possibilities can be conceived as actual in the
case of the heavens. As to that which is moved, we have
shown that it is primary and simple and ungenerated and 288^b
indestructible and generally unchanging; and the mover
has an even better right to these attributes. It is the
primary that moves the primary, the simple the simple,
the indestructible and ungenerated that which is indestructible and ungenerated. Since then that which is moved, 5
being a body, is nevertheless unchanging, how should the
mover, which is incorporeal, be changed?

It follows then, further, that the motion cannot be
irregular. For if irregularity occurs, there must be change
either in the movement as a whole, from fast to slow and
slow to fast, or in its parts. That there is no irregularity in
the parts is obvious, since, if there were, some divergence 10
of the stars would have taken place[1] before now in the
infinity of time, as one moved slower and another faster:
but no alteration of their intervals is ever observed. Nor
again is a change in the movement as a whole admissible.
Retardation is always due to incapacity, and incapacity is
unnatural. The incapacities of animals, age, decay, and the 15
like, are all unnatural, due, it seems, to the fact that the

cannot be said to be attained at either terminus, since neither terminus
is involved, but only 'between the two'. This means that in the case
of natural motion 'goal' must be taken to be the natural place of the
body, which is also the 'starting-point' of unnatural motion in the
same body. In 'throwing', therefore, there is neither starting-point
nor goal, but all is in the intermediate region.

[1] For γεγόνει read ἐγεγόνει with FHLMJ.

whole animal complex is made up of materials which differ
in respect of their proper places, and no single part occupies
its own place. If therefore that which is primary contains
20 nothing unnatural, being simple and unmixed and in its
proper place and having no contrary, then it has no place
for incapacity, nor, consequently, for retardation or (since
acceleration involves retardation) for acceleration. Again,
it is inconceivable that the mover should first show incapacity for an infinite time, and capacity afterwards for
another infinity. For clearly nothing which, like incapacity,
25 is unnatural ever continues for an infinity of time ; nor does
the unnatural endure as long as the natural, or any form of
incapacity as long as the capacity.¹ But if the movement
is retarded it must necessarily be retarded for an infinite
time.² Equally impossible is perpetual acceleration or
perpetual retardation. For such movement would be infinite and indefinite,³ but every movement, in our view,
30 proceeds from one point to another and is definite in
character. Again, suppose one assumes a minimum time
in less than which the heaven could not complete its movement. For, as a given walk or a given exercise on the harp
cannot take any and every time, but every performance has
its definite minimum time which is unsurpassable, so, one
might suppose, the movement of the heaven could not be
289ª completed in any and every time. But in that case perpetual acceleration is impossible (and, equally, perpetual
retardation : for the argument holds of both and each),⁴

¹ Reading οὐδ' ὅλως, with all MSS. except E, which Prantl follows
in reading οὐδ' ἄλλως.—The effect of ἄλλως is to make the unnatural
one species or department within the general notion of incapacity.
ὅλως has much more varied uses and enables one to avoid this
implication.
² i. e. equality of duration must be supposed between the incapacity
(retardation) and the preceding capacity, as assumed in the foregoing
argument, in which infinity (sc. in *one* direction) is attributed to each.
For if the speed of movement has been everlastingly increasing, and
now begins to decrease, it is impossible to suppose anything else but
that it will decrease everlastingly.
³ viz. in respect of its speed. The hypothesis now considered is
retardation or acceleration not balanced by its opposite but having
neither beginning nor end, i. e. infinite in *both* directions.
⁴ Prantl's stopping needs correction. The words εἰ δὲ μή . . . θάτερον
should be enclosed within brackets.

if we may take acceleration to proceed by identical or increasing additions of speed and for an infinite time. The remaining alternative is to say that the movement exhibits 5 an alternation of slower and faster: but this is a mere fiction and quite inconceivable. Further, irregularity of this kind would be particularly unlikely to pass unobserved, since contrast makes observation easy.

That there is one heaven, then, only, and that it is ungenerated and eternal, and further that its movement is regular, has now been sufficiently explained. 10

7 We have next to speak of the stars, as they are called, of their composition, shape, and movements. It would be most natural and consequent upon what has been said that each of the stars should be composed of that substance in 15 which their path lies,[1] since, as we said, there is an element whose natural movement is circular. In so saying we are only following the same line of thought as those who say that the stars are fiery because they believe the upper body to be fire, the presumption being that a thing is composed of the same stuff as that in which it is situated. The warmth and light which proceed from them are caused by the friction 20 set up in the air by their motion. Movement tends to create fire in wood, stone, and iron ; and with even more reason should it have that effect on air, a substance which is closer to fire than these.[2] An example is that of missiles, which as they move are themselves fired so strongly that leaden balls are melted ; and if they are fired the surround- 25 ing air must be similarly affected. Now while the missiles are heated by reason of their motion in air, which is turned into fire by the agitation produced by their movement,[3] the upper bodies are carried on a moving sphere, so that, though they are not themselves fired, yet the air underneath 30 the sphere of the revolving body is necessarily heated by its

[1] i. e. of the same substance as the spheres to which their motion is due.

[2] A colon is required after the word ἀήρ in l. 23.

[3] πληγή seems to stand here for the continuous beating of the missile upon the air rather than for a single blow. Cf. Simpl. 439. 25 ὑπὸ τῆς . . . πληγῆς καὶ παρατρίψεως. The same use recurs below, 291ᵃ 17.

motion, and particularly in that part where the sun is attached to it.[1] Hence warmth increases as the sun gets nearer or higher or overhead. Of the fact, then, that the
35 stars are neither fiery nor move in fire, enough has been said.

289^b Since changes evidently occur not only in the position of **8** the stars but also in that of the whole heaven, there are three possibilities. Either (1) both are at rest, or (2) both are in motion, or (3) the one is at rest and the other in motion.

(1) That both should be at rest is impossible; for, if the
5 earth is at rest, the hypothesis does not account for the observations; and we take it as granted that the earth is at rest. It remains either that both are moved, or that the one is moved and the other at rest.

(2) On the view, first, that both are in motion, we have the absurdity that the stars and the circles move with the same speed, i. e. that the pace of every star is that of the circle in
10 which it moves. For star and circle are seen to come back to the same place at the same moment; from which it follows that the star has traversed the circle and the circle has completed its own movement, i. e. traversed its own circumference, at one and the same moment. But it is difficult to conceive that the pace of each star should be
15 exactly proportioned to the size of its circle. That the pace of each circle should be proportionate to its size is not absurd but inevitable: but that the same should be true of the movement of the stars contained in the circles is quite

---

[1] The stars are not themselves ignited because the substance of which they are composed cannot be transmuted into any other as fire, air, and the other sublunary substances can. It is, however, legitimate to object to the above account that fire, not air, is the substance in contact with the spheres, and that only with the innermost. How, then, is air ignited by the movement of the spheres? Alex. and Simpl. agree that 'air' must in some sense include fire (or ὑπέκκαυμα, the 'fuel of fire' which occupies the outer place); but that, even if true, will not solve the difficulties. The view here advanced is nowhere fully worked out; but some further suggestions are made in *Meteor.* I. iii and iv. Cf. Heath, *Aristarchus,* pp. 241–2. It seems certain that what Aristotle meant was that the 'fire' which is in contact with the spheres is ignited and agitated by their motion and the air beneath by it (341^a 2–3 and 30–31).

incredible. For if, on the one hand, we suppose that the star which moves on the greater circle is necessarily swifter, clearly we also admit that if stars shifted their position so as to exchange circles, the slower would become swifter and [20] the swifter slower. But this would show that their movement was not their own, but due to the circles. If, on the other hand, the arrangement was a chance combination, the coincidence in every case of a greater circle with a swifter movement of the star contained in it is too much to believe. In one or two cases it might not inconceivably fall out so, [25] but to imagine it in every case alike is a mere fiction. Besides, chance has no place in that which is natural, and what happens everywhere and in every case is no matter of chance.

(3) The same absurdity is equally plain[1] if it is supposed that the circles stand still and that it is the stars themselves which move. For it will follow that the outer stars are the swifter, and that the pace of the stars corresponds to [30] the size of their circles.

Since, then, we cannot reasonably suppose either that both are in motion or that the star alone moves, the remaining alternative is that the circles should move, while the stars are at rest and move with the circles to which they are attached. Only on this supposition are we involved in no absurd consequence. For, in the first place, the quicker movement of the larger circle is natural when all the circles [35] are attached to the same centre. Whenever bodies are **290**[a] moving with their proper motion, the larger moves quicker. It is the same here with the revolving bodies: for the arc intercepted by two radii will be larger in the larger circle, and hence it is not surprising that the revolution of the larger circle should take the same time as [5] that of the smaller. And secondly, the fact that the heavens do not break in pieces follows not only from this

---

[1] Bekker and Prantl read ταῦτα instead of τὰ αὐτά, which is the reading of all MSS. and of Simpl. The alteration is unnecessary. The difficulty is the same as that pointed out in the preceding argument—an unaccountable correspondence between the size of the circle and the speed of the star's movement.

but also from the proof already given[1] of the continuity of the whole.

Again, since the stars are spherical, as our opponents assert and we may consistently admit, inasmuch as we construct them out of the spherical body, and since the spherical body has two movements proper to itself, namely rolling and spinning,[2] it follows that if the stars have a movement of their own, it will be one of these. But neither is observed. (1) Suppose them to *spin*. They would then stay where they were, and not change their place, as, by observation and general consent, they do. Further, one would expect them all to exhibit the same movement: but the only star which appears to possess this movement is the sun, at sunrise or sunset, and this appearance is due not to the sun itself but to the distance from which we observe it. The visual ray being excessively prolonged becomes weak and wavering.[3] The same reason probably accounts for the apparent twinkling of the fixed stars and the absence of twinkling in the planets. The planets are near, so that the visual ray reaches them in its full vigour, but when it comes to the fixed stars it is quivering because of the distance and its excessive extension; and its tremor produces an appearance of movement in the star: for it makes no difference whether movement is set up in the ray or in the object of vision.

(2) On the other hand, it is also clear that the stars do not *roll*. For rolling involves rotation: but the 'face',

---

[1] Cf. c. iv. But there is no attempt to prove continuity in the *De Caelo*.

[2] By 'spinning' is meant rotation on a stationary axis, by 'rolling' a forward movement in which a body turns completely round in a distance equal to its own circumference. See Heath, *Aristarchus*, pp. 233-5.

[3] The term ὄψις (= visual ray) belongs to pre-Aristotelian psychology. Cf. Plato, *Meno*, 76 C-D. Aristotle's use of it here and elsewhere (e. g. *Meteor.* III. iv, 373ᵇ 2) seems to commit him 'to the view that the eye sees by rays issuing from a native fire within it' (Beare, *Greek Theories of Elementary Cognition*, p. 66, n. 1). But his own argument, when dealing with vision, is to the contrary effect. 'In seeing we take something in, not give something out' (*Top.* 105ᵇ 6); and the process is 'from object to eye, not conversely' (Beare, p. 86). Aristotle must be supposed here to be adopting popular or Platonic terminology.

as it is called, of the moon is always seen.[1] Therefore, since any movement of their own which the stars possessed would presumably be one proper to themselves, and no such movement is observed in them, clearly they have no movement of their own.

There is, further, the absurdity that nature has bestowed 30 upon them no organ appropriate to such movement. For nature leaves nothing to chance, and would not, while caring for animals, overlook things so precious. Indeed, nature seems deliberately to have stripped them of everything which makes self-originated progression possible, and to have removed them as far as possible from things which have organs of movement. This is just why it seems 35 proper that the whole heaven and every star should be **290^b** spherical. For while of all shapes the sphere is the most convenient for movement in one place, making possible, as it does, the swiftest and most self-contained motion, for forward movement it is the most unsuitable, least of all 5 resembling shapes which are self-moved, in that it has no dependent or projecting part, as a rectilinear figure has, and is in fact as far as possible removed in shape from ambulatory bodies. Since, therefore, the heavens have to move in one place, and the stars are not required to move themselves forward, it is natural that both should be spherical— 10 a shape which best suits the movement of the one and the immobility of the other.

9   From all this it is clear that the theory that the movement of the stars produces a harmony, i. e. that the sounds they make are concordant, in spite of the grace and originality with which it has been stated, is nevertheless 15 untrue.[2] Some thinkers suppose that the motion of bodies

---

[1] It has been objected to Aristotle that if the moon always shows the same side to us it is thereby proved that it does rotate upon its axis. But such rotation (incidental, in Aristotle's view, to the movement of the sphere) is quite different from the rotation involved in 'rolling', which Aristotle is here concerned to deny. See Heath, p. 235.

[2] The doctrine of the 'harmony of the spheres' is no doubt, as Simpl. says, Pythagorean. The most famous statement of the doctrine is in Plato's *Republic* (Myth of Er, 617B), and the ratios given to the planets in *Timaeus*, 35B, seem to have a musical significance. For a discussion of the doctrine see Heath, *Aristarchus*, pp. 105-15.

of that size must produce a noise, since on our earth the
motion of bodies far inferior in size and in speed of movement has that effect. Also, when the sun and the moon,
they say, and all the stars, so great in number and in size,
20 are moving with so rapid a motion, how should they not
produce a sound immensely great? Starting from this
argument and from the observation that their speeds, as
measured by their distances, are in the same ratios as
musical concordances, they assert that the sound given
forth by the circular movement of the stars is a harmony.
Since, however, it appears unaccountable that we should
25 not hear this music, they explain this by saying that the
sound is in our ears from the very moment of birth and is
thus indistinguishable from its contrary silence, since sound
and silence are discriminated by mutual contrast. What
happens to men, then, is just what happens to coppersmiths,
who are so accustomed to the noise of the smithy that it
30 makes no difference to them. But, as we said before,
melodious and poetical as the theory is, it cannot be a true
account of the facts. There is not only the absurdity of our
hearing nothing, the ground of which they try to remove,
but also the fact that no effect other than sensitive is
produced upon us. Excessive noises, we know, shatter the
35 solid bodies even of inanimate things: the noise of thunder,
291^a for instance, splits rocks and the strongest of bodies. But
if the moving bodies are so great, and the sound which
penetrates to us is proportionate to their size, that sound
must needs reach us in an intensity many times that of
thunder, and the force of its action must be immense.
5 Indeed the reason why we do not hear, and show in our
bodies none of the effects of violent force, is easily given:
it is that there is no noise. But not only is the explanation
evident; it is also a corroboration of the truth of the views
we have advanced. For the very difficulty which made
the Pythagoreans say that the motion of the stars produces
10 a concord corroborates our view. Bodies which are themselves in motion, produce noise and friction: but those
which are attached or fixed to a moving body, as the parts
to a ship, can no more create noise, than a ship on a river

moving with the stream. Yet by the same argument one might say it was absurd that on a large vessel the motion of mast and poop should not make a great noise, and the like 15 might be said of the movement of the vessel itself. But sound is caused when a moving body is enclosed in an unmoved body, and cannot be caused by one enclosed in, and continuous with, a moving body which creates no friction. We may say, then, in this matter that if the heavenly bodies moved in a generally diffused mass of air or fire, as every one supposes, 20 their motion would necessarily cause a noise of tremendous strength and such a noise would necessarily reach and shatter us.[1] Since, therefore, this effect is evidently not produced, it follows that none of them can move with the motion either of animate nature or of constraint.[2] It is as though nature had foreseen the result, that if their move- 25 ment were other than it is, nothing on this earth could maintain its character.

That the stars are spherical and are not self-moved, has now been explained.

10   With their order—I mean the position of each, as 30 involving the priority of some and the posteriority of others, and their respective distances from the extremity— with this astronomy may be left to deal, since the astro- nomical discussion is adequate.[3] This discussion shows that the movements of the several stars depend, as regards the varieties of speed which they exhibit, on the distance

---

[1] Prantl misprints διακναίεν for διακναίειν.

[2] If the stars moved in a non-moving medium either with a self-originated motion, like that of an animal, or with a motion imposed on them by external force, like that of a stone thrown, a great and destructive noise would result. There is no such noise or destruction. Therefore they do not so move. The Pythagorean doctrine is thus used to corroborate a conclusion already reached. It might be objected that Aristotle has already postulated friction with another substance to account for the brightness of the stars, and that this friction might well be expected to be accompanied with noise as in the case of missiles on the earth.

[3] The tone of this reference to 'astronomy', as well as the present tense in the verb λέγεται, suggest that Aristotle is not here referring to other works of his own but to contemporary works on astronomy, current in the school, by other writers. These sentences also clearly imply that 'astronomy' is more empirical in its methods than the De Caelo. Cf. infra, 291ᵇ21.—In l. 29 Prantl's ὅ is a misprint for ὄν.

35 of each from the extremity. It is established that the outermost revolution of the heavens is a simple movement 291^b and the swiftest of all, and that the movement of all other bodies is composite and relatively slow, for the reason that each is moving on its own circle with the reverse motion to that of the heavens. This at once leads us to expect that the body which is nearest to that first simple revolution 5 should take the longest time to complete its circle, and that which is farthest from it the shortest, the others taking a longer time the nearer they are and a shorter time the farther away they are. For it is the nearest body which is most strongly influenced, and the most remote, by reason of its distance, which is least affected, the influence on the intermediate bodies varying, as the mathematicians show, 10 with their distance.[1]

With regard to the shape of each star, the most reasonable 11 view is that they are spherical. It has been shown [2] that it is not in their nature to move themselves, and, since nature is no wanton or random creator, clearly she will have 15 given things which possess no movement a shape particularly unadapted to movement. Such a shape is the sphere, since it possesses no instrument of movement. Clearly then their mass will have the form of a sphere.[3] Again, what

---

[1] In regard to 'order' Aristotle only seeks to explain one point which might present a difficulty. It would be natural to expect the moon, which is the nearest planet to the earth, to have the slowest motion; but in fact it is the swiftest of the planets. His answer is that the movement of the planets, being the reverse of that of the outer heaven, is hampered by proximity to it; and the planet nearest to the earth is least influenced and therefore moves swiftest. Simpl. raises the objection: is not the planetary motion then in some degree constrained or unnatural? He quotes with approval from Alex. the reply: 'No: for the planetary sphere is not unwilling. This accords with its purpose and desire. It may be necessity, but it is also good, and recognized as such.' Simpl. is not altogether satisfied by this solution.

[2] Ch. viii.

[3] Simpl. notes a circle in Aristotle's argument, since he has already used the spherical shape of the stars to prove that they have no independent motion (c. viii). (The same charge is brought against Aristotle by Dreyer, *Planetary Systems*, p. 111.) He is not satisfied with Alex.'s rejoinder that neither of these arguments stands alone. The true answer is that the argument of c. viii is explicitly based, in respect of the spherical shape of the stars, on a premise borrowed from the opposition: see 290^a 7. Aristotle's own proof of the matter precedes it. This argument is therefore in order.

holds of one holds of all, and the evidence of our eyes shows us that the moon is spherical. For how else should the moon as it waxes and wanes show for the most part 20 a crescent-shaped or gibbous figure, and only at one moment a half-moon? And astronomical arguments[1] give further confirmation; for no other hypothesis accounts for the crescent shape of the sun's eclipses. One, then, of the heavenly bodies being spherical, clearly the rest will be spherical also.

12   There are two difficulties, which may very reasonably here be raised, of which we must now attempt to state the 25 probable solution:[2] for we regard the zeal of one whose thirst after philosophy leads him to accept even slight indications where it is very difficult to see one's way, as a proof rather of modesty than of over-confidence.

Of, many such problems one of the strangest is the problem why we find the greatest number of movements in 30 the intermediate bodies, and not, rather, in each successive body a variety of movement proportionate to its distance from the primary motion. For we should expect, since the primary body shows one motion only, that the body which is nearest to it should move with the fewest movements, say two, and the one next after that with three, or some similar arrangement. But the opposite is the case. The 35 movements of the sun and moon are fewer than those of 292ᵃ some of the planets. Yet these planets are farther from the centre and thus nearer to the primary body than they, as observation has itself revealed. For we have seen the moon, half-full, pass beneath the planet Mars, which 5 vanished on its shadow side and came forth by the bright and shining part.[3] Similar accounts of other stars are

---

[1] See note on 291ᵃ 32.

[2] See note on 288ᵃ 2.

[3] Brandis (Berlin Aristotle, vol. IV, 497ᵇ 13) quotes a scholium to the effect that Alexander in his Commentary said it was Mercury, not Mars. Both Simpl. and Them., however, give Mars without question. If it was Mars, a calculation of Kepler's (*Astronomia Nova*, 1609, p. 323) fixes the date. 'Inveni,' he writes, 'longissima inductione per annos L, ab anno quindecimo ad finem vitae Aristotelis, non potuisse esse alio die, quam in vespera diei IV Aprilis, anno ante CHRISTI vulgarem epocham CCCLVII, cum Aristoteles XXI annorum audiret

given by the Egyptians and Babylonians, whose observations have been kept for very many years past, and from
whom much of our evidence about particular stars is
derived.[1]

10 A second difficulty which may with equal justice be
raised is this. Why is it that the primary motion includes
such a multitude of stars that their whole array seems to
defy counting, while of the other stars[2] each one is separated
off, and in no case do we find two or more attached to the
same motion?[3]

On these questions, I say, it is well that we should seek
15 to increase our understanding, though we have but little to
go upon, and are placed at so great a distance from the
facts in question. Nevertheless there are certain principles
on which if we base our consideration we shall not find this
difficulty by any means insoluble. We may object that we
have been thinking of the stars as mere bodies, and as units
20 with a serial order indeed but entirely inanimate; but
should rather conceive them as enjoying life and action.
On this view the facts cease to appear surprising. For it is
natural that the best-conditioned of all things should have
its good without action, that that which is nearest to it
should achieve it by little and simple action, and that which
is farther removed by a complexity of actions, just as with
25 men's bodies one is in good condition without exercise at
all, another after a short walk, while another requires
running and wrestling and hard training,[4] and there are yet

Eudoxum, ut ex Diogene Laërtio constat.' Diogenes' date for
Aristotle's birth is in fact Ol. 99, 1 (384–3 B.C.): Aristotle would
therefore be 27 at the date arrived at. The calculation for Mercury
does not appear to have been made.

[1] See note on 270ᵇ 14.

[2] i.e. the planets.

[3] The term φορά (motion) is transferred from the motion itself to the
sphere which imparts the motion.

[4] There seems to be no parallel for the use of the word κόνισις
(tr. 'hard training') in connexion with the exercises of the palaestra,
though κονίστρα is used in post-Aristotelian writers for the arena.
Simpl. says the term stands for the training of the wrestler, διὰ τὸ ἐν
κόνει γυμνάζεσθαι τὰ παλαιστρικά. Bywater (*J. of Phil.* xxviii, p. 241)
objects that the third term in the phrase should be a distinct form of
exercise from running or wrestling, and suggests κἀκοντίσεως. Perhaps
it is best to keep the text, though there can be no certainty that it is
right.

others who however hard they worked themselves could
never secure this good, but only some substitute for it.   To
succeed often or in many things is difficult.   For instance,
to throw ten thousand Coan throws with the dice would be 30
impossible, but to throw one or two is comparatively easy.[1]
In action, again, when A has to be done to get B, B to
get C, and C to get D, one step or two present little
difficulty, but as the series extends the difficulty grows· 292ᵇ
We must, then, think of the action of the lower stars as
similar to that of animals and plants.   For on our earth
it is man that has the greatest variety of actions—for there
are many goods that man can secure; hence his actions are
various[2] and directed to ends beyond them—while the
perfectly conditioned has no need of action, since it is itself 5
the end, and action always requires two terms, end and
means.   The lower animals have less variety of action than
man; and plants perhaps have little action and of one kind
only.[3]   For either they have but one attainable good (as
indeed man has), or, if several, each contributes directly to 10
their ultimate good.[4]   One thing then has and enjoys the

---

[1] Prantl's Κῴους rests on one MS. (H) and was known as an alternative reading to Simpl.   Two MSS. (EL) give Χίους, two others (FM)
χίους ἢ κώους.   J has χιλίους χωλούς, with χίους ἢ κωίους in the margin.
Simpl. thinks the point is the size of the dice (ὡς μεγάλων ἀστραγάλων
ἐν ἀμφοτέραις γινομένων ταῖς νήσοις).   Prantl takes the impossibility to
be a succession of good throws or 'sixes', and therefore prefers
'Coan' to 'Chian', which according to Pollux was used for the worst
throw.   The impossibility is clearly the same whether the worst throw
or the best is intended; but, since success is implied by the context,
I have followed Prantl.   The double reading Χίους ἢ Κῴους may however be right.

[2] Reading πράττει, with FHMJ and Bekker, for Prantl's πράττειν
(EL).

[3] The long parenthesis (l. 3 πολλῶν γάρ to l. 7 ἕνεκα) in Prantl's text
breaks the structure of the sentence and should be removed.   The
succession of colons which results (for a colon must be marked after
πράξεις in l. 3) is best broken by placing full-stops after φυτῶν (l. 2),
ἕνεκα (l. 4), ἕνεκα (l. 7).

[4] If there is more than one good, e. g. nutriment and propagation,
each is a constituent of the plant's 'good' in the final sense.   To be
able to accept something merely as a means to something else, i. e. as
indirectly good, is a distinctive mark of a higher development.   Thus
the variety here indicated as characteristic of human action lies not
so much in the superior range of human desires (though that also is
a fact) as in the variety and complexity of the means by which man
effects their satisfaction.

ultimate good, other things attain to it, one immediately[1]
by few steps, another by many, while yet another does not
even attempt to secure it but is satisfied to reach a point
not far removed from that consummation.　Thus, taking
health as the end, there will be one thing that always
possesses health, others that attain it, one by reducing
flesh, another by running and thus reducing flesh, another
15 by taking steps to enable himself to run, thus further
increasing the number of movements, while another cannot
attain health itself, but only running or reduction of flesh,
so that one or other of these is for such a being the end.[2]
For while it is clearly best for any being to attain the real
end, yet, if that cannot be, the nearer it is to the best the
20 better will be its state.　It is for this reason that the earth
moves not at all and the bodies near to it with few movements.　For they do not attain the final end, but only come
as near to it as their share in the divine principle permits.[3]
But the first heaven finds it immediately with a single
25 movement, and the bodies intermediate between the first
and last heavens attain it indeed, but at the cost of a multiplicity of movement.[4]

As to the difficulty that into the one primary motion
is crowded a vast multitude of stars, while of the other
stars each has been separately given special movements
of its own, there is in the first place this reason for regarding
the arrangement as a natural one.　In thinking of the life

---

[1] Reading εὐθύς for ἐγγύς. Cf. l. 20 below. ἐγγύς is in all the
MSS., but is quite intolerable in view of the general contrast between
attainment and approximation made here and repeated below.　The
influence of ἐγγύς in the following line may be supposed to have
caused its substitution for εὐθύς here.　Simpl. paraphrases τὸ δὲ δι᾽
ὀλίγων κινήσεων ἀφικνεῖται πρὸς τὸ ἑαυτοῦ τέλος, and therefore appears
not to have had ἐγγύς in his text.　Them., however, has it : 'ad illud
prope per pauca accedit.'

[2] Place a full-stop after ἐλθεῖν (l. 13), delete bracket, comma after
ἰσχνανθῆναι (l. 17).　'Running' or 'reduction of flesh' becomes in such
a case the 'end', i. e. the content of purpose, as soon as the true end
or good is recognized as unattainable.

[3] Simpl. finds this sentence difficult.　He did not see that Aristotle
here, as frequently elsewhere, uses ἀλλά where ἀλλ᾽ ἤ would be
expected.　See Bonitz, Ind. Ar. 33^b 15.

[4] The upshot of the argument seems to be this, that the earth and
the bodies nearest to it move simply, or not at all, because they are
content with little, and perfection is beyond their reach.

and moving principle of the several heavens one must regard the first as far superior to the others. Such 30 a superiority would be reasonable. For this single first motion has to move many of the divine bodies, while the numerous other motions move only one each, since each **293**^{a} single planet moves with a variety of motions. Thus, then, nature makes matters equal and establishes a certain order, giving to the single motion many bodies and to the single body many motions. And there is a second reason why the other motions have each only one body, in that each of 5 them except the last, i. e. that which contains the one star,[1] is really moving many bodies. For this last sphere moves with many others, to which it is fixed, each sphere being actually a body; so that its movement will be a joint product. Each sphere, in fact, has its particular natural motion, to which the general movement is, as it were, 10 added. But the force of any limited body is only adequate to moving a limited body.[2]

The characteristics of the stars which move with a circular motion, in respect of substance and shape, movement and order, have now been sufficiently explained.

13   It remains to speak of the earth, of its position, of the 15 question whether it is at rest or in motion, and of its shape.

I. As to its *position* there is some difference of opinion. Most people—all, in fact, who regard the whole heaven as finite—say it lies at the centre. But the Italian philoso- 20 phers known as Pythagoreans take the contrary view. At the centre, they say, is fire, and the earth is one of the stars, creating night and day by its circular motion about the

---

[1] The movements of each planet are analysed into the combination of a number of simple spherical motions each contributed by a single sphere. The 'last' sphere or motion means the outermost, viz. that to which the planet is actually attached. The inner spheres have really bodies to move even though they carry no planet: for they have to communicate their motion to the sphere or spheres in which they are included.

[2] Prantl seems to find unnecessary difficulty in this sentence. These spheres, says Aristotle, have only a limited force, and they have enough to do to impart their motion to the outer spheres, and through it to the planet: the burden of several planets would be too much for them.

centre. They further construct another earth in opposition
25 to ours to which they give the name counter-earth.[1] In all
this they are not seeking for theories and causes to account
for observed facts, but rather forcing their observations and
trying to accommodate them to certain theories and
opinions of their own. But there are many others who
would agree that it is wrong to give the earth the central
30 position, looking for confirmation rather to theory than to
the facts of observation. Their view is that the most
precious place befits the most precious thing: but fire, they
say, is more precious than earth, and the limit than the
intermediate, and the circumference and the centre are
limits. Reasoning on this basis they take the view that it
is not earth that lies at the centre of the sphere, but rather
293^b fire. The Pythagoreans have a further reason. They hold
that the most important part of the world, which is the
centre, should be most strictly guarded, and name it, or
rather the fire which occupies that place, the ' Guard-house
of Zeus ', as if the word ' centre ' were quite unequivocal,
5 and the centre of the mathematical figure were always the
same with that of the thing or the natural centre. But it is
better to conceive of the case of the whole heaven as
analogous to that of animals, in which the centre of the
animal and that of the body are different. For this reason
they have no need to be so disturbed about the world, or to
10 call in a guard for its centre: rather let them look for the
centre in the other sense and tell us what it is like and
where nature has set it. That centre will be something
primary and precious; but to the mere position we should
give the last place rather than the first. For the middle is
what is defined, and what defines it is the limit, and that
which contains or limits is more precious than that which
15 is limited, seeing that the latter is the matter and the
former the essence of the system.

II. As to the position of the earth, then, this is the view
which some advance, and the views advanced concerning
its *rest or motion* are similar. For here too there is no
general agreement. All who deny that the earth lies at

[1] ὄνομα is omitted by FHMJ, but is probably right.

the centre think that it revolves about the centre,[1] and not the earth only but, as we said before, the counter-earth as 20 well. Some of them even consider it possible that there are several bodies so moving, which are invisible to us owing to the interposition of the earth. This, they say, accounts for the fact that eclipses of the moon are more frequent than eclipses of the sun : for in addition to the earth each of these moving bodies can obstruct it. Indeed, 25 as in any case the surface of the earth is not actually a centre but distant from it a full hemisphere, there is no more difficulty, they think, in accounting for the observed facts on their view that we do not dwell at the centre, than on the common view that the earth is in the middle.[2] Even as it is, there is nothing in the observations to suggest that we are removed from the centre by half the diameter of the 30 earth. Others, again, say that the earth, which lies at the centre, is 'rolled', and thus in motion, about the axis of the whole heaven. So it stands written in the *Timaeus*.[3]

III. There are similar disputes about the *shape* of the earth. Some think it is spherical, others that it is flat and drum-shaped. For evidence they bring the fact that, as the 294[a]

---

[1] μηδ' in l. 18 appears to prove that the comma should be put after κεῖσθαι instead of after αὐτήν, and that φασιν governs both infinitives.

[2] Prantl's insertion of μή in the last clause rests on a misunderstanding of the passage. The text is quite sound.—Dreyer (*Planetary Systems*, p. 45) thinks that the supposed movement would seriously affect observations of the sun and the moon.

[3] *Timaeus*, 40 B. For a discussion of this vexed passage see Heath, *Aristarchus*, pp. 174-8. J has εἰλεῖσθαι καὶ κινεῖσθαι (in 296[a] 26, however, where the same pair of words recur, it has εἴλλεσθαι κ. κ.), which decreases the probability, not antecedently very great, that the words καὶ κινεῖσθαι are an insertion. Unless the idea of movement is contained in the phrase, the quotation would seem to be out of place here. It seems plain that Aristotle considered the word ἴλλεσθαι ('rolled' in the text) obscure or ambiguous, and added the words καὶ κινεῖσθαι to indicate his interpretation of it. Alex. (*apud* Simpl.) says that the word used in the *Timaeus* means 'pressed' (βιάζεσθαι), but that it is difficult to contradict Aristotle on a point on which he was so much better informed. Simpl. says that, spelt with the diphthong ει and a single λ, the word does connote rotation. He points out that Aristotle promised to speak of the earth's motion *and rest*; and suggests that, taking καὶ κινεῖσθαι to be a later insertion, one might suppose that Aristotle passes in this sentence to the consideration of the view that the earth is at rest. But this will hardly do.

sun rises and sets, the part concealed by the earth shows
a straight and not a curved edge, whereas if the earth were
spherical the line of section would have to be circular. In
5 this they leave out of account the great distance of the sun
from the earth and the great size of the circumference,
which, seen from a distance on these apparently small
circles appears straight. Such an appearance ought not to
make them doubt the circular shape of the earth. But they
have another argument. They say that because it is at
10 rest, the earth must necessarily have this shape. For there
are many different ways in which the movement or rest of
the earth has been conceived.

The difficulty must have occurred to every one. It would
indeed be a complacent mind that felt no surprise that,
while a little bit of earth, let loose in mid-air, moves and
15 will not stay still, and the more there is of it the faster it
moves, the whole earth, free in mid-air, should show no
movement at all. Yet here is this great weight of earth,
and it is at rest. And again, from beneath one of these
moving fragments of earth, before it falls, take away the
earth, and it will continue its downward movement with
nothing to stop it. The difficulty then, has naturally passed
20 into a commonplace of philosophy; and one may well
wonder that the solutions offered are not seen to involve
greater absurdities than the problem itself.

By these considerations some have been led to assert
that the earth below us is infinite, saying, with Xenophanes
of Colophon, that it has 'pushed its roots to infinity',[1]—in
order to save the trouble of seeking for the cause. Hence
25 the sharp rebuke of Empedocles, in the words 'if the deeps
of the earth are endless and endless the ample ether—such
is the vain tale told by many a tongue, poured from the
mouths of those who have seen but little of the whole'[2]

---

[1] Diels, *Vorsokratiker*³, 11 A 47 (53, 38 ff.), B 28 (63, 8). Ritter and
Preller, 103 b. Simpl. cannot find the quotation in the writings of
Xenophanes, and doubts whether τὸ κάτω τῆς γῆς means 'the under-
parts of the earth' or 'the ether under the earth'. A fragment
corroborating the former interpretation survives (no. 28 in Diels).
Cf. Burnet, E.G.P.³ § 60.

[2] Diels, *Vors.*³ 21 B 39 (241, 16). Ritter and Preller, 103 b. Burnet,
E.G.P.³ p. 212.

Others say the earth rests upon water. This, indeed, is the
oldest theory that has been preserved, and is attributed to
Thales of Miletus. It was supposed to stay still because it 30
floated like wood and other similar substances, which are
so constituted as to rest upon water but not upon air. / As
if the same account had not to be given of the water which
carries the earth as of the earth itself! It is not the nature
of water, any more than of earth, to stay in mid-air: it
must have something to rest upon. Again, as air is lighter 294^b
than water, so is water than earth: how then can they think
that the naturally lighter substance lies below the heavier?
Again, if the earth as a whole is capable of floating upon
water, that must obviously be the case with any part of it.
But observation shows that this is not the case. Any piece 5
of earth goes to the bottom, the quicker the larger it is.
[These thinkers seem to push their inquiries some way into
the problem, but not so far as they might. It is what we
are all inclined to do, to direct our inquiry not by the
matter itself, but by the views of our opponents: and even
when interrogating oneself one pushes the inquiry only 10
to the point at which one can no longer offer any opposition. Hence a good inquirer will be one who is ready in
bringing forward the objections proper to the genus, and
that he will be when he has gained an understanding of all
the differences.[1]

Anaximenes and Anaxagoras and Democritus give the
flatness of the earth as the cause of its staying still. Thus, 15
they say, it does not cut, but covers like a lid, the air
beneath it. This seems to be the way of flat-shaped
bodies: for even the wind can scarcely move them because
of their power of resistance. The same immobility, they
say, is produced by the flatness of the surface which the
earth presents to the air which underlies it ; while the air,

[1] The objections must be ‘proper to the kind’ or class to which the
subject of investigation belongs, i.e. scientific, not dialectical or
sophistical. These thinkers, as Simpl. observes, have failed to investigate the peculiar characteristics of wood and earth in the genus
‘body’, and therefore think that, because wood floats, earth may.
For the importance of a study of the ‘differences’ Simpl. refers to
Top. I. xviii.

20 not having room enough to change its place because it is underneath the earth, stays there in a mass, like the water in the case of the water-clock.[1] And they adduce an amount of evidence to prove that air, when cut off and at rest, can bear a considerable weight.

Now, first, if the shape of the earth is not flat, its flatness cannot be the cause of its immobility. But in their 25 own account it is rather the size of the earth than its flatness that causes it to remain at rest. For the reason why the air is so closely confined that it cannot find a passage, and therefore stays where it is, is its great amount: and this amount is great because the body which isolates it, the earth, is very large. This result, then, will follow, even if 30 the earth is spherical, so long as it retains its size. So far as their arguments go, the earth will still be at rest.

In general, our quarrel with those who speak of movement in this way cannot be confined to the parts[2]; it concerns the whole universe. One must decide at the outset whether bodies have a natural movement or not, whether there is no natural but only constrained movement. Seeing, **295**[a] however, that we have already decided this matter to the best of our ability, we are entitled to treat our results as representing fact. Bodies, we say, which have no natural movement, have no constrained movement; and where there is no natural and no constrained movement there will 5 be no movement at all. This is a conclusion, the necessity of which we have already decided,[3] and we have seen further that rest also will be inconceivable, since rest, like

---

[1] Reading ὥσπερ with the MSS. Diels (*Vors.*[3] 25, 32) inserts τοῦ before μεταστῆναι (l. 19), a conjecture which has some support in L, which has που in that place.—Experiments with the water-clock are frequently mentioned. See esp. Emped. fr. 100 (Diels), Arist. *Probl.* 914[b] 26, Burnet, E.G.P.[3] Index I s.v. Klepsydra. 'The water-clock', says Simpl., 'is a vessel with a narrow mouth and a flattish base pierced with small holes, what we now call a *hydrarpax*. If this vessel is dipped in water while the mouth at the top is kept closed, no water runs in through the holes. The massed air inside resists the water and prevents its ingress, being unable to change its own place. When the mouth at the top is opened the water runs in, the air making way for it.' The position of the water beneath the water-clock is analogous to that of the air beneath the earth.

[2] i. e. to the single element earth or to earth and air.

[3] I. ii–iv.

movement, is either natural or constrained.   But if there is
any natural movement, constraint will not be the sole principle of motion or of rest.   If, then, it is by constraint that
the earth now keeps its place, the so-called 'whirling'
movement by which its parts came together at the centre 10
was also constrained.   (The form of causation supposed
they all borrow from observations of liquids and of air,
in which the larger and heavier bodies always move
to the centre of the whirl.   This is thought by all those
who try to generate the heavens to explain why the earth
came together at the centre.   They then seek a reason for its 15
staying there; and some say, in the manner explained, that
the reason is its size and flatness, others, with Empedocles,
that the motion of the heavens, moving about it at a higher
speed, prevents movement of the earth, as the water in
a cup, when the cup is given a circular motion, though it is 20
often underneath the bronze, is for this same reason pre-
vented from moving with the downward movement which
is natural to it.[1])   But suppose both the 'whirl' and its
flatness (the air beneath being withdrawn[2]) cease to prevent the earth's motion, where will the earth move to then?
Its movement to the centre was constrained, and its rest at
the centre is due to constraint; but there must be some
motion which is natural to it.   Will this be upward motion 25
or downward or what?   It must have some motion; and if
upward and downward motion are alike to it, and the air
above the earth does not prevent upward movement, then
no more could air below it prevent downward movement.
For the same cause must necessarily have the same effect
on the same thing.[3]

Further, against Empedocles there is another point which 30
might be made.   When the elements were separated off by

---

[1] Simplicius seems to be right in considering the portion included
within brackets in the text as a parenthetic note on δίνησις, interrupt-
ing Aristotle's argument.

[2] The sense required is 'withdrawn', as above, but there is no
parallel to the use of ὑπελθεῖν in this sense.   The MSS. offer no
variant, and Simpl. paraphrases ἐκστάντος.   In the absence of a better
suggestion I should read ὑπεξελθόντος.

[3] The suggestion clearly is that, consciously or unconsciously, these
thinkers attributed a natural motion downward to the earth, since
they gave it a reason for not moving in that direction only.

Hate, what caused the earth to keep its place? Surely the
'whirl' cannot have been then also the cause. It is absurd
too not to perceive that, while the whirling movement may
have been responsible for the original coming together of
the parts of earth at the centre, the question remains, why
35 *now* do all heavy bodies move to the earth. For the whirl
295ᵇ surely does not come near us. Why, again, does fire move
upward? Not, surely, because of the whirl. But if fire is
naturally such as to move in a certain direction, clearly the
same may be supposed to hold of earth. Again, it cannot
be the whirl which determines the heavy and the light.[1]
5 Rather that movement caused the pre-existent heavy and
light things to go to the middle and stay on the surface
respectively. Thus, before ever the whirl began, heavy and
light existed; and what can have been the ground of their
distinction, or the manner and direction of their natural
movements? In the infinite chaos there can have been
neither above nor below, and it is by these that heavy and
light are determined.

10　It is to these causes that most writers pay attention: but
there are some, Anaximander, for instance, among the
ancients, who say that the earth keeps its place because of
its indifference.[2] Motion upward and downward and side-
ways were all, they thought, equally inappropriate to that
which is set at the centre and indifferently related to every
15 extreme point; and to move in contrary directions[3] at the
same time was impossible: so it must needs remain still.
This view is ingenious but not true. The argument would
prove that everything, whatever it be, which is put at the

---

[1] Read καὶ τὸ κοῦφον with all MSS. except E.

[2] Literally 'likeness'. Kranz, Index to Diels, *Vors.*, s. v. ὁμοιότης,
translates 'gleichmässige Lage'. Burnet (who formerly took a different view) now accepts 'indifference' as the equivalent of ὁμοιότης
in this passage. (E.G.P.³ p. 66, n. 1.) Cf. Burnet's note on Plato,
Phaedo, 109 A 2, where he proposes the translation 'equiformity',
and the phrase πρὸς ὁμοίας γωνίας below (296ᵇ 20). From Aristotle's wording it seems probable that he had the *Phaedo* in mind
here. The full phrase there is: τὴν ὁμοιότητα τοῦ οὐρανοῦ αὐτοῦ
ἑαυτῷ πάντῃ καὶ τῆς γῆς αὐτῆς τὴν ἰσορροπίαν. It is to be observed that
Plato makes ὁμοιότης an attribute of the whole heaven or universe, not
of the earth.

[3] Prantl's ἐναντίον is a misprint for ἐναντίον.

centre, must stay there. Fire, then, will rest at the centre:
for the proof turns on no peculiar property of earth. But
this does not follow. The observed facts about earth are 20
not only that it remains at the centre, but also that it moves
to the centre. The place to which any fragment of earth
moves must necessarily be the place to which the whole
moves; and in the place to which a thing naturally moves,
it will naturally rest. The reason then is not in the fact
that the earth is indifferently related to every extreme
point: for this would apply to any body, whereas move- 25
ment to the centre is peculiar to earth. Again it is absurd
to look for a reason why the earth remains at the centre
and not for a reason why fire remains at the extremity. If
the extremity is the natural place of fire, clearly earth must
also have a natural place. But suppose that the centre is
not its place, and that the reason of its remaining there is this 30
necessity of indifference—on the analogy of the hair which,
it is said, however great the tension, will not break under
it, if it be evenly distributed, or of the man who, though
exceedingly hungry and thirsty, and both equally,[1] yet
being equidistant from food and drink, is therefore bound
to stay where he is—even so, it still remains to explain why 35
fire stays at the extremities. It is strange, too, to ask **296^{a}**
about things staying still but not about their motion,—why,
I mean, one thing, if nothing stops it, moves up, and another
thing to the centre. Again, their statements are not true.
It happens, indeed, to be the case that a thing to which 5
movement this way and that is equally inappropriate is
obliged to remain at the centre.[2] But so far as their argument goes, instead of remaining there, it will move, only not
as a mass but in fragments. For the argument applies
equally to fire. Fire, if set at the centre, should stay there,
like earth, since it will be indifferently related to every point 10
on the extremity. Nevertheless it will move, as in fact it
always does move when nothing stops it, away from the
centre to the extremity. It will not, however, move in a

---

[1] The structure of the sentence would be made clearer if commas
were placed after μέν and after δέ in l. 33.

[2] The principle is in fact true, if it is properly understood, i.e. seen
to apply, as explained in what follows, only to indivisible bodies.

mass to a single point on the circumference—the only possible result on the lines of the indifference theory—but
15 rather each corresponding portion of fire to the corresponding part of the extremity, each fourth part, for instance, to
a fourth part of the circumference. For since no body is
a point, it will have parts. The expansion, when the body
increased the place occupied, would be on the same principle as the contraction, in which the place was diminished.
Thus, for all the indifference theory shows to the contrary,
20 earth also would have moved in this manner away from the
centre, unless the centre had been its natural place.

We have now outlined the views held as to the shape,
position, and rest or movement of the earth.

Let us first decide the question whether the earth moves 14
25 or is at rest. For, as we said, there are some who make it
one of the stars, and others who, setting it at the centre,
suppose it to be 'rolled' and in motion about the pole as
axis.[1] That both views are untenable will be clear if we
take as our starting-point the fact that the earth's motion,
whether the earth be at the centre or away from it, must
30 needs be a constrained motion. It cannot be the movement
of the earth itself. If it were, any portion of it would have
this movement; but in fact every part moves in a straight
line to the centre. Being, then, constrained and unnatural,
the movement could not be eternal. But the order of the
universe is eternal. Again, everything that moves with the
35 circular movement, except the first sphere, is observed to
296ᵇ be passed, and to move with more than one motion. The
earth, then, also, whether it move about the centre or as
stationary at it, must necessarily move with two motions.
But if this were so, there would have to be passings and
5 turnings of the fixed stars. Yet no such thing is observed.
The same stars always rise and set in the same parts of the
earth.[2]

---

[1] For ἴλλεσθαι J has εἴλλεσθαι. See note on 293ᵇ 31.
[2] This passage is examined in Heath, *Aristarchus*, pp. 240-1. The
necessity for two motions appears to rest only on the analogy of the
planets, which are 'passed' or left behind by the motion of the sphere
of the fixed stars. The consequence, that there would be variety in

Further, the natural movement of the earth, part and whole alike, is to the centre of the whole—whence the fact that it is now actually situated at the centre—but it might be questioned, since both centres are the same, which centre 10 it is that portions of earth and other heavy things move to. Is this their goal because it is the centre of the earth or because it is the centre of the whole? The goal, surely, must be the centre of the whole. For fire and other light things move to the extremity of the area which contains the centre. It happens, however, that the centre of the 15 earth and of the whole is the same. Thus they do move to the centre of the earth, but accidentally, in virtue of the fact that the earth's centre lies at the centre of the whole. That the centre of the earth is the goal of their movement is indicated by the fact that heavy bodies moving towards the earth do not move parallel but so as to make equal 20 angles,[1] and thus to a single centre, that of the earth. It is clear, then, that the earth must be at the centre and immovable, not only for the reasons already given, but also because heavy bodies forcibly thrown quite straight upward return to the point from which they started, even if they are thrown to an infinite distance.[2] From these considera- 25 tions then it is clear that the earth does not move and does not lie elsewhere than at the centre.

From what we have said the explanation of the earth's immobility is also apparent. If it is the nature of earth, as observation shows, to move from any point to the centre, as

the places of rising and setting of the fixed stars, follows from the assumption of a second motion, if the second is taken to be oblique to the first (Heath, *loc. cit.*).

[1] i.e. at right angles to a tangent: if it fell otherwise than at right angles, the angles on each side of the line of fall would be unequal. Cf. *inf.* 311^b 34, where the argument is repeated. The phrase πρὸς ὁμοίας γωνίας, 'at *like* angles', appears to strike Simpl. as a rather strange equivalent for πρὸς ἴσας γωνίας, 'at *equal* angles', borrowed, as he says, from those who referred 'angle' to the category of quality— ὁμοίας δὲ ἐκάλουν τὰς ἴσας γωνίας οἱ τὴν γωνίαν ὑπὸ τὸ ποιὸν ἀνάγοντες (538, 22). Cf. Burnet's remarks on ὁμοιότης in *Phaedo*, 109 A 2, quoted in part above in note on 295^b 11.

[2] It seems plain that the words κατὰ στάθμην ('quite straight') refer to the line of the throw, not, as Simpl. supposes, to the line of return. But it is difficult to see what independent test Aristotle had of the straightness of the throw.

of fire contrariwise to move from the centre to the extremity,
30 it is impossible that any portion of earth should move away
from the centre except by constraint. For a single thing
has a single movement, and a simple thing a simple: contrary movements cannot belong to the same thing, and
movement away from the centre is the contrary of movement
to it. If then no portion of earth can move away from the
centre, obviously still less can the earth as a whole so move.
35 For it is the nature of the whole to move to the point to
297ª which the part naturally moves. Since, then, it would
require a force greater than itself to move it, it must needs
stay at the centre. This view is further supported by the
contributions of mathematicians to astronomy, since the
5 observations made as the shapes change by which the order
of the stars is determined,[1] are fully accounted for on the
hypothesis that the earth lies at the centre. Of the position
of the earth and of the manner of its rest or movement, our
discussion may here end.

Its shape must necessarily be spherical. For every por-
10 tion of earth has weight until it reaches the centre, and the
jostling of parts greater and smaller would bring about not
a waved surface, but rather compression and convergence[2]
of part and part until the centre is reached. The process
should be conceived by supposing the earth to come into
being in the way that some of the natural philosophers
15 describe.[3] Only they attribute the downward movement
to constraint, and it is better to keep to the truth and say
that the reason of this motion is that a thing which possesses

---

[1] The sense of the sentence is, clearly, 'the phenomena are accounted
for on the present hypothesis: why change it?' But the precise
relevance of (apparent) changes of shape does not seem clear. Simpl.
illustrates by changes which would be necessitated by the hypothesis
of a moving earth; but his own paraphrase of Aristotle's words
implies that the changes in question are *observed* changes. The
Greek implies (1) that the order of the stars is settled by the apparent
shapes or patterns which they make in combination; (2) that the
changes of these shapes are accounted for on the hypothesis of a
stationary earth.

[2] συγχωρεῖν is clearly used here of 'convergence', not, as Prantl
translates, of 'making way'. So Simpl. paraphrases, συμπλάττεται
ἢ συγχωρεῖ ἕτερον ἑτέρῳ.

[3] The cosmogony which follows is in principle that of Anaxagoras
(Burnet, E.G.P.³ § 133).

weight is naturally endowed with à centripetal movement.
When the mixture, then, was merely potential, the things
that were separated off moved similarly from every side
towards the centre. Whether the parts which came together
at the centre were distributed at the extremities evenly, or 20
in some other way, makes no difference. If, on the one
hand, there were a similar movement from each quarter of
the extremity to the single centre, it is obvious that the
resulting mass would be similar on every side. For if an
equal amount is added on every side the extremity of the
mass will be everywhere equidistant from its centre, i.e. the 25
figure will be spherical. But neither will it in any way
affect the argument if there is not a similar accession of
concurrent fragments from every side. For the greater
quantity, finding a lesser in front of it, must necessarily
drive it on, both having an impulse whose goal is the centre,
and the greater weight driving the lesser forward till this 30
goal is reached. In this we have also the solution of a possible difficulty. The earth, it might be argued, is at the
centre and spherical in shape : if, then, a weight many times
that of the earth were added to one hemisphere, the centre
of the earth and of the whole will no longer be coincident.
So that either the earth will not stay still at the centre, or
if it does, it will be at rest without having its centre at the 297ᵇ
place to which it is still its nature to move.[1] Such is the
difficulty. A short consideration will give us an easy
answer, if we first give precision to our postulate that any
body endowed with weight, of whatever size, moves towards
the centre. Clearly it will not stop when its edge touches 5
the centre. The greater quantity must prevail until the
body's centre occupies the centre. For that is the goal of
its impulse. Now it makes no difference whether we apply

---

[1] The words 'at the centre' in the first clause seem intrusive at first
sight ; and logically they are indefensible. 'Either the earth will not
stay still at the centre, or, if it does stay still at the centre, it will not
have its (new) centre at the centre which is its natural goal !' The
words ἐπὶ τοῦ μέσου, then, may be an insertion. They are, however,
more probably due to the desire for a direct contradictory. The view
is μένει ἐπὶ τοῦ μέσου : the contradictory is therefore οὐ μένει ἐπὶ τοῦ
μέσου : and the εἴπερ recalls only the μένει. 'Either it does not stay
still at the centre or it doesn't stay still at the centre.'

this to a clod or common fragment of earth or to the earth
as a whole. The fact indicated does not depend upon
10 degrees of size but applies universally to everything that
has the centripetal impulse. Therefore earth in motion,
whether in a mass or in fragments, necessarily continues to
move until it occupies the centre equally every way, the
less being forced to equalize itself by the greater owing to
the forward drive of the impulse.[1]

If the earth was generated, then, it must have been
15 formed in this way, and so clearly its generation was
spherical; and if it is ungenerated and has remained so
always, its character must be that which the initial generation, if it had occurred, would have given it. But the
spherical shape, necessitated by this argument, follows also
from the fact that the motions of heavy bodies always
20 make equal angles,[2] and are not parallel. This would be
the natural form of movement towards what is naturally
spherical. Either then the earth is spherical or it is at
least naturally spherical.[3] And it is right to call anything
that which nature intends it to be, and which belongs to it,
rather than that which it is by constraint and contrary to
nature. The evidence of the senses further corroborates
this. How else would eclipses of the moon show segments
25 shaped as we see them? As it is, the shapes which the
moon itself each month shows are of every kind—straight,
gibbous, and concave—but in eclipses the outline is always
curved: and, since it is the interposition of the earth that

---

[1] The argument is quite clear if it is understood that 'greater' and
'less' here and in ᵃ 30 and in ᵇ 5 stand for greater and smaller portions
of one body, the line of division passing through the centre which is
the goal. Suppose the earth so placed in regard to the centre. The
larger and heavier division would 'drive the lesser forward', i.e.
beyond the centre (ᵃ 30); it would 'prevail until the body's centre
occupied the centre' (ᵇ 5); it would 'force the less to equalize itself',
i.e. to move on until the line passing through the central goal divided
the body equally. Simpl. fails to see this.—Alex. (*ap*. Simpl. 543, 15)
raises the difficulty that the final movement of the 'less' will be away
from the centre, or upward, and hence unnatural. But this is to make
a perverse abstraction of part from whole. The desire of earth to
reach the centre can never be fully satisfied, since the centre is
a geometrical point.
[2] See note on 296ᵇ 20.
[3] Allowing for scruples due to the evident inequalities of the earth's
surface.

makes the eclipse, the form of this line will be caused by 30
the form of the earth's surface, which is therefore spherical.
Again, our observations of the stars make it evident, not
only that the earth is circular, but also that it is a circle of
no great size. For quite a small change of position to
south or north causes a manifest alteration of the horizon.
There is much change, I mean, in the stars which are over- 298^{a}
head, and the stars seen are different, as one moves north-
ward or southward. Indeed there are some stars seen in
Egypt and in the neighbourhood of Cyprus which are not
seen in the northerly regions; and stars, which in the north 5
are never beyond the range of observation, in those regions
rise and set. All of which goes to show not only that the
earth is circular in shape, but also that it is a sphere of no
great size: for otherwise the effect of so slight a change of
place would not be so quickly apparent. Hence one should
not be too sure of the incredibility of the view of those who 10
conceive that there is continuity between the parts about
the pillars of Hercules and the parts about India, and that
in this way the ocean is one. As further evidence in favour
of this they quote the case of elephants, a species occurring
in each of these extreme regions, suggesting that the
common characteristic of these extremes is explained by 15
their continuity. Also, those mathematicians who try to
calculate the size of the earth's circumference arrive at the
figure 400,000 stades.[1] This indicates not only that the
earth's mass is spherical in shape, but also that as compared
with the stars it is not of great size.   20

[1] Simpl. gives, for the benefit of 'those who doubt the wisdom of
the ancients', a summary account of the methods by which this result
was attained.—This appears to be the oldest recorded estimate of the
size of the earth. 400,000 stades = 9,987 geographical miles. Other
estimates (in miles) are: Archimedes, 7,495; Eratosthenes and Hip-
parchus, 6,292; Poseidonius, 5,992 or 4,494; present day, 5,400.
(These figures are borrowed from Prantl's note on the passage in his
translation, p. 319.)

BOOK III

WE have already discussed the first heaven and its parts, **I**
25 the moving stars within it, the matter of which these are
composed and their bodily constitution, and we have also
shown that they are ungenerated and indestructible. Now
things that we call natural are either substances or functions
and attributes of substances. As substances I class the
30 simple bodies—fire, earth, and the other terms of the
series—and all things composed of them; for example,
the heaven as a whole and its parts, animals, again, and
plants and their parts. By attributes and functions I mean
the movements of these and of all other things in which
they have power in themselves to cause movement, and
298^b also their alterations and reciprocal transformations. It is
obvious, then, that the greater part of the inquiry into
nature concerns bodies: for a natural substance is either
a body or a thing which cannot come into existence without
5 body and magnitude. This appears plainly from an analysis
of the character of natural things, and equally from an
inspection of the instances of inquiry into nature. Since,
then, we have spoken of the primary element, of its bodily
constitution, and of its freedom from destruction and
generation, it remains to speak of the other two.¹ In
speaking of them we shall be obliged also to inquire into
10 generation and destruction. For if there is generation
anywhere, it must be in these elements and things composed of them.

This is indeed the first question we have to ask: is
generation a fact or not? Earlier speculation was at
variance both with itself and with the views here put for-
15 ward as to the true answer to this question. Some removed
generation and destruction from the world altogether.

---

¹ Aristotle speaks of the four sublunary elements as two, because
generically they are two. Two are heavy, two light: two move up
and two down. Books III and IV of this treatise deal solely with
these elements.

Nothing that is, they said, is generated or destroyed, and our conviction to the contrary is an illusion. So maintained the school of Melissus and Parmenides. But however excellent their theories may otherwise be, anyhow they cannot be held to speak as students of nature. There may be things not subject to generation or any kind of movement, but if so they belong to another and a higher inquiry 20 than the study of nature. They, however, had no idea of any form of being other than the substance of things perceived; and when they saw, what no one previously had seen, that there could be no knowledge or wisdom without some such unchanging entities, they naturally transferred what was true of them to things perceived. Others, perhaps intentionally, maintain precisely the contrary opinion to 25 this. It had been asserted that everything in the world was subject to generation and nothing was ungenerated, but that after being generated some things remained indestructible while the rest were again destroyed. This had been asserted in the first instance by Hesiod and his followers, but afterwards outside his circle by the earliest natural philosophers.[1] But what these thinkers maintained was that all else has been generated and, as they said, 'is 30 flowing away', nothing having any solidity, except one single thing which persists as the basis of all these transformations. So we may interpret the statements of Heraclitus of Ephesus and many others.[2] And some[3] subject all bodies whatever to generation, by means of the composition and separation of planes.   299^a

Discussion of the other views may be postponed.[4] But this last theory which composes every body of planes is, as

[1] The reference, according to Simplicius, is to Orphic writings ('the school of Orpheus and Musaeus').

[2] e.g. Thales, Anaximander, Anaximenes.

[3] 'The view of Timaeus the Pythagorean, recorded by Plato in the dialogue named after him' (Simpl.). The theory criticized is certainly that advanced in the *Timaeus*, and is usually attributed to Plato, as by Zeller, *Ph. d. Gr.*[4] II. i, p. 804, but Aristotle probably has also in mind certain members of the Academy, particularly Xenocrates (*ib.*, pp. 1016 ff.).

[4] The promised discussion is not to be found in the *De Caelo* nor in its sequel, the *De Generatione et Corruptione*. But Aristotle has already devoted some attention to these views at the beginning of the *Physics*, and there is also the discussion of *Met.* A.

the most superficial observation shows, in many respects in
plain contradiction with mathematics. It is, however, wrong
5 to remove the foundations of a science unless you can replace
them with others more convincing. And, secondly, the same
theory which composes solids of planes clearly composes
planes of lines and lines of points, so that a part of a line
need not be a line. This matter has been already considered
10 in our discussion of movement, where we have shown that
an indivisible length is impossible.[1] But with respect to
natural bodies there are impossibilities involved in the
view which asserts indivisible lines, which we may briefly
consider at this point. For the impossible consequences
which result from this view in the mathematical sphere will
reproduce themselves when it is applied to physical bodies,
15 but there will be difficulties in physics which are not present
in mathematics; for mathematics deals with an abstract
and physics with a more concrete object. There are many
attributes necessarily present in physical bodies which are
necessarily excluded by indivisibility; all attributes, in fact,
which are divisible.[2] There can be nothing divisible in an
indivisible thing, but the attributes of bodies are all divisible
20 in one of two ways. They are divisible into kinds, as colour
is divided into white and black, and they are divisible *per
accidens* when that which has them is divisible. In this
latter sense attributes which are simple[3] are nevertheless
divisible. Attributes of this kind will serve, therefore, to
illustrate the impossibility of the view. It is impossible, if
25 two parts of a thing have no weight, that the two together
should have weight. But either all perceptible bodies
or some, such as earth and water, have weight, as these
thinkers would themselves admit. Now if the point has no
weight, clearly the lines have not either, and, if they have
not, neither have the planes. Therefore no body has
30 weight. It is, further, manifest that their point cannot have

---

[1] *Phys.* VI. i.
[2] The reading διαιρετόν, though preserved only in one rather inferior
manuscript, must be preferred on grounds of sense to the ἀδιαίρετον
of the other manuscripts. The silence of Simplicius seems to corroborate the reading διαιρετόν. Possibly the clause is a gloss.
[3] i.e. not divisible into kinds.

weight. For while a heavy thing may always be heavier than something and a light thing lighter than something, **299**[b] a thing which is heavier or lighter than something need not be itself heavy or light, just as a large thing is larger than others, but what is larger is not always large. A thing which, judged absolutely, is small may none the less be larger than other things. Whatever, then, is heavy 5 and also heavier than something else, must exceed this by something which is heavy. A heavy thing therefore is always divisible. But it is common ground that a point is indivisible. Again, suppose that what is heavy is a dense body, and what is light rare. Dense differs from rare in containing more matter in the same cubic area. A point, then, if it may be heavy or light, may be dense or rare. 10 But the dense is divisible while a point is indivisible. And if what is heavy must be either hard or soft, an impossible consequence is easy to draw. For a thing is soft if its surface can be pressed in, hard if it cannot; and if it can be pressed in it is divisible.

Moreover, no weight can consist of parts not possessing 15 weight. For how, except by the merest fiction, can they specify the number and character of the parts which will produce weight? And, further, when one weight is greater than another, the difference is a third weight; from which it will follow that every indivisible part possesses weight. For suppose that a body of four points possesses weight. A body composed of more than four points[1] will be superior in weight to it, a thing which has weight. But the 20 difference between weight and weight must be a weight, as the difference between white and whiter is white. Here the difference which makes the superior weight heavier[2] is the single point which remains when the common number, four, is subtracted. A single point, therefore, has weight.

Further, to assume, on the one hand, that the planes can

---

[1] Prantl's conjecture ἢ τουδί is unsatisfactory. The alternatives are (1) to keep the reading of the manuscripts (ἢ τοδί), (2) to read τουδί, omitting ἢ. In the latter case the sense remains the same but the construction becomes rather easier.

[2] Prantl's conjectural duplication of the words μιᾷ στιγμῇ, though harmless, is unnecessary.

25 only be put in linear contact[1] would be ridiculous. For just as there are two ways of putting lines together, namely, end to end and side by side, so there must be two ways of putting planes together. Lines can be put together so that contact is linear by laying one along the other, though not by putting them end to end.[2] But if, similarly, in putting the planes together, superficial contact is allowed as an 30 alternative to linear, that method will give them bodies which are not any element nor composed of elements.[3] Again, if it is the number of planes in a body[4] that makes 300[a] one heavier than another, as the *Timaeus*[5] explains, clearly the line and the point will have weight. For the three cases are, as we said before, analogous.[6] But if the reason of differences of weight is not this, but rather the 5 heaviness of earth and the lightness of fire, then some of the planes will be light and others heavy (which involves a similar distinction in the lines and the points); the earth-plane, I mean, will be heavier than the fire-plane. In general, the result is either that there is no magnitude at all, or that all magnitude could be done away with. For 10 a point is to a line as a line is to a plane and as a plane is to a body. Now the various forms in passing into one another will each be resolved into its ultimate constituents. It might happen therefore that nothing existed except points, and that there was no body at all. A further consideration is that if time is similarly constituted, there would be, or might be, a time at which it was done away with. For 15 the indivisible now is like a point in a line. The same consequences follow from composing the heaven of numbers, as some of the Pythagoreans do who make all nature out of numbers. For natural bodies are manifestly endowed with weight and lightness, but an assemblage of units can neither be composed to form a body nor possess weight.

[1] i. e. so as to form pyramids, cubes, &c.

[2] Grammar requires the readings ἐπιτιθεμένη, προστιθεμένη instead of the ἐπιτιθεμένην, προστιθεμένην of all manuscripts but one (M).

[3] Because they will not be pyramids or instances of any other recognized figure.

[4] Omitting the τά before τῶν ἐπιπέδων, which got into E by a simple dittography and is found in no other manuscript.

[5] Plato, *Tim.* 56 B.

[6] i. e. point : line :: line : plane :: plane : body (as below).

2 The necessity that each of the simple bodies should have 20 a natural movement may be shown as follows. They manifestly move, and if they have no proper movement they must move by constraint: and the constrained is the same as the unnatural. Now an unnatural movement presupposes a natural movement which it contravenes, and which, how- 25 ever many the unnatural movements, is always one. For naturally a thing moves in one way, while its unnatural movements are manifold.[1] The same may be shown from the fact of rest. Rest, also, must either be constrained or natural, constrained in a place to which movement was constrained, natural in a place movement to which was natural. Now manifestly there is a body which is at rest at the 30 centre. If then this rest is natural to it, clearly motion to this place is natural to it. If, on the other hand, its rest is constrained, what is hindering its motion? Something, perhaps, which is at rest: but if so, we shall simply repeat the same argument; and either we shall come to an ultimate something to which rest where it is is natural, or we shall 300^{b} have an infinite process, which is impossible. The hindrance to its movement, then, we will suppose, is a moving thing— as Empedocles says that it is the vortex which keeps the earth still— : but in that case we ask, where would it have moved to but for the vortex?[2] It could not move infinitely; for to traverse an infinite is impossible, and im- 5 possibilities do not happen. So the moving thing must stop somewhere, and there rest not by constraint but naturally. But a natural rest proves a natural movement

---

[1] This is in verbal contradiction with the doctrine of Book I, which asserts that the unnatural movement is single since it is the contrary of the natural, which is single. But it is not difficult to conceive of all movements of a body divergent from the one natural path as unnatural according to the degree of their divergence, even though, strictly construed, the unnatural path is also one.

[2] This question, though relevant to the general problem, is not *specially* relevant to the hypothesis that the obstacle is in movement. There is therefore something to be said for an interpretation which, like that attributed by Simplicius to Alexander, makes the question refer to the supposed moving obstacle instead of to the earth. But Alexander's interpretation turns out on examination to create more difficulties than it removes: and there is no great objection, after all, to supposing that Aristotle refutes the second alternative by an argument which refutes both.

to the place of rest. Hence Leucippus and Democritus,
who say that the primary bodies are in perpetual movement
10 in the void or infinite, may be asked to explain the manner
of their motion and the kind of movement which is natural
to them. For if the various elements are constrained by
one another to move as they do, each must still have
a natural movement which the constrained contravenes, and
the prime mover must cause motion not by constraint but
15 naturally. If there is no ultimate natural cause of movement and each preceding term in the series is always moved
by constraint, we shall have an infinite process. The same
difficulty is involved even if it is supposed, as we read in
the *Timaeus*,[1] that before the ordered world was made the
elements moved without order. Their movement must
have been due either to constraint or to their nature. And
20 if their movement was natural, a moment's consideration
shows that there was already an ordered world. For the
prime mover must cause motion in virtue of its own natural
movement,[2] and the other bodies, moving without constraint,
as they came to rest in their proper places, would fall into
the order in which they now stand, the heavy bodies moving
25 towards the centre and the light bodies away from it. But
that is the order of their distribution in our world. There
is a further question, too, which might be asked. Is it possible or impossible that bodies in unordered movement
should combine in some cases into combinations like those
of which bodies of nature's composing are composed, such,
I mean, as bones and flesh? Yet this is what Empedocles
30 asserts to have occurred under Love. 'Many a head', says

---

[1] Plato, *Tim.* 30 a.

[2] Taking the reading for which Alexander argued—κινεῖν αὐτὸ κινούμενον κατὰ φύσιν. I should put a comma after κινεῖν and take κατὰ φ.
with κινούμενον. The hypothesis is that the elements have their
natural movements; and the dependent clause αὐτὸ κιν. κ. φ. applies
this hypothesis to the prime mover, as τὰ κινούμενα μὴ βίᾳ applies it to
the other bodies. Aristotle shows that, on this hypothesis, the present
world-order would exist: the prime mover would be imparting movement to the bodies within it, as it does now, and the four elements
would be moving towards or resting in their proper places, as now.
If αὐτό is read, we have a more disputable description of this κόσμος
and less use for the words κινούμενον κατὰ φύσιν. αὐτό is said to be
the reading of the manuscripts, but neither copyists nor collators are
to be trusted with a breathing. J has αὐτό (*sic*).

he, 'came to birth without a neck.'[1] The answer to the
view that there are infinite bodies moving in an infinite is
that, if the cause of movement is single, they must move
with a single motion, and therefore not without order; and
if, on the other hand, the causes are of infinite variety, their 301^a
motions too must be infinitely varied. For a finite number
of causes would produce a kind of order, since absence of
order is not proved by diversity of direction in motions:
indeed, in the world we know, not all bodies, but only
bodies of the same kind, have a common goal of movement.
Again, disorderly movement means in reality unnatural 5
movement, since the order proper to perceptible things is
their nature. And there is also absurdity and impossibility
in the notion that the disorderly movement is infinitely continued. For the nature of things is the nature which most
of them possess for most of the time. Thus their view
brings them into the contrary position[2] that disorder is 10
natural, and order or system unnatural. But no natural
fact can originate in chance. This is a point which Anaxagoras seems to have thoroughly grasped; for he starts his
cosmogony from unmoved things. The others, it is true,
make things collect together somehow before they try to
produce motion and separation. But there is no sense in
starting generation from an original state in which bodies 15
are separated and in movement. Hence Empedocles
begins after the process ruled by Love: for he could not
have constructed the heaven by building it up out of
bodies in separation, making them to combine by the power
of Love, since our world has its constituent elements in
separation, and therefore presupposes a previous state of
unity and combination.[3] 20

These arguments make it plain that every body has its
natural movement, which is not constrained or contrary to
its nature. We go on to show that there are certain bodies[4]

---

[1] Emped. fr. 57, l. 1 (Diels, *Vors.*³ 245, 20).
[2] Reading συμβαίνει, with HMJ, for συμβαίνειν.
[3] Putting a comma instead of a full-stop after στοιχείων (l. 19).
[4] The proposition to be proved is that *some* bodies have *necessarily*
this kind of impetus. The introduction of necessity shows that we are
dealing with a universal. Below in 301^b 16, and again in 301^b 30, we

whose necessary impetus is that of weight and lightness.
Of necessity, we assert, they must move, and a moved thing
25 which has no natural impetus cannot move either towards
or away from the centre. Suppose a body *A* without weight,
and a body *B* endowed with weight. Suppose the weightless body to move the distance *CD*, while *B* in the same
time moves the distance *CE*, which will be greater since the
heavy thing must move further. Let the heavy body then
30 be divided in the proportion *CE* : *CD* (for there is no reason
why a part of *B* should not stand in this relation to the
whole). Now if the whole moves the whole distance *CE*,
the part must in the same time move the distance *CD*.
A weightless body, therefore, and one which has weight
301ᵇ will move the same distance, which is impossible. And
the same argument would fit the case of lightness. Again,
a body which is in motion but has neither weight nor lightness, must be moved by constraint, and must continue its
constrained movement infinitely. For there will be a force
5 which moves it, and the smaller and lighter a body is the
further will a given force move it. Now let *A*, the weightless body, be moved the distance *CE*, and *B*, which has
weight, be moved in the same time the distance *CD*.
Dividing the heavy body in the proportion *CE* : *CD*, we
10 subtract from the heavy body a part which will in the same
time move the distance *CE*, since the whole moved *CD* :
for the relative speeds of the two bodies will be in inverse
ratio to their respective sizes. Thus the weightless body
will move the same distance as the heavy in the same time.
15 But this is impossible. Hence, since the motion of the
weightless body will cover a greater distance than any that
is suggested,[1] it will continue infinitely. It is therefore
obvious that every body must have a definite[2] weight or

are told that *every* body is either light or heavy. Aristotle's readers
would of course understand that the disjunction only applied universally 'beneath the moon'. The more cautious statement in this
passage allows for the exception of the heavenly body.
    [1] Reading προτεθέντος, which is given by all manuscripts except M
and by Simplicius.
    [2] i.e. not infinite. διωρισμένον is here equivalent to ὡρισμένον.
A similar tendency is observable in other derivatives of διορίζειν, e.g.
ἀδιόριστος. Alexander and Simplicius made great, but not very

lightness. But since 'nature' means a source of movement within the thing itself, while a force is a source of movement in something other than it or in itself *quâ* other,[1] and since movement is always due either to nature or to constraint, movement which is natural, as downward movement is to a stone, will be merely accelerated by an external force, while an unnatural movement will be due to the force alone.[2] In either case the air is as it were instrumental to the force. For air is both light and heavy, and thus *quâ* light produces upward motion, being propelled and set in motion by the force, and *quâ* heavy produces a downward motion. In either case the force transmits the movement to the body by first, as it were, impregnating the air.[3] That is why a body moved by constraint continues to move when that which gave the impulse ceases to accompany it. Otherwise, i. e. if the air were not endowed with this function, constrained movement would be impossible. And the natural movement of a body may be helped on in the same way. This discussion suffices to show[4] (1) that all bodies are either light or heavy, and (2) how unnatural movement takes place.

From what has been said earlier[5] it is plain that there

successful, efforts to interpret the word as qualifying 'body': they do not consider the possibility of its qualifying βάρος ἢ κουφότητα. Probably their manuscripts, like FHMJ, had τό before διωρισμένον, which would make it difficult or impossible to take διωρισμένον in that way.

[1] Reading ἢ ᾗ ἄλλο. It looks as if Simplicius had this reading (see critical note to Heiberg's edition, p. 595, 22): his interpretation requires it.

[2] Reading θάττω in l. 20, with all manuscripts except F and with Simplicius. αὐτή in 22 is somewhat vague in reference, but must stand for ἡ δύναμις αὐτή.

[3] ll. 23–5, πέφυκε . . . βαρύς, are grammatically a parenthesis, and should be so printed, with a colon in 23 after βαρύς. For the doctrine cf. *Phys.* IV. 8 and VIII. 10.

[4] Simplicius and Alexander, with three of our manuscripts (FHM), have ἐν τούτοις for ἐκ τούτων. ἐν τούτοις would go with ἔχουσι rather than with φανερόν, qualifying the application of the second clause. The qualification, however, cannot be made very precise, and it is best to follow the other three manuscripts.

[5] The γάρ which introduces the next sentence shows that the justification of the statement is to come. The thesis follows from what was 'said earlier', because in *Phys.* IV. 6-9 the hypothesis of a void was investigated and refuted, and it is here shown that absolute generation, or generation of body out of not-body, requires a void.

cannot be generation either of everything or in an absolute
sense of anything.　It is impossible that everything should
302^a be generated, unless an extra-corporeal [1] void is possible.
For, assuming generation, the place which is to be occupied
by that which is coming to be, must have been previously
occupied by void in which no body was.[2]　Now it is quite
possible for one body to be generated out of another, air
5 for instance out of fire, but in the absence of any pre-
existing mass generation is impossible.　That which is
potentially a certain kind of body may, it is true, become
such in actuality.　But if the potential body was not already
in actuality some other kind of body, the existence of an
extra-corporeal void must be admitted.

10　　It remains to say what bodies are subject to generation, 3
and why.　Since in every case knowledge depends on what
is primary, and the elements are the primary constituents
of bodies, we must ask which of such bodies [3] are elements,
and why; and after that what is their number and character.
15 The answer will be plain if we first explain what kind of
substance an element is.　An element, we take it, is a body
into which other bodies may be analysed, present in them
potentially or in actuality (which of these, is still disputable),
and not itself divisible into bodies different in form.　That,
or something like it, is what all men in every case mean by
20 element.　Now if what we have described is an element,
clearly there must be such bodies.　For flesh and wood
and all other similar bodies contain potentially fire and
earth, since one sees these elements exuded from them;
and, on the other hand, neither in potentiality nor in actuality
25 does fire contain flesh or wood, or it would exude them.

The nature of the heavenly body and the views of Parmenides and
Melissus, referred to by Simplicius, are not here in point.
　[1] i.e. a void outside bodies, as distinct from the fragments of void
which are supposed to be distributed throughout the texture of every
body.　Simplicius attributes the distinction of two kinds of void to the
authors of the theory themselves.
　[2] Reading in l. 2 τὸ γινόμενον, εἰ ἐγένετο with Bekker.　The manuscripts are confused, and offer many variánts.
　[3] viz. bodies subject to generation.　We read ποῖα τῶν τοιούτων with
the manuscripts, taking τῶν τοιούτων as a partitive genitive (after
Simplicius).

Similarly, even if there were only one elementary body, it would not contain them. For though it will be either flesh or bone or something else, that does not at once show that it contained these in potentiality: the further question remains, in what manner it becomes them. Now Anaxagoras opposes Empedocles' view of the elements. Empedocles says that fire and earth and the related bodies 30 are elementary bodies of which all things are composed; but this Anaxagoras denies. His elements are the homoeomerous things,[1] viz. flesh, bone, and the like. Earth and 302^b fire are mixtures, composed of them and all the other seeds, each consisting of a collection of all the homoeomerous bodies, separately invisible; and that explains why from these two bodies all others are generated. (To him fire and *aither* are the same thing.[2]) But since every natural 5 body has its proper movement, and movements are either simple or mixed, mixed in mixed bodies and simple in simple, there must obviously be simple bodies; for there are simple movements. It is plain, then, that there are elements, and why.

4   The next question to consider is whether the elements 10 are finite or infinite in number, and, if finite, what their number is. Let us first show reason for denying that their number is infinite, as some suppose. We begin with the view of Anaxagoras that all the homoeomerous bodies are elements.[3] Any one who adopts this view misapprehends 15 the meaning of element. Observation shows that even mixed bodies are often divisible into homoeomerous parts; examples are flesh, bone, wood, and stone. Since then the composite

---

[1] 'Homoeomerous' means 'having parts like one another and like the whole of which they are parts'. Some confusion is here caused by the fact that Aristotle sometimes uses 'homoeomerous' as an attribute of the parts of a homoeomerous whole, i.e. as meaning 'like one another and like the whole of which they are parts'. That is what he means when he says of a body (302^b 16) that it is 'divisible into homoeomerous parts' or (*ib.* 25) that it is 'composed of homoeomerous bodies'. The use of the term λεπτομερές (= μικρομερές) is complicated by a similar transference from whole to part (cp. 304^b 9, note).

[2] Cp. Book I, 270^b 24.

[3] τοὺς ... ποιοῦντας must be construed (by a kind of zeugma) with θεωρητέον.

cannot be an element, not every homoeomerous body can
be an element; only, as we said before,[1] that which is
20 not divisible into bodies different in form.[2] But even
taking 'element' as they do, they need not assert an
infinity of elements, since the hypothesis of a finite number
will give identical results. Indeed even two or three such
bodies serve the purpose as well, as Empedocles' attempt
shows. Again, even on their view it turns out that all
25 things are not composed of homoeomerous bodies. They
do not pretend that a face is composed of faces, or that any
other natural conformation is composed of parts like itself.[3]
Obviously then it would be better to assume a finite number
of principles. They should, in fact, be as few as possible,
consistently with proving what has to be proved. This is
30 the common demand of mathematicians, who always assume
as principles things finite either in kind or in number.[4]
Again, if body is distinguished from body by the appropriate qualitative difference, and there is a limit to
303^a the number of differences (for the difference lies in qualities
apprehended by sense, which are in fact finite in number,
though this requires proof[5]), then manifestly there is necessarily a limit to the number of elements.

There is, further, another view—that of Leucippus and
Democritus of Abdera—the implications of which are also

---

[1] Above, 302^a 18.

[2] 'Divisible into homoeomerous parts' = 'homoeomerous wholes'
(cp. note on 'homoeomerous' at 302^a 31). The argument is therefore
as follows: 'homoeomerous' includes mixed as well as simple bodies;
but any one who understood the meaning of the term 'element' would
have seen that a mixed body cannot be an element: instead of
regarding all homoeomerous bodies as elements, he would have
confined the term to such homoeomerous bodies as are simple.—As
an argument against Anaxagoras this is ineffective; for he (a) denied
that flesh, bone, &c., are mixed; (b) denied that earth, air, fire, and
water—cited by Simplicius as simple and homoeomerous—are simple.
Aristotle is content to argue from what he regards as established fact,
whether Anaxagoras admits it or not. Anaxagoras would have
claimed that the suggested criterion of indivisibility κατ' εἶδος was
satisfied by his ὁμοιομερῆ, and could therefore plead not guilty to the
charge of misapprehending the meaning of 'element'.

[3] All bodies should be either elements or composed of elements.
But Anaxagoras, though he makes his elements infinite, is still not
able to show that every whole is composed of parts like itself.

[4] Reading τὰ πεπερασμένα (so J, as well as three of Bekker's manuscripts).

[5] The proof of the proposition is given in De Sensu, 6 (445^b 20 ff.).

unacceptable. The primary masses, according to them, [5]
are infinite in number and indivisible in mass: one cannot
turn into many nor many into one; and all things are
generated by their combination and involution. Now this
view in a sense makes things out to be numbers or composed
of numbers.[1] The exposition is not clear, but this is its [10]
real meaning. And further, they say that since the atomic
bodies differ in shape, and there is an infinity of shapes,
there is an infinity of simple bodies. But they have never
explained in detail the shapes of the various elements,
except so far as to allot the sphere to fire. Air, water, [15]
and the rest they distinguished by the relative size of
the atom, assuming that the atomic substance was a sort
of master-seed for each and every element. Now, in
the first place, they make the mistake already noticed.
The principles which they assume are not limited in
number, though such limitation would necessitate no other
alteration in their theory. Further, if the differences of
bodies are not infinite, plainly the elements will not be [20]
an infinity.[2] Besides, a view which asserts atomic bodies
must needs come into conflict with the mathematical
sciences, in addition to invalidating many common opinions
and apparent data of sense perception. But of these things
we have already spoken in our discussion of time and movement.[3] They are also bound to contradict themselves. [25]
For if the elements are atomic, air, earth, and water cannot
be differentiated by the relative sizes of their atoms, since
then they could not be generated out of one another. The
extrusion of the largest atoms is a process that will in time
exhaust the supply; and it is by such a process that they
account for the generation of water, air, and earth from one
another.[4] Again, even on their own presuppositions it does [30]

---

[1] Because the atom is practically a mathematical unit, out of which
bodies are formed by simple addition. Cp. *Met.* Z. 13, 1039ᵃ 3 ff.

[2] Cp. 303ᵃ 1.   [3] Esp. *Phys.* VI. 1-2 (231ᵃ 18 ff.).

[4] Suppose water is being formed out of air; and suppose that the
water-atom is larger than the air-atom: what is required on this
theory is the extrusion from the air of the larger atoms. Conversely,
if air were being formed out of water, the smaller atoms would be
extruded from the water. But the supply of large (or small) atoms
will soon run out, and air not reducible to water (or water not reducible
to air) will be left.

not seem as if the elements would be infinite in number.
The atoms differ in figure, and all figures are composed of
303ᵇ pyramids, rectilinear in the case of rectilinear figures, while
the sphere has eight pyramidal parts.[1] The figures must
have their principles,[2] and, whether these are one or two
or more, the simple bodies must be the same in number
as they. Again, if every element has its proper movement,
5 and a simple body has a simple movement, and the number
of simple movements is not infinite, because the simple
motions are only two and the number of places is not
infinite,[3] on these grounds also we should have to deny
that the number of elements is infinite.

Since the number of the elements must be limited, it 5
10 remains to inquire whether there is more than one element.
Some assume one only, which is according to some [4] water,
to others [5] air, to others [6] fire, to others [7] again something
finer than water and denser than air, an infinite body—
so they say—embracing all the heavens.

Now those who decide for a single element, which is
either water or air or a body finer than water and denser
15 than air, and proceed to generate other things out of it
by use of the attributes density and rarity, all alike fail
to observe the fact that they are depriving the element
of its priority. Generation out of the elements is, as they
say, synthesis, and generation into the elements is analysis,

---

[1] The pyramids are tetrahedrons; and those produced by triple
section of a sphere are irregular, having a spherical base.

[2] i. e. there must be a limited number of primary figures to which all
other figures are reducible.

[3] There are only two places to which movement can be directed,
viz. the circumference and the centre. By the two simple motions
Aristotle probably here means motions towards these two places,
motion up and motion down. Circular motion is not possible beneath
the moon.

[4] Thales and Hippon.

[5] Anaximenes and Diogenes of Apollonia.

[6] Heracleitus and Hippasus: but see below, 304ᵃ 18, note.

[7] Anaximander. This identification has been rejected by many
modern scholars. See Bonitz, *Ind.* 50ᵃ 33, Diels, *Vors.*³ 18, 10 and
416, 1, Burnet, *E.G.P.*³ § 15. Diels follows Zeller in attributing the
view to a certain Idaios of Himera, whom Aristotle never mentions
by name and of whom hardly anything is known. Burnet refers the
passage to Anaximander.

so that the body with the finer parts must have priority
in the order of nature. But they say that fire is of all 20
bodies the finest. Hence fire will be first in the natural
order. And whether the finest body is fire or not makes
no difference; anyhow it must be one of the other bodies
that is primary and not that which is intermediate.[1] Again,
density and rarity, as instruments of generation, are equivalent to fineness and coarseness, since the fine is rare, and
coarse in their use means dense. But fineness and coarse- 25
ness, again, are equivalent to greatness and smallness, since
a thing with small parts is fine and a thing with large parts
coarse. For that which spreads itself out widely is fine,
and a thing composed of small parts is so spread out. In
the end, then, they distinguish the various other substances
from the element by the greatness and smallness of their 30
parts. This method of distinction makes all judgement relative. There will be no absolute distinction between fire, water,
and air, but one and the same body will be relatively to
this fire, relatively to something else air.[2] The same 304^a
difficulty is involved equally in the view which recognizes
several elements and distinguishes them by their greatness
and smallness. The principle of distinction between bodies
being quantity, the various sizes will be in a definite ratio,
and whatever bodies are in this ratio to one another must be 5
air, fire, earth, and water respectively. For the ratios of
smaller bodies may be repeated among greater bodies.[3]

Those who start from fire as the single element, while
avoiding this difficulty, involve themselves in many others.
Some of them give fire a particular shape, like those who 10
make it a pyramid, and this on one of two grounds. The
reason given may be—more crudely—that the pyramid is
the most piercing of figures as fire is of bodies,[4] or—more

---

[1] i.e. the rarest or finest body is the true element, as being the true
starting-point of the process of generation or synthesis; and a body
denser than fire and rarer than earth, like air or water, or finer than
water and denser than air, like Anaximander's infinite, will not do.

[2] For the attributes great and small belong to the category of
relation (*Cat.* 5^b 10 ff.).

[3] i.e. what is really asserted is a ratio, and ratio is independent
of size.

[4] Simplicius observes that the argument is justly called crude, since

ingeniously—the position may be supported by the following argument. As all bodies are composed of that which
15 has the finest parts, so all solid figures are composed of
pyramids: but the finest body is fire, while among figures
the pyramid is primary and has the smallest parts;[1] and
the primary body must have the primary figure: therefore
fire will be a pyramid.[2] Others, again, express no opinion on
the subject of its figure, but simply regard it as the body
20 of the finest parts, which in combination will form other
bodies, as the fusing of gold-dust produces solid gold.
Both of these views involve the same difficulties. For (1)
if, on the one hand, they make the primary body an atom,
the view will be open to the objections already advanced
against the atomic theory. And further the theory is incon
25 sistent with a regard for the facts of nature. For if all
bodies are quantitatively commensurable, and the relative
size of the various homoeomerous masses and of their
several elements are in the same ratio, so that the total
mass of water,[3] for instance, is related to the total mass
of air as the elements of each are to one another, and
30 so on, and if there is more air than water and, generally,
more of the finer body than of the coarser, obviously the
element of water will be smaller than that of air.[4] But
the lesser quantity is contained in the greater. Therefore

it involves an undistributed middle: 'fire is piercing', 'the pyramid
is piercing': they attempt to draw an affirmative conclusion in the
second figure.

[1] Reading μικρομερέστατον with FHMJ. The word is used as
equivalent to λεπτομερέστατον, which is the reading of EL and (probably) of Simplicius.—The pyramid is presumably said to have the
smallest parts because it contains fewer of the primary triangles than
any other regular solid. But the assertion is not thereby justified.
Given a certain size of triangle, the pyramid would be the smallest of
the solids in cubic content; thus the body composed of pyramids
would be the body with the smallest parts. The epithet λεπτομερές,
in short, seems to be transferred from the whole to the part, just as
ὁμοιομερές was (above, 302[a] 31, note).

[2] To whom is this 'more ingenious' version to be attributed?
'Heracleitus made fire the universal element but did not say it was
a pyramid, and the Pythagoreans, who said that fire was composed
of pyramids, did not make it the universal element' (Simpl.).

[3] Perhaps οἷον τό should be read for οἷον τά.

[4] The ascertained fact on which this argument is based is that
when (e. g.) water turns into air, the volume of the resultant air is

the air element is divisible. And the same could be shown 304^b
of fire and of all bodies whose parts are relatively fine.
(2) If, on the other hand, the primary body is divisible, then
(*a*) those who give fire a special shape will have to say
that a part of fire is not fire, because a pyramid is not
composed of pyramids,[1] and also that not every body 5
is either an element or composed of elements, since a
part of fire will be neither fire nor any other element.
And (*b*) those whose ground of distinction is size will
have to recognize an element prior to the element, a
regress which continues infinitely, since every body is divisible and that which has the smallest parts is the element.[2]
Further, they too will have to say that the same body is
relatively to this fire and relatively to that air, to others 10
again water and earth.

The common error of all views which assume a single
element is that they allow only one natural movement,
which is the same for every body. For it is a matter
of observation that a natural body possesses a principle
of movement. If then all bodies are one, all will have 15
one movement. With this motion the greater their quantity
the more they will move, just as fire, in proportion as its
quantity is greater, moves faster with the upward motion
which belongs to it. But the fact is that increase of quantity
makes many things move the faster downward. For these
reasons, then, as well as from the distinction already 20
established[3] of a plurality of natural movements, it is
impossible that there should be only one element. But
if the elements are not an infinity and not reducible to
one, they must be several and finite in number.

greater than that of the original water. This increase of volume can
only be accounted for (since the hypothesis of a void has been refuted)
by supposing an increase in the volume of the atom proportionate to
the observed increase in the volume of the total mass. But the
enlarged atom would be divisible, and therefore no atom.

[1] i. e. a pyramid cannot be divided so that *every* part is a pyramid.

[2] If every body is infinitely divisible, it is difficult to give a precise
meaning to 'that which has the smallest parts'. Further, the phrase,
as used, is somewhat illogical; for the argument would point to the
smallest part of any body, rather than the body with the smallest
parts, as the element. But the use of λεπτομερές (and μικρομερές) as
an epithet of the part instead of the whole occurs elsewhere (cf. note
on 304^a 16).   [3] Book I, c. ii.

First we must inquire whether the elements are eternal **6**
or subject to generation and destruction; for when this
25 question has been answered their number and character will
be manifest. In the first place, they cannot be eternal.
It is a matter of observation that fire, water, and every
simple body undergo a process of analysis, which must [1]
either continue infinitely or stop somewhere. (1) Suppose
it infinite. Then the time occupied by the process will be
infinite, and also that occupied by the reverse process of
30 synthesis. For the processes of analysis and synthesis
succeed one another in the various parts. It will follow
that there are two infinite times which are mutually exclusive, the time occupied by the synthesis, which is infinite,
being preceded by the period of analysis. There are thus
305^a two mutually exclusive infinites, which is impossible.
(2) Suppose, on the other hand, that the analysis stops
somewhere. Then the body at which it stops will be either
atomic or, as Empedocles seems to have intended, a divisible
body which will yet never be divided. The foregoing argu-
5 ments [2] show that it cannot be an atom; but neither can it
be a divisible body which analysis will never reach.. For
a smaller body is more easily destroyed than a larger;
and a destructive process which succeeds in destroying,
that is, in resolving into smaller bodies, a body of some
size, cannot reasonably be expected to fail with the smaller
10 body. Now in fire we observe a destruction of two kinds:
it is destroyed by its contrary when it is quenched, and
by itself when it dies out. [3] But the effect is produced by
a greater quantity upon a lesser, and the more quickly the
smaller it is. The elements of bodies must therefore be
subject to destruction and generation.

Since they are generated, they must be generated either
15 from something incorporeal or from a body, and if from
a body, either from one another or from something else.
The theory which generates them from something in-

---

[1] Reading ἀνάγκη δέ with the MSS.　　　　　　　　[2] c. iv.
[3] i.e. it may die out 'of itself'. Aristotle does not develop this, but
his point is only the simple one that the smaller the fire is, the sooner,
by either process, it is destroyed.

corporeal requires an extra-corporeal void.[1] For everything that comes to be comes to be in something,[2] and that
in which the generation takes place must either be incorporeal or possess body; and if it has body, there will be
two bodies in the same place at the same time, viz. that
which is coming to be and that which was previously there, 20
while if it is incorporeal, there must be an extra-corporeal
void. But we have already shown[3] that this is impossible.
But, on the other hand, it is equally impossible that the
elements should be generated from some kind of body.
That would involve a body distinct from the elements and
prior to them. But if this body possesses weight or lightness, it will be one of the elements; and if it has no 25
tendency to movement, it will be an immovable or mathematical entity, and therefore not in a place at all. A place
in which a thing is at rest is a place in which it might move,
either by constraint, i. e. unnaturally, or in the absence of
constraint, i. e. naturally. If, then, it is in a place and
somewhere,[4] it will be one of the elements; and if it is
not in a place, nothing can come from it, since that which 30
comes into being and that out of which it comes must
needs be together. The elements therefore cannot be
generated from something incorporeal nor from a body
which is not an element, and the only remaining alternative
is that they are generated from one another.

7 We must, therefore, turn to the question, what is the
manner of their generation from one another? Is it as
Empedocles and Democritus say, or as those who resolve 35
bodies into planes say, or is there yet another possibility? 305^b

---

[1] γεννώμενον is found only in EL, and the other four manuscripts
offer no substitute. It was clearly not in Simplicius' text. κεχωρισμένον,
or another word of similar meaning, must be read.

[2] The words ἐν τινι γίνεται καί are a conjectural addition suggested
by Simplicius (after Alexander). They occur (without the καί) in one
of our manuscripts, M, whose original readings are mostly either
errors or conjectures. Without these words it is almost impossible
to make any sense of the passage; but they are not intrinsically
a probable conjecture and are only accepted because a better remedy
remains to be suggested.

[3] *Phys.* IV. 8.

[4] Placing the comma after που (1 29) instead of after τόπῳ (1. 28).
To be 'somewhere' is to be 'in a place'.

(1) What the followers of Empedocles do, though without observing it themselves, is to reduce the generation of elements out of one another to an illusion. They make it a process of excretion from a body of what was in it all the time—as though generation required a vessel rather than 5 a material—so that it involves no change of anything. And even if this were accepted, there are other implications equally unsatisfactory. We do not expect a mass of matter to be made heavier by compression. But they will be bound to maintain this, if they say that water is a body present in air and excreted from air, since air becomes 10 heavier when it turns into water.[1] Again, when the mixed body is divided, they can show no reason why one of the constituents must by itself take up more room than the body did: but when water turns into air, the room occupied is increased. The fact is that the finer body takes up more room, as is obvious in any case of transforma- 15 tion. As the liquid is converted into vapour or air the vessel which contains it is often burst because it does not contain room enough. Now, if there is no void at all, and if, as those who take this view say, there is no expansion of bodies,[2] the impossibility of this is manifest: and if there is void and expansion, there is no accounting for the fact that the body which results from division occupies of 20 necessity a greater space. It is inevitable, too, that generation of one out of another should come to a stop, since a finite quantum cannot contain an infinity of finite quanta. When earth produces water something is taken away from the earth, for the process is one of excretion. The same thing happens again when the residue produces water. 25 But this can only go on for ever, if the finite body contains an infinity, which is impossible. Therefore the generation of elements out of one another will not always continue.[3]

[1] More accurately, becomes heavy, since air rises and water falls. Lightness is treated here as a low degree of heaviness.

[2] The words καθάπερ φασὶν οἱ τ. λ. must be taken to refer only to expansion, since Democritus of course believed in a void.

[3] In the end the elements will be sorted out, and there will remain several homogeneous masses between which no interchange is possible.

(2) We have now explained that the mutual transformations of the elements cannot take place by means of excretion. The remaining alternative is that they should be generated by changing into one another. And this in one of two ways, either by change of shape, as the same wax takes 30 the shape both of a sphere and of a cube, or, as some assert, by resolution' into planes. (a) Generation by change of shape would necessarily involve the assertion of atomic bodies. For if the particles were divisible there would be a part of fire which was not fire and a part of earth which was not earth, for the reason that not every part of a 35 pyramid is a pyramid nor of a cube a cube. But if **306^a** (b) the process is resolution into planes, the first difficulty is that the elements cannot all be generated out of one another. This they are obliged to assert, and do assert. It is absurd, because it is unreasonable that one element alone should have no part in the transformations, and also contrary to the observed data of sense, according to which all 5 alike change into one another. In fact their explanation of the observations is not consistent with the observations. And the reason is that their ultimate principles are wrongly assumed : they had certain predetermined views, and were resolved to bring everything into line with them. It seems that perceptible things require perceptible principles, 10 eternal things eternal principles, corruptible things corruptible principles; and, in general, every subject matter principles homogeneous with itself. But they, owing to their love for their principles, fall into the attitude of men who undertake the defence of a position in argument. In the confidence that the principles are true they are ready to accept any consequence of their application. As though some principles did not require to be judged 15 from their results, and particularly from their final issue! And that issue, which in the case of productive knowledge[1] is the product, in the knowledge of nature is the unimpeachable evidence of the senses as to each fact.

The result of their view is that earth has the best right to the name element, and is alone indestructible ; for that

---

[1] i. e. in the case of art.

20 which is indissoluble is indestructible and elementary, and earth alone cannot be dissolved into any body but itself. Again, in the case of those elements which do suffer dissolution, the 'suspension' of the triangles is unsatisfactory. But this takes place whenever one is dissolved into another, because of the numerical inequality of the triangles which compose them.[1] Further, those who hold these views must needs suppose that generation does not 25 start from a body. For what is generated out of planes cannot be said to have been generated from a body. And they must also assert that not all bodies are divisible, coming thus into conflict with our most accurate sciences, namely the mathematical, which assume that even the intelligible is divisible, while they, in their anxiety to save 30 their hypothesis, cannot even admit this of every perceptible thing. For any one who gives each element a shape of its own, and makes this the ground of distinction between the substances, has to attribute to them indivisibility; since division of a pyramid or a sphere must leave somewhere at least a residue which is not a sphere or a pyramid. Either, then, a part of fire is not fire, so that 306^b there is a body prior to the element—for every body is either an element or composed of elements—or not every body is divisible.

In general, the attempt to give a shape to each of the 8 simple bodies is unsound, for the reason, first, that they 5 will not succeed in filling the whole. It is agreed that there are only three plane figures which can fill a space, the triangle, the square, and the hexagon, and only two solids, the pyramid and the cube.[2] But the theory needs more than these because the elements which it recognizes are more in number. Secondly, it is manifest that the simple 10 bodies are often given a shape by the place in which they are included, particularly water and air. In such a case the shape of the element cannot persist; for, if it did, the

---

[1] e. g. the εἰκοσάεδρον of water, with its twenty triangles, has to be converted into the ὀκτάεδρον of air, with eight triangles. Four of the twenty component triangles of the water-particle will be 'suspended'.

[2] Only regular figures are included.

contained mass would not be in continuous contact with the containing body; while, if its shape is changed, it will cease to be water, since the distinctive quality is shape. Clearly, then, their shapes are not fixed.[1] Indeed, nature 15 itself seems to offer corroboration of this theoretical conclusion. Just as in other cases the substratum must be formless and unshapen—for thus the 'all-receptive', as we read in the *Timaeus*,[2] will be best for modelling—so the elements should be conceived as a material for composite 20 things; and that is why they can put off their qualitative distinctions and pass into one another. Further, how can they account for the generation of flesh and bone or any other continuous body? The elements alone cannot produce them because their collocation cannot produce a continuum. 25 Nor can the composition of planes; for this produces the elements themselves, not bodies made up of them. Any one then who insists upon an exact statement of this kind of theory,[3] instead of assenting after a passing glance at it, will see that it removes generation from the world.

Further, the very properties, powers, and motions, to 30 which they paid particular attention in allotting shapes, show the shapes not to be in accord with the bodies. Because fire is mobile and productive of heat[4] and combustion, some made it a sphere, others a pyramid. These shapes, they thought, were the most mobile because they offer the fewest points of contact and are the least stable of 307^a any; they were also the most apt to produce warmth and combustion, because the one is angular throughout[5] while the other has the most acute angles, and the angles, they say, produce warmth and combustion. Now, in the first place, with regard to movement both are in error. These may be the figures best adapted to movement; they are 5

---

[1] Reading αὐτῶν for αὐτοῦ, with LMJ.

[2] Plato, *Tim.* 51 A. At Mr. Ross's suggestion, I have altered the stopping of the sentence. Delete comma after ἄλλοις (l. 17), and enclose the words μάλιστα γὰρ . . . τὸ πανδεχές (ll. 18-19) within brackets.

[3] Reading τοὺς τοιούτους with FHMJ.

[4] Prantl's text (presumably by accident) omits the καί before θερμαντικόν.

[5] Cf. below, 307^a 16.

not, however, well adapted to the movement of fire, which is an upward and rectilinear movement, but rather to that form of circular movement which we call rolling. Earth, again,[1] they call a cube because it is stable and at rest. But it rests only in its own place, not anywhere; from 10 any other it moves if nothing hinders, and fire and the other bodies do the same. The obvious inference, therefore, is that fire and each several element is in a foreign place a sphere or a pyramid, but in its own a cube. Again, if the possession of angles makes a body produce 15 heat and combustion, every element produces heat, though one may do so more than another. For they all possess angles, the octahedron and dodecahedron as well as the pyramid; and Democritus makes even the sphere a kind of angle, which cuts things because of its mobility.[2] The difference, then, will be one of degree: and this is plainly false. They must also accept the inference that the mathe- 20 matical solids produce heat and combustion, since they too possess angles and contain atomic spheres[3] and pyramids, especially if there are, as they allege, atomic figures.[4] Any- how if these functions belong to some of these things and not to others, they should explain the difference, instead of speaking in quite general terms as they do. Again, 25 combustion of a body produces fire, and fire is a sphere or a pyramid. The body, then, is turned into spheres or pyramids. Let us grant that these figures may reasonably be supposed to cut and break up bodies as fire does; still it remains quite inexplicable that a pyramid must needs produce pyramids or a sphere spheres. One might as well 30 postulate that a knife or a saw divides things into knives or saws. It is also ridiculous to think only of division when allotting fire its shape. Fire is generally thought of as combining and connecting rather than as separating.

---

[1] Prantl has εἶπειτ' for ἔπειτ' by a misprint.

[2] Though it has a low degree of angularity, it is highly mobile and therefore extremely piercing. But the double ὡς is awkward, and perhaps the tradition is at fault. (J has τέμνει ὡς εὐκίνητον, supporting E against the other MSS.)

[3] Prantl's σφαῖρα is a misprint for σφαῖραι.

[4] i. e. indivisible units of line, of which the geometrical figures are composed.

For though it separates bodies different in kind, it combines 307^b those which are the same; and the combining is essential to it, the functions of connecting and uniting being a mark of fire, while the separating is incidental. For the expulsion of the foreign body is an incident in the compacting of the homogeneous. In choosing the shape, then, they should have thought either of both functions or preferably of the 5 combining function. In addition, since hot and cold are contrary powers, it is impossible to allot any shape to the cold. For the shape given must be the contrary of that given to the hot, but there is no contrariety between figures. That is why. they have all left the cold out, though properly either all or none should have their dis- 10 tinguishing figures. Some of them, however, do attempt to explain this power, and they contradict themselves. A body of large particles, they say, is cold because instead of penetrating through the passages it crushes. Clearly, then, that which is hot is that which penetrates these passages, or in other words that which has fine particles. It results that hot and cold are distinguished not by the 15 figure but by the size of the particles. Again, if the pyramids are unequal in size, the large ones will not be fire, and that figure will produce not combustion but its contrary.

From what has been said it is clear that the difference of the elements does not depend upon their shape. Now their most important differences are those of property, 20 function, and power; for every natural body has, we maintain, its own functions, properties, and powers. Our first business, then, will be to speak of these, and that inquiry will enable us to explain the differences of each from each.

BOOK IV

307ᵇ WE have now to consider the terms 'heavy' and 'light'. 1
We must ask what the bodies so called are, how they are
30 constituted, and what is the reason of their possessing these
powers. The consideration of these questions is a proper
part of the theory of movement, since we call things heavy
and light because they have the power of being moved
naturally in a certain way. The activities corresponding
to these powers have not been given any name, unless
308ᵃ it is thought that 'impetus' is such a name. But because
the inquiry into nature is concerned with movement,[1] and
these things have in themselves some spark (as it were)
of movement, all inquirers avail themselves of these powers,
though in all but a few cases without exact discrimination.
5 We must then first look at whatever others have said, and
formulate the questions which require settlement in the
interests of this inquiry, before we go on to state our own
view of the matter.

Language recognizes (a) an absolute, (b) a relative heavy
and light. Of two heavy things, such as wood and bronze,
we say that the one is relatively light, the other relatively
10 heavy. Our predecessors have not dealt at all with the
absolute use of the terms, but only with the relative. I mean,
they do not explain what the heavy is or what the light
is, but only the relative heaviness and lightness of things
possessing weight. This can be made clearer as follows.
There are things whose constant nature it is to move away
15 from the centre, while others move constantly towards the
centre; and of these movements that which is away from
the centre I call upward movement and that which is
towards it I call downward movement. (The view, urged
by some,[2] that there is no up and no down in the heaven,
is absurd. There can be, they say, no up and no down, since

---

[1] Read φυσικὴν μὲν εἶναι (E alone omits μέν).
[2] The digression is directed against Plato, *Tim.* 62 E; but the view
was held by others besides Timaeus.

⟩ the universe is similar every way, and from any point on 20
the earth's surface a man by advancing far enough will
come to stand foot to foot with himself. But the extremity
of the whole, which we call 'above', is in position above and
in nature primary. And since the universe has an extremity
and a centre, it must clearly have an up and down. Common
usage is thus correct,[1] though inadequate. And the reason 25
of its inadequacy is that men think that the universe is not
similar every way. They recognize only the hemisphere
which is over us. But if they went on to think of the
world as formed on this pattern all round, with a centre
identically related to each point on the extremity, they
would have to admit that the extremity was above and
the centre below.) By absolutely light, then, we mean that
which moves upward or to the extremity, and by absolutely 30
heavy that which moves downward or to the centre. By
lighter or relatively light we mean that one, of two bodies
endowed with weight and equal in bulk, which is exceeded
by the other in the speed of its natural downward movement.[2]

2   Those of our predecessors who have entered upon this
inquiry have for the most part spoken of light and heavy 35
things only in the sense in which one of two things both 308^b
endowed with weight is said to be the lighter. And this
treatment they consider a sufficient analysis also of the
notions of absolute heaviness and absolute lightness, to
which their account does not apply. This, however, will
become clearer as we advance. One use of the terms
'lighter' and 'heavier' is that which is set forth in writing 5
in the *Timaeus*,[3] that the body which is composed of the
greater number of identical parts is relatively heavy, while
that which is composed of a smaller number is relatively

---

[1] Read ὥσπερ with FHMJ.
[2] Accepting Prantl's first correction, οὖ (for ὅ), which seems to be
necessary to the sense. His second correction, ἴσων (for ἴσον), is to
be rejected as unnecessary. Bywater (*J. of Phil.* xxviii, p. 242)
suggests θατέρου, keeping ὅ and ἴσον; but the phrase, so emended,
seems to be descriptive of the heavy rather than of the light.
[3] 63 C.

light. As a larger quantity of lead or of bronze is heavier than a smaller—and this holds good of all homogeneous masses, the superior weight always depending upon a
10 numerical superiority of equal parts—in precisely the same way, they assert, lead is heavier than wood.[1] For all bodies, in spite of the general opinion to the contrary, are composed of identical parts and of a single material. But this analysis says nothing of the absolutely heavy and light. The facts are that fire is always light and moves upward, while earth and all earthy things move downwards or
15 towards the centre. It cannot then be the fewness of the triangles (of which, in their view, all these bodies are composed)[2] which disposes fire to move upward. If it were, the greater the quantity of fire the slower it would move, owing to the increase of weight due to the increased number of triangles. But the palpable fact, on the contrary, is that the greater the quantity, the lighter the mass is and
20 the quicker its upward movement: and, similarly, in the reverse movement from above downward, the small mass will move quicker and the large slower. Further, since to be lighter is to have fewer of these homogeneous parts and to be heavier is to have more, and air, water, and fire are composed of the same triangles, the only difference being
25 in the number of such parts, which must therefore explain any distinction of relatively light and heavy between these bodies, it follows that there must be a certain quantum of air which is heavier than water. But the facts are directly opposed to this. The larger the quantity of air the more readily it moves upward, and any portion of air without exception will rise up out of the water.

So much for one view of the distinction between light
30 and heavy. To others[3] the analysis seems insufficient; and their views on the subject, though they belong to an older generation than ours, have an air of novelty. It is apparent

---

[1] I put a colon in l. 6 after ἐλαττόνων and mark ll. 8-9, ὁμοίως δέ . . . ἐστιν, as parenthetical. This leaves an asyndeton at ὥσπερ in l. 7, but it seems to give the sequence of thought better than the stopping of Bekker and Prantl does.

[2] There should be a comma after τριγώνων in l. 15.

[3] The atomists, Democritus and Leucippus.

that there are bodies which, when smaller in bulk than others, yet exceed them in weight. It is therefore obviously insufficient to say that bodies of equal weight are composed of an equal number of primary parts: for that would give 35 equality of bulk. Those who maintain that the primary or atomic parts, of which bodies endowed with weight are composed, are planes, cannot so speak without absurdity;[1] 309ᵃ but those who regard them as solids are in a better position to assert that of such bodies the larger is the heavier. But since in composite bodies the weight obviously does not correspond in this way to the bulk, the lesser bulk being often superior in weight (as, for instance, if one be wool 5 and the other bronze), there are some who think and say that the cause is to be found elsewhere. The void, they say, which is imprisoned in bodies, lightens them and sometimes makes the larger body the lighter. The reason is that there is more void. And this would also account for the fact that a body composed of a number of solid parts equal to, or even smaller than, that of another is sometimes larger in bulk than it. In short, generally and in every 10 case a body is relatively light when it contains a relatively large amount of void. This is the way they put it themselves, but their account requires an addition. Relative lightness must depend not only on an excess of void, but also on a defect of solid: for if the ratio of solid to void exceeds a certain proportion, the relative lightness will 15 disappear. Thus fire, they say, is the lightest of things just for this reason that it has the most void. But it would follow that a large mass of gold, as containing more void than a small mass of fire, is lighter than it, unless it also contains many times as much solid. The addition is therefore necessary.

Of those who deny the existence of a void some, like Anaxagoras and Empedocles, have not tried to analyse the notions of light and heavy at all; and those who, while still 20 denying the existence of a void, have attempted this,[2] have

---

[1] For, since the planes have no weight, their number cannot affect the weight of a body.

[2] Plato, in the *Timaeus.*

failed to explain why there are bodies which are absolutely
heavy and light, or in other words why some move upward
and others downward. The fact, again, that the body of
25 greater bulk is sometimes lighter than smaller bodies is one
which they have passed over in silence, and what they have
said gives no obvious suggestion for reconciling their views
with the observed facts.

But those who attribute the lightness of fire to its containing so much void are necessarily involved in practically
the same difficulties. For though fire be supposed to
30 contain less solid than any other body, as well as more
void, yet there will be a certain quantum of fire in which
the amount of solid or plenum is in excess of the solids
contained in some small quantity of earth. They may
reply that there is an excess of void also. But the question
is, how will they discriminate the absolutely heavy? Presumably, either by its excess of solid or by its defect
309ᵇ of void. On the former view there could be an amount of
earth so small as to contain less solid than a large mass of
fire. And similarly, if the distinction rests on the amount
of void, there will be a body, lighter than the absolutely
light, which nevertheless moves downward as constantly as
5 the other moves upward. But that cannot be so, since the
absolutely light is always lighter than bodies which have
weight and move downward, while, on the other hand, that
which is lighter need not be light, because in common
speech we distinguish a lighter and a heavier (viz. water
and earth) among bodies endowed with weight. Again,
the suggestion of a certain ratio between the void and the
solid in a body is no more equal to solving the problem
10 before us. This manner of speaking will issue in a similar
impossibility. For any two portions of fire, small or great,
will exhibit the same ratio of solid to void; but the upward
movement of the greater is quicker than that of the less,
just as the downward movement of a mass of gold or lead,
15 or of any other body endowed with weight, is quicker in
proportion to its size. This, however, should not be the
case if the ratio is the ground of distinction between heavy
things and light. There is also an absurdity in attributing

the upward movement of bodies to a void which does not itself move. If, however, it is the nature of a void to move upward and of a plenum to move downward, and therefore each causes a like movement in other things,[1] there was 20 no need to raise the question why composite bodies are some light and some heavy; they had only to explain why these two things are themselves light and heavy respectively, and to give, further, the reason why the plenum and the void are not eternally separated. It is also unreasonable to imagine a place for the void, as if the void were not 25 itself a kind of place.[2] But if the void is to move, it must have a place out of which and into which the change carries it. Also what is the cause of its movement? Not, surely, its voidness: for it is not the void only which is moved, but also the solid.[3]

Similar difficulties are involved in all other methods of distinction, whether they account for the relative lightness 30 and heaviness of bodies by distinctions of size, or proceed on any other principle, so long as they attribute to each the same matter, or even if they recognize more than one matter, so long as that means only a pair of contraries. If there is a single matter, as with those who compose things of triangles, nothing can be absolutely heavy or light: and if there is one matter and its contrary—the void, for 310[a] instance, and the plenum—no reason can be given for the relative lightness and heaviness of the bodies intermediate between the absolutely light and heavy when compared either with one another or with these themselves.[4] The

---

[1] Read φορᾶς ἑκατέρας. ἑκατέρας is in all MSS. except E, and is implied in Simplicius' paraphrase.

[2] Read αὐτό with FHMJ and the corrector of E. The construction is certainly loose, but the other reading (αὐτῷ) does not give the required sense. To give void a motion is to give it a 'place', i.e. a natural place to which it moves. But it is itself nothing but a place where no body is (cf. *Phys.* IV. 7): and, as Simplicius punningly remarks, 'it is out of place to give a place a place' (τοῦ δὲ τόπου τόπον ποιεῖν τῶν ἀτοπωτάτων ἐστίν).

[3] If movement is natural to both void and solid, the cause of movement must lie in something common to both and not in the peculiar nature of either, i.e. not in voidness or solidity.

[4] Aristotle's argument is that the observed diversity of movement necessarily involves a corresponding diversity of bodies: hence any view which makes the four elements one in substance fails to account

view which bases the distinction upon differences of size is
5 more like a mere fiction than those previously-mentioned,
but, in that it is able to make distinctions between the four
elements, it is in a stronger position for meeting the foregoing difficulties. Since, however,[1] it imagines that these
bodies which differ in size are all made of one substance,
it implies, equally with the view that there is but one
matter, that there is nothing absolutely light and nothing
10 which moves upward (except as being passed by other
things or forced up by them);[2] and since a multitude of
small atoms are heavier than a few large ones, it will follow
that much air or fire is heavier than a little water or earth,
which is impossible.

These, then, are the views which have been advanced by 3
15 others and the terms in which they state them. We may
begin our own statement by settling a question which to
some has been the main difficulty—the question why some
bodies move always and naturally upward and others downward, while others again move both upward and downward.
After that we will inquire into light and heavy and the
20 explanation of the various phenomena connected with
them.[3] The local movement of each body into its own
place must be regarded as similar to what happens in connexion with other forms of generation and change. There

for the facts of movement. He here adds that it is not enough to
recognize two kinds of substance or two contrary attributes. For
there are four bodies to be accounted for. A single pair of opposites
may yield an account of fire and earth, but they cannot account also
for the 'intermediate bodies', water and air. Two pairs of opposites
will be required, such as those which he uses himself (warm, cold:
dry, moist).—In l. 3 τῶν ἁπλῶν must refer to the things also called τῶν
ἁπλῶς βαρέων καὶ κούφων. Simplicius tells us that Alexander read
τῶν ἁπλῶν, but found in some MSS. τῶν ἁπλῶς. ἁπλῶς is tempting,
but ἁπλῶν may be allowed to stand: for (a) the absolutely heavy and
light are, on the theory criticized, pure solid and pure void respectively: thus τὰ ἁπλῶς are τὰ ἁπλᾶ: (b) all other bodies whatever will
be composed of these in combination, and may therefore be opposed
to them as composite to simple.

  [1] Reading τῷ with HMLJ. Simplicius' paraphrase supports this.
  [2] i.e. upward movement is either (a) illusory: as all things race
downward, some, moving slower, are left behind, and thus appear to
move up: or (b) unnatural: due to pressure applied from without by
other bodies pushing downward.
  [3] Prantl misprints γένεται for γίνεται.

are, in fact, three kinds of movement, affecting respectively
the size, the form, and the place of a thing, and in each it
is observable that change proceeds from a contrary to 25
a contrary or to something intermediate: it is never the
change of any chance subject in any chance direction, nor,
similarly, is the relation of the mover to its object fortuitous: the thing altered is different from the thing
increased, and precisely the same difference holds between
that which produces alteration and that which produces
increase. In the same manner it must be thought that 30
that which produces local motion and that which is so
moved are not fortuitously related. Now,[1] that which produces upward and downward movement is that which
produces weight and lightness, and that which is moved
is that which is potentially heavy or light, and the movement of each body to its own place is motion towards
its own form. (It is best to interpret in this sense the 310ᵇ
common statement of the older writers that 'like moves to
like'. For the words are not in every sense true to fact.
If one were to remove the earth to where the moon now is,
the various fragments of earth would each move not towards
it but to the place in which it now is. In general, when 5
a number of similar and undifferentiated bodies are moved
with the same motion this result is necessarily produced,
viz. that the place which is the natural goal of the movement of each single part is also that of the whole.[2] But
since the place of a thing is the boundary of that which
contains it, and the continent of all things that move
upward or downward is the extremity and the centre, and
this boundary comes to be, in a sense, the form of that 10
which is contained, it is to its like that a body moves when

---

[1] Reading εἰ οὖν εἰς with EL (Simplicius' MSS. had, some εἰ μὲν εἰς,
and some εἰ μέν. J has εἰς οὖν). The apodosis does not begin till
310ᵇ 16 τὸ δὲ ζητεῖν, the argument being interrupted by a long note on
the meaning of the saying ὅμοιον πρὸς ὅμοιον, which should be marked
as a parenthesis.

[2] ὥσθ' ὅπου . . . τὸ πᾶν is explanatory of τοῦτο συμβαίνειν. Grammatically the predicate to be supplied to τὸ πᾶν is πέφυκε φέρεσθαι,
though this in the context creates a slight illogicality. Aristotle's
point is that a fragment of earth moves to the mass called the earth,
not because it loves its like, but *per accidens* in the effort to reach the
centre. It is the effort of numberless such fragments to reach
the centre which has formed the mass, not the presence of the mass
at the centre which causes the effort.

it moves to its own place. For the successive members of
the series[1] are like one another: water, I mean, is like air
and air like fire, and between intermediates the relation
may be converted, though not between them and the
extremes; thus air is like water, but water is like earth:[2]
15 for the relation of each outer body to that which is next
within it is that of form to matter.[3]) Thus[4] to ask why fire

[1] ἐφεξῆς should be read, with the other MSS. and Simplicius, rather
than E's ἑξῆς. Cf. *de Gen. et Corr.* 331^b 4, 26, 34.

[2] i. e. though air is like fire, fire is not like air; and though water is
like earth, earth is not like water. See next note. Prantl proposes
to take μέσοις and ἄκροις in l. 13 to mean inner and outer respectively,
i. e. to make the former stand for earth and water, the latter for fire
and air. His reason is grammatical: μέσοις is in the dative and so
are ὕδατι and γῇ. Thus a construction is provided for μέσοις. He
omits to observe that τοῖς δ' ἄκροις οὐ becomes meaningless: which,
with the admitted difficulty of taking the terms in this sense, is
sufficient reason for rejecting the proposal. It is no doubt due to
ὅμοια that μέσοις is in the dative: *likeness to* a μέσον is convertible,
likeness to an ἄκρον not.

[3] The connexion is difficult, and may be explained as follows.
Aristotle's argument is formally concluded at φέρεσθαι in l. 11 ('to its
own place'). The 'place' (centre and extremity, as explained) gives
form to the body, and the body in reaching its place attains its form,
i. e. completes the transition from potentiality to actuality. In a sense,
then, if the potential is like the actual, it moves 'to its like'. The γάρ
in l. 11 forestalls an objection. 'There remain the intermediate
bodies: what of them?' These are given form or determined by
the extreme bodies, and thus mediately determined by the 'place'.
Instead of saying 'are given form' or 'are determined' Aristotle says
'are like'; being entitled to do so by the meaning just given to 'like'.
The like to which earth moves is that from which it receives its form,
and the like to which water and air move is the extreme body—earth
in the one case, fire in the other—from which each receives its form.
Thus 'like' means 'receptive of form from'. In this sense water
is like air which is like fire, and air is like water which is like earth;
but the extremes themselves, earth and fire, are like nothing but their
places. The relation of likeness is reciprocal (i. e. determination is
mutual) only between the intermediates; and the chain of resemblance
breaks off in each direction short of the extreme. Starting from the
centre, we find in the three terms, water, air, fire, a gradual approximation (ἀεὶ τὸ ἀνώτερον . . .) to the form realized in fire; starting from the
extremity, we find in the terms air, water, earth, a gradual approximation to the form realized in earth. (Of these two complementary
statements Aristotle gives only the first; but the second is necessary
to complete the argument.) Therefore the intermediate bodies, as
well as the extremes, may be said in moving to their places to attain
their form.—The above account agrees in principle with that of
Simplicius, who, however, is not very clear. Alexander, he tells us,
took another view, based on a different interpretation of ἀεὶ τὸ
ἀνώτερον κτλ. As reported the view is not easy to fit into the
context.—For the relation of upper to lower bodies, cf. 312^a 15 and
De Gen. et Corr. 335^a 18.

[4] Alexander's δή for δέ here, like his τῶν ἄλλων for τούτων in l. 22,

moves upward and earth downward is the same as to ask
why the healable, when moved and changed *quâ* healable,
attains health and not whiteness; and similar questions
might be asked concerning any other subject of alteration.
Of course the subject of increase, when changed *quâ* in- 20
creasable, attains not health but a superior size. The same
applies in the other cases. One thing changes in quality,
another in quantity: and so in place, a light thing goes
upward, a heavy thing downward. The only difference is
that in the last case, viz. that of the heavy and the light,
the bodies are thought to have a spring of change within 25
themselves, while the subjects of healing and increase are
thought to be moved purely from without. Sometimes,
however, even they change of themselves, i.e. in response
to a slight external movement reach health or increase, as
the case may be. And since the same thing which is healable is also receptive of disease, it depends on whether it is 30
moved *quâ* healable or *quâ* liable to disease whether the
motion is towards health or towards disease. But the
reason why the heavy and the light appear more than
these things to contain within themselves the source of
their movements is that their matter is nearest to being.
This is indicated by the fact that locomotion belongs to
bodies only when isolated from other bodies,[1] and is generated
last of the several kinds of movement; in order of being
then it will be first. Now whenever air comes into being 311^a
out of water, light out of heavy, it goes to the upper place.
It is forthwith light: becoming is at an end, and in that
place it has being.[2] Obviously, then, it is a potentiality,

---

was advanced as a conjecture unsupported by MSS. None of our
MSS. have either. The apodosis to the protasis introduced by εἰ in
310ᵃ 31 begins here. δή is therefore attractive, but δέ *in apodosi*
is easily excused in view of the long intervening parenthesis.

[1] The use of ἀπολελυμένων ('isolated') is interesting, as Prantl
points out, because of its later technical use (= *absolutus*, absolute).
Simplicius here takes it to stand for complete substances (ὁλοκλήρων
κατ᾽ οὐσίαν ὄντων) not involved in any process of γένεσις, αὔξησις, or
ἀλλοίωσις. Prantl says ἀπολελυμένα means 'independent beings'
(unabhängige Wesen). Bonitz, *Ind.* 84ᵃ 26, says '*idem fere ac* ἀπο-
κεκριμένον, χωριστόν'. The 'independence' intended is rather physical
than metaphysical.

[2] Read ἐκεῖ ἔστιν.

5 which, in its passage to actuality, comes into that place and quantity and quality which belong to its actuality.[1] And the same fact explains why what is already actually fire or earth moves, when nothing obstructs it, towards its own place. For motion is equally immediate in the case of nutriment, when nothing hinders, and in the case of the thing healed, when nothing stays the healing. But the 10 movement is also due to the original creative force and to that which removes the hindrance or off which the moving thing rebounded, as was explained in our opening discussions, where we tried to show how none of these things moves itself.[2] The reason of the various motions of the various bodies, and the meaning of the motion of a body to its own place, have now been explained.

15 We have now to speak of the distinctive properties of **4** these bodies and of the various phenomena connected with them. In accordance with general conviction we may distinguish the absolutely heavy, as that which sinks to the bottom of all things, from the absolutely light, which is that which rises to the surface of all things. I use the term 'absolutely', in view of the generic character of 'light' and 'heavy',[3] in order to confine the application to bodies which do not combine lightness and heaviness. It is 20 apparent, I mean, that fire, in whatever quantity, so long as there is no external obstacle, moves upward, and earth downward; and, if the quantity is increased, the movement is the same, though swifter. But the heaviness and lightness of bodies which combine these qualities is different from this, since while they rise to the surface of some bodies they sink to the bottom of others. Such are air and water. Neither of them is absolutely either light or heavy. Both 25 are lighter than earth—for any portion of either rises to the surface of it—but heavier than fire, since a portion of either, whatever its quantity, sinks to the bottom of fire; compared together, however, the one has absolute weight, the other

---

[1] Omitting, with F, the words καὶ ὅπου, which I assume to have been inserted by some one who mistook οὗ = *ubi* for the genitive of the relative.

[2] *Phys.* VII. 1, 241ᵇ 24; VIII. 4, 254ᵇ 7.

[3] i. e. because there are distinct species of light and heavy.

absolute lightness, since air in any quantity rises to the surface of water, while water in any quantity sinks to the
bottom of air.   Now other bodies are severally light and 30
heavy, and evidently in them the attributes are due to the
difference of their uncompounded parts: that is to say,
according as the one or the other happens to preponderate
the bodies will be heavy and light respectively.   Therefore
we need only speak of these parts, since they are primary
and all else consequential: and in so doing we shall be 35
following the advice which we gave[1] to those who attribute
heaviness to the presence of plenum and lightness to that of 311ᵇ
void.   It is due to the properties of the elementary bodies
that a body which is regarded as light in one place is
regarded as heavy in another, and vice versa.   In air, for
instance, a talent's weight of wood is heavier than a mina
of lead, but in water the wood is the lighter.   The reason
is that all the elements except fire have weight and all but 5
earth lightness.   Earth, then, and bodies in which earth
preponderates, must needs have weight everywhere, while
water is heavy anywhere but in earth, and air is heavy
when not in water or earth.   In its own place each of these
bodies has weight except fire, even air.   Of this we have
evidence in the fact that a bladder when inflated weighs 10
more than when empty.   A body, then, in which air preponderates over earth and water, may well be lighter than
something in water and yet heavier than it in air, since such
a body does not rise in air but rises to the surface in water.

   The following account will make it plain that there is an 15
absolutely light and an absolutely heavy body.   And by
absolutely light I mean one which of its own nature always
moves upward, by absolutely heavy one which of its own
nature always moves downward, if no obstacle is in the
way.   There are, I say, these two kinds of body,[2] and it is
not the case, as some[3] maintain, that all bodies have weight.

---

   [1] Above, 309ᵇ 20: if they would only give an account of the simple
bodies, their questions as to the composite would answer themselves.
   [2] Read ἐστί τινα (E and Simpl. omit τινα).
   [3] This view is maintained in its most unqualified form by those
(atomists, probably) who distinguish the four elements by the size of
their particles (cf. c. ii. 310ᵃ 9).

Different views are in fact agreed that there is a heavy
body, which moves uniformly towards the centre. But
20 there is also similarly a light body.[1]   For we see with our
eyes, as we said before,[2] that earthy things sink to the
bottom of all things and move towards the centre. But
the centre is a fixed point.   If therefore there is some body
which rises to the surface of all things—and we observe
fire to move upward even in air itself, while the air remains
at rest[3]—clearly this body is moving towards the extremity.
It cannot then have any weight.   If it had, there would be
25 another body in which it sank: and if that had weight,
there would be yet another which moved to the extremity
and thus rose to the surface of all moving things.[4]   In fact,
however, we have no evidence of such a body.   Fire, then,
has no weight.   Neither has earth any lightness, since it
sinks to the bottom of all things, and that which sinks
moves to the centre.   That there is a centre[5] towards which
30 the motion of heavy things, and away from which that
of light things is directed, is manifest in many ways.   First,
because no movement can continue to infinity.   For what
cannot be can no more come-to-be than be, and movement
is a coming-to-be in one place from another.   Secondly,
like the upward movement of fire, the downward movement
35 of earth and all heavy things makes equal angles on every
side with the earth's surface[6] : it must therefore be directed
312[a] towards the centre.   Whether it is really the centre of the
earth and not rather that of the whole to which it moves,
may be left to another inquiry, since these are coincident.[7]

---

[1] It cannot be right to print ll. 14–19, λέγω δ' . . . κοῦφον, as a
parenthesis, with Prantl.   The sentences are not sufficiently self-
contained nor closely enough inter-connected to justify such treatment.
The argument which begins in l. 19 with ὁρῶμεν γάρ is a justification
of the statement last preceding : as there is, by general admission
and by the evidence of observation, a heavy body, so there is a light
body.

[2] Above, 311[a] 20.

[3] Since the air is at rest, the explanation that the fire is 'forced up'
(ἐκθλιβόμενον, 310[a] 10) is inadmissible.

[4] Reading ὅ with the MSS.   Prantl's conjecture, οὗ, is unnecessary.

[5] Read ἔστι for ἐστί.

[6] i. e. the line of movement is at right angles to any tangent.
Cf. above, 296[b] 20, 297[b] 19.

[7] The question is discussed in II. xiv, 296[b] 9.

But since that which sinks to the bottom of all things moves to the centre, necessarily that which rises to the surface moves to the extremity of the region in which the move- 5 ment of these bodies takes place. For the centre is opposed as contrary to the extremity, as that which sinks is opposed to that which rises to the surface. This also gives a reasonable ground for the duality of heavy and light in the spatial duality centre and extremity. Now there is also the intermediate region to which each name is given in opposition to the other extreme. For that which is intermediate 10 between the two is in a sense both extremity and centre.[1] For this reason there is another heavy and light; namely, water and air. But in our view the continent pertains to form and the contained to matter: and this distinction is present in every genus.[2] Alike in the sphere of quality and in that of quantity there is that which corresponds 15 rather to form and that which corresponds to matter. In the same way, among spatial distinctions, the above belongs to the determinate, the below to matter. The same holds, consequently, also of the matter itself of that which is heavy and light: as potentially possessing the one character, it is matter for the heavy, and as potentially possessing the other, for the light. It is the same matter, but its being is different, as that which is receptive of disease is the same as 20 that which is receptive of health, though in being different from it, and therefore diseasedness is different from healthiness.[3]

5   A thing then which has the one kind of matter is light and always moves upward, while a thing which has the

---

[1] Read ἔστι γὰρ ὡς, omit ἐστί after ἀμφοτέρων, and put a colon after μεταξύ. (J has an erasure in the position of the second ἐστί.)

[2] i.e. in every category. For this use of γένος see Bonitz, *Ind.* 152ᵃ 16.

[3] The doctrine here expressed is the same as that expressed in the last chapter (310ᵇ 15, note). A single matter is receptive of two opposed forms, weight and lightness or health and disease. But Aristotle here adds the new point that of two such alternative forms one is always more formal and the other more material. Weight and lightness, disease and health, are not true coordinates. *A* form, we may say, is realized in disease, in weight, in the female; but *the* form is realized in health, in lightness, and in the male. The principle is stated in the *Metaphysics* in the form τῶν ἐναντίων ἡ ἑτέρα συστοιχία στέρησις (1004ᵇ 27).

opposite matter is heavy and always moves downward.
Bodies composed of kinds of matter different from these
but having relatively to each other the character which
²⁵ these have absolutely, possess both the upward and the
downward motion.[1] Hence air and water each have both
lightness and weight, and water sinks to the bottom of
all things except earth, while air rises to the surface of all·
things except fire. But since there is one body only which
rises to the surface of all things and one only which sinks
to the bottom of all things, there must needs be two other
³⁰ bodies which sink in some bodies and rise to the surface of
others. The kinds of matter, then, must be as numerous as
these bodies, i. e. four, but though they are four there must
be a common matter of all—particularly if they pass into
one another—which in each is in being different. There
312ᵇ is no reason why[2] there should not be one or more intermediates between the contraries, as in the case of colour ;
for 'intermediate' and 'mean' are capable of more than
one application.[3]

Now in its own place every body endowed with both
weight and lightness has weight—whereas earth has weight
5 everywhere—but they only have lightness among bodies to
whose surface they rise. Hence when a support is withdrawn such a body moves downward until it reaches the
body next below it, air to the place of water and water to
that of earth. But if the fire above air is removed, it will
not move upward to the place of fire, except by constraint ;
and in that way water also may be drawn up, when the up-
10 ward movement of air which has had a common surface with
it is swift enough to overpower the downward impulse of
the water. Nor does water move upward to the place of
air, except in the manner just described. Earth is not so
affected at all, because a common surface is not possible to

---

[1] In l. 24 put the comma *after*, not before, ἁπλῶς. (The correction
is due to Mr. Ross.) The intermediates, air and water, are only
relatively light and heavy. In the absolute sense these characters
belong only to fire and water.

[2] οὐδέ in Bekker and Prantl must surely be. a misprint for οὐδέν
(so J).

[3] 'Intermediate' stands for a region, not a point, and includes as
a rule a variety of things.

it.[1] Hence water is drawn up into the vessel to which fire is applied, but not earth. As earth fails to move upward, so fire fails to move downward when air is withdrawn 15 from beneath it: for fire has no weight even in its own place, as earth has no lightness. The other two move downward when the body beneath is withdrawn because, while the absolutely heavy is that which sinks to the bottom of all things,[2] the relatively heavy sinks to its own place or to the surface of the body in which it rises, since it is similar in matter to it.[3]

It is plain that one must suppose as many distinct species 20 of matter as there are bodies. For if, *first*, there is a single matter of all things, as, for instance, the void or the plenum or extension or the triangles, either all things will move upward or all things will move downward, and the second motion will be abolished. And so, either there will be no absolutely light body, if superiority of weight is due to superior size or number of the constituent bodies or to the 25 fullness of the body: but the contrary is a matter of observation, and it has been shown that the downward and upward movements are equally constant and universal: or, if the matter in question is the void or something similar, which moves uniformly upward, there will be nothing to move uniformly downward.[4] Further, it will follow that

---

[1] The surface of earth is too rough to allow of the necessary σύμφυσις (Simpl.), or continuity of surface, with another body.

[2] Read ἐστιν ὅ (not ἐστιν, ὅ with Bekker). Prantl's ingenious conjecture, εἰς τὴν ὑπό, is not quite convincing.

[3] The downward movement of earth (absolute weight) is quite determinate, having its limit at the centre. But the downward movement of air and water (relative weight) is not equally determinate: it is limited only by the surface of the body next beneath, air by that of water, water by that of earth, the upper body being attracted to the lower by similarity of matter. This admission inflicts some damage on the doctrine of 'places'—for where a body has weight it cannot be said to 'rest naturally' or to 'be in its place'—and also on the symmetry of the elements—for if the fire above air were removed the air would not move upward, but if the earth below water were removed the water would move downward.—In l. 18 εἰς must be construed with φέρεται, and in l. 19 ἢ οἷς, more fully expressed, would be ἢ εἰς τὴν ἐκείνων οἷς. The construction is difficult, and the passage may be corrupt.

[4] The stopping of this sentence requires alteration. ἐὰν δέ in l. 27 is an irregular second limb to the disjunction introduced by ἢ κοῦφον in l. 23. Put a colon at πλήρη (l. 25) and at ἄνω (l. 27), and delete the comma after πλειόνων (l. 25).

the intermediate bodies move downward in some cases
quicker than earth: for air in sufficiently large quantity
30 will contain a larger number of triangles or solids or
particles. It is, however, manifest that no portion of air
whatever moves downward.[1] And the same reasoning
applies to lightness, if that is supposed to depend on
superiority of quantity of matter.[2] But if, *secondly*, the
kinds of matter are two, it will be difficult to make the
intermediate bodies behave as air and water behave.
313^a Suppose, for example, that the two asserted are void and
plenum. Fire, then, as moving upward, will be void, earth,
as moving downward, plenum ; and in air, it will be said,
fire preponderates, in water, earth.[3] There will then be
a quantity of water containing more fire than a little air,
and a large amount of air will contain more earth than
5 a little water: consequently we shall have to say that air
in a certain quantity moves downward more quickly than
a little water. But such a thing has never been observed
anywhere. Necessarily, then, as fire goes up because it has
something, e. g. void, which other things do not have, and
earth goes downward because it has plenum, so air goes to
10 its own place above water because it has something else,
and water goes downward because of some special kind
of body. But if the two bodies[4] are one matter, or two
matters both present in each,[5] there will be a certain quantity
of each at which water will excel a little air in the upward
movement and air excel water in the downward movement, as we have already often said.

The shape of bodies will not account for their moving 6
15 upward or downward in general, though it will account
for their moving faster or slower. The reasons for this

---

[1] *sc.* in earth.

[2] On the somewhat absurd theory that the universal 'matter' is
void or absolute lightness.

[3] 312^b 33—313^a 3, οἷον . . . γῆς, is a parenthesis and should be so
printed, with a colon, instead of a full-stop, at πλῆρες and at κάτω.
This is proved by the infinitive ἔχειν (after φαίη) in l. 3, as well as by
the γάρ which follows.

[4] viz. air and water.

[5] Prantl's ἑκατέρω is a misprint for ἑκατέρῳ.

are not difficult to see. For the problem thus raised is why a flat piece of iron or lead floats upon water, while smaller and less heavy things, so long as they are round or long—a needle, for instance—sink down; and sometimes a thing floats because it is small, as with gold 20 dust and the various earthy and dusty materials which throng the air. With regard to these questions, it is wrong to accept the explanation offered by Democritus. He says that the warm bodies moving up[1] out of the water hold up heavy bodies which are broad, while the **313^b** narrow ones fall through, because the bodies which offer this resistance are not numerous. But this would be even more likely to happen in air—an objection which he himself raises. His reply to the objection is feeble. In the air, he says, the 'drive' (meaning by drive the move- 5 ment of the upward moving bodies) is not uniform in direction. But since some continua are easily divided and others less easily, and things which produce division differ similarly in the ease with which they produce it, the explanation must be found in this fact. It is the easily bounded,[2] in proportion as it is easily bounded, which is easily divided; and air is more so than water, water than 10 earth. Further, the smaller the quantity in each kind, the more easily it is divided and disrupted. Thus the reason why broad things keep their place is because they cover so wide a surface and the greater quantity is less easily disrupted. Bodies of the opposite shape sink down because they occupy so little of the surface, which is there- 15 fore easily parted. And these considerations apply with far greater force to air, since it is so much more easily divided than water. But since there are two factors, the force responsible for the downward motion of the heavy body and the disruption-resisting force of the continuous surface, there must be some ratio between the two. For in proportion as the force applied by the heavy thing

---

[1] ἀναφερόμενα is the better-attested reading (ELMJ Simpl.) and should be preferred to ἄνω φερόμενα. The word is elsewhere used of upward movement by Aristotle.

[2] i. e. the fluid or moist. Cp. *de Gen. et Corr.* 329^b 30.

20 towards disruption and division exceeds that which resides in the continuum, the quicker will it force its way down; only if the force of the heavy thing is the weaker, will it ride upon the surface.

We have now finished our examination of the heavy and the light and of the phenomena connected with them.

[The sign + following a reference means that many other references could be given.]

68-13 = 268-313.

INDEX II. Greek

[The reference is to the foot-note in which the word is cited.]

DE GENERATIONE

ET

CORRUPTIONE

DE GENERATIONE
ET
CORRUPTIONE

BY

HAROLD H. JOACHIM

FELLOW OF NEW COLLEGE, HONORARY FELLOW OF MERTON COLLEGE, AND
WYKEHAM PROFESSOR OF LOGIC IN THE UNIVERSITY OF OXFORD

OXFORD
AT THE CLARENDON PRESS
1922

Oxford University Press

London   Edinburgh   Glasgow   Copenhagen
New York   Toronto   Melbourne   Cape Town
Bombay   Calcutta   Madras   Shanghai
Humphrey Milford Publisher to the UNIVERSITY

PREFACE

'THIS translation has been made from a revised text, which is now being published for me by the Delegates of the Clarendon Press as part of an edition of Aristotle's περὶ γενέσεως καὶ φθορᾶς. I have indicated in a few brief footnotes the chief passages in which the readings I have adopted differ from those of Bekker; a full explanation, and a defence of my interpretation in detail, will be found in my edition.

To Mr. W. D. Ross, Fellow of Oriel College, I am greatly indebted for many most valuable criticisms and suggestions. The references in the footnotes to Burnet are to the third edition of that author's *Early Greek Philosophy* (London, 1920); and the references to Diels are to the second edition of *Die Fragmente der Vorsokratiker* (Berlin, 1906).

H. H. J.

BOOK II.

ON COMING-TO-BE AND PASSING-AWAY

BOOK I

1 OUR next task is to study coming-to-be and passing- 314ᵃ
away. We are to distinguish the causes, and to state the
definitions, of these processes considered in general—as
changes predicable uniformly of all the things that come-to-
be and pass-away by nature. Further, we are to study
growth and 'alteration'. We must inquire what each of
them is; and whether 'alteration' is to be identified with 5
coming-to-be, or whether to these different names there
correspond two separate processes with distinct natures.

On this question, indeed, the early philosophers are
divided. Some of them assert that the so-called 'unqualified
coming-to-be' is 'alteration', while others maintain that
'alteration' and coming-to-be are distinct. For those who
say that the universe is one something (i. e. those who
generate all things out of one thing) are bound to assert
that coming-to-be is 'alteration', and that whatever 'comes- 10
to-be' in the proper sense of the term is 'being altered':
but those who make the matter of things more than one 2
must distinguish coming-to-be from 'alteration'. To this
latter class belong Empedokles, Anaxagoras, and Leukippos.
And yet Anaxagoras himself failed to understand his own
utterance. He *says*, at all events, that coming-to-be and
passing-away are the same as 'being altered':[1] yet, in 15
common with other thinkers, he affirms that the elements
are many. Thus Empedokles holds that the corporeal
elements are four, while all the elements—including those
which initiate movement—are six in number; whereas

[1] Cf. fr. 17 (Diels, pp. 320–1).

Anaxagoras agrees with Leukippos and Demokritos that the elements are infinite.

(Anaxagoras posits as elements the 'homoeomeries', viz.
20 bone, flesh, marrow, and everything else which is such that part and whole are the same in name and nature; while Demokritos and Leukippos say that there are indivisible bodies, infinite both in number and in the varieties of their shapes, of which everything else is composed—the compounds differing one from another according to the shapes, 'positions', and 'groupings' of their constituents.)

25 For the views of the school of Anaxagoras seem diametrically opposed to those of the followers of Empedokles. Empedokles says that Fire, Water, Air, and Earth are four elements, and are thus 'simple' rather than flesh, bone, and bodies which, like these, are 'homoeomeries'. But the followers of Anaxagoras regard the 'homoeomeries' as 'simple' and elements, whilst they affirm that Earth, Fire, Water, and Air are composite; for each of these is (accord-
314ᵇ ing to them) a 'common seminary' of all the 'homoeomeries'.[1]

Those, then, who construct all things out of a single element, must maintain that coming-to-be and passing-away are 'alteration'. For they must affirm that the underlying something always remains identical and one; and change of such a *substratum* is what we call 'altering'. Those, on the other hand, who make the ultimate kinds of
5 things more than one, must maintain that 'alteration' is distinct from coming-to-be: for coming-to-be and passing-away result from the consilience and the dissolution of the many kinds. That is why Empedokles too[2] uses language to this effect, when he says 'There is no coming-to-be of anything, but only a mingling and a divorce of what has been mingled'.[3] Thus it is clear (i) that to describe coming-

---

[1] Aristotle's point (from 314ª 11 to 314ᵇ 1) is that Anaxagoras, Empedokles, Leukippos, and Demokritos are all pluralists, and therefore logically bound (whatever they may say) to distinguish coming-to-be and 'alteration'. They are all pluralists, though their theories differ, and though the theory of Anaxagoras is actually 'contrary' to that of Empedokles.

[2] i.e. as well as Anaxagoras: cf. above, 314ª 13–15.

[3] Cf. fr. 8 (Diels, p. 175), and the paraphrase in MXG 975ª36–ᵇ16.

to-be and passing-away in these terms is in accordance
with their fundamental assumption, and (ii) that they do in 10
fact so describe them : nevertheless, they too [1] must recognize 'alteration' as a fact distinct from coming-to-be,
though it is impossible for them to do so consistently with
what they say.

That we are right in this criticism is easy to perceive.
For 'alteration' is a fact of observation. While the substance of the thing remains unchanged, we *see* it 'altering'
just as we *see* in it the changes of magnitude called 'growth' 15
and 'diminution'. Nevertheless, the statements of those
who posit more 'original reals' than one make 'alteration'
impossible. For 'alteration', as we assert, takes place in
respect to certain qualities : and these qualities (I mean,
e. g., hot-cold, white-black, dry-moist, soft-hard, and so
forth) are, all of them, differences characterizing the 20
'elements'. The actual words of Empedokles may be
quoted in illustration—

> The sun everywhere bright to see, and hot;
> The rain everywhere dark and cold; [2]

and he distinctively characterizes his remaining elements in
a similar manner. Since, therefore, it is not possible [3] for
Fire to become Water, or Water to become Earth, neither
will it be possible for anything white to become black, or
anything soft to become hard; and the same argument 25
applies to all the other qualities. Yet this is what 'alteration'
essentially is.

It follows, as an obvious corollary, that a single matter
must always be assumed as underlying the contrary 'poles'
of any change—whether change of place, or growth and
diminution, or 'alteration'; further, that the being of this
matter and the being of 'alteration' stand and fall together.
For if the change is 'alteration', then the *substratum* is 315^a
a single element; i. e. all things which admit of change
into one another have a single matter. And, conversely, if
the *substratum* of the changing things is one, there is
'alteration'.

---

[1] i. e. as well as ordinary people : cf. ^b 13 ff.
[2] Cf. fr. 21, ll. 3 and 5 (Diels, p. 180).
[3] i. e. according to Empedokles.

Empedokles, indeed, seems to contradict his own state-
5 ments as well as the observed facts.   For he denies that any
one of his elements comes-to-be out of any other, insisting
on the contrary that they are the things out of which everything else comes-to-be; and yet (having brought the
entirety of existing things, except Strife, together into one)
he maintains, simultaneously with this denial, that each
thing once more comes-to-be out of the One.   Hence it was
clearly out of a One that *this* came-to-be Water, and *that*
10 Fire, various portions of it being separated off by certain
characteristic differences or qualities—as indeed he calls the
sun 'white and hot', and the earth 'heavy and hard'.   If,
therefore, these characteristic differences be taken away (for
they can be taken away, since they came-to-be), it will
clearly be inevitable for Earth to come-to-be out of Water
and Water out of Earth, and for each of the other elements
to undergo a similar transformation—not only *then*,[1] but
15 also *now*—if, and because, they change their qualities.   And,
to judge by what he says, the qualities are such that they
can be 'attached' to things and *can* again be 'separated'
from them, especially since Strife and Love are still fighting
with one another for the mastery.   It was owing to this
same conflict that the elements were generated from a One
at the former period.   I say 'generated', for presumably
Fire, Earth, and Water had no distinctive existence at all
while merged in one.

There is another obscurity in the theory of Empedokles.
20 Are we to regard the One as his 'original real'?   Or is it
the Many—i.e. Fire and Earth, and the bodies co-ordinate
with these?   For the One is an 'element' in so far as it
underlies the process as matter—as that out of which Earth
and Fire come-to-be through a change of qualities due to
'the motion'.[2]   On the other hand, in so far as the One
results from *composition* (by a consilience of the Many),
whereas they result from *disintegration*, the Many are more
25 'elementary' than the One, and prior to it in their nature.

---

[1] i.e. at the period when Empedokles himself appears to recognize
that his 'elements' come-to-be.

[2] i.e. the motion of dissociation initiated by Strife.

2   We have therefore to discuss the whole subject of 'un-qualified' coming-to-be and passing-away; we have to inquire whether these changes do or do not occur and, if they occur, to explain the precise conditions of their occur-rence. We must also discuss the remaining forms of change, viz. growth and 'alteration'. For though, no doubt, Plato investigated the conditions under which things come-to-be and pass-away, he confined his inquiry to these changes ; 30 and he discussed not *all* coming-to-be, but only that of the elements. He asked no questions as to how flesh or bones, or any of the other similar compound things, come-to-be ; nor again did he examine the conditions under which 'alteration' or growth are attributable to things.

A similar criticism applies to all our predecessors with the single exception of Demokritos. Not one of them pene- 35 trated below the surface or made a thorough examination of a single one of the problems. Demokritos, however, does seem not only to have thought carefully about all the problems, but also to be distinguished from the outset by 315^b his method. For, as we are saying, none of the other philo-sophers made any definite statement about growth, except such as any amateur might have made. They said that things grow 'by the accession of like to like', but they did not proceed to explain the manner of this accession. Nor did they give any account of 'combination': and they neg-lected almost every single one of the remaining problems, offering no explanation, e. g., of 'action' or 'passion'—how 5 in physical actions one thing acts and the other undergoes action. Demokritos and Leukippos, however, postulate the 'figures', and make 'alteration' and coming-to-be result from them. They explain coming-to-be and passing-away by their 'dissociation' and 'association', but 'alteration' by their 'grouping' and 'position'. And since they thought that the truth lay in the appearance, and the appearances 10 are conflicting and infinitely many, they made the 'figures' infinite in number.[1] Hence—owing to the changes of the compound—*the same* thing seems different and conflicting to different people : it is 'transposed' by a small additional

---

[1] And in variety of shape also: cf. above, 314^a 22–3.

ingredient, and appears utterly other by the 'transposition'
15 of a single constituent. For Tragedy and Comedy are both
composed of *the same* letters.

Since almost all our predecessors think (i) that coming-
to-be is distinct from 'alteration', and (ii) that, whereas
things 'alter' by change of their qualities, it is by 'association' and 'dissociation' that they come-to-be and pass-
away, we must concentrate our attention on these theses.
For they lead to many perplexing and well-grounded
20 dilemmas. If, on the one hand, coming-to-be *is* 'association',
many impossible consequences result: and yet there are
other arguments, not easy to unravel, which force the conclusion upon us that coming-to-be cannot possibly be anything else. If, on the other hand, coming-to-be *is not*
'association', either there is no such thing as coming-to-be
at all or it is 'alteration': or else[1] we must endeavour to
unravel this dilemma too—and a stubborn one we shall
find it.

25   The fundamental question, in dealing with all these difficulties, is this: 'Do things come-to-be and "alter" and
grow, and undergo the contrary changes, because the
primary "reals" are indivisible magnitudes? Or is no magnitude indivisible?' For the answer we give to this question
makes the greatest difference. And again, if the primary
30 'reals' are indivisible magnitudes, are these *bodies*, as Demokritos and Leukippos maintain? Or are they *planes*, as is
asserted in the *Timaeus*?

To resolve bodies into planes and no further—this, as
we have also remarked elsewhere,[2] is in itself a paradox.
Hence there is more to be said for the view that there are
indivisible bodies. Yet even these involve much of paradox.
Still, as we have said, it is possible to construct 'alteration'
35 and coming-to-be with them, if one 'transposes' *the same*
316^a by 'turning' and 'intercontact', and by 'the varieties of the
figures', as Demokritos does. (His denial of the reality of
colour is a corollary from this position: for, according to

---

[1] i. e. if we still wish to maintain that coming-to-be (though it
actually occurs and is distinct from 'alteration') is not 'association'
[2] Cf. e. g. *de Caelo* 299^a 6-11.

him, things get coloured by 'turning' of the 'figures'.) But the possibility of such a construction no longer exists for those who divide bodies into planes. For nothing except solids results from putting planes together: they do not even attempt to generate any quality from them.

Lack of experience diminishes our power of taking 5 a comprehensive view of the admitted facts. Hence those who dwell in intimate association with nature and its phenomena grow more and more able to formulate, as the foundations of their theories, principles such as to admit of a wide and coherent development: while those whom devotion to abstract discussions has rendered unobservant of the facts are too ready to dogmatize on the basis of a few 10 observations. The rival treatments of the subject now before us will serve to illustrate how great is the difference between a 'scientific' and a 'dialectical' method of inquiry. For, whereas the Platonists argue that there must be atomic magnitudes 'because otherwise "The Triangle" will be more than one', Demokritos would appear to have been convinced by arguments appropriate to the subject, i.e. drawn from the science of nature. Our meaning will become clear as we proceed.

For to suppose that a body (i. e. a magnitude) is divisible 15 through and through, and that this division is possible, involves a difficulty. What will there be in the body which escapes the division?

If it is divisible through and through, and if this division is possible, then it might *be*, at one and the same moment, *divided* through and through, even though the dividings had not been effected simultaneously: and the actual occurrence of this result would involve no impossibility. Hence the same principle will apply whenever a body is 20 by nature divisible through and through, whether by bisection,[1] or generally by any method whatever: nothing impossible will have resulted if it has actually been divided— not even if it has been divided into innumerable parts, themselves divided innumerable times. Nothing impossible

---

[1] i. e. by progressive bisection *ad infinitum.*

will have resulted, though perhaps nobody in fact could so divide it.

Since, therefore, the body is divisible through and through, let it have been divided. What, then, will remain? A magnitude? No: that is impossible, since then there
25 will be something not divided, whereas *ex hypothesi* the body was divisible *through and through*. But if it be admitted that neither a body nor a magnitude will remain, and yet division[1] is to take place, the constituents of the body will *either* be points (i.e. without magnitude) *or* absolutely nothing. If its constituents are nothings, then it might both come-to-be out of nothings and exist as a composite of nothings: and thus presumably the whole body will be nothing but an appearance. But if it consists
30 of points, a similar absurdity will result: it will not possess any magnitude. For when the points were in contact and coincided to form a single magnitude, they did not make the whole any bigger (since, when the body was divided into two or more parts, the whole[2] was not a bit smaller or bigger than it was before the division): hence, even if all the points[3] be put together, they will not make any magnitude.

But suppose that, as the body is being divided, a minute
316^b section—a piece of sawdust, as it were—is extracted, and that in this sense a body 'comes away' from the magnitude, evading the division. Even then the same[4] argument applies. For in what sense is that section divisible? But if what 'came away' was not a body but a separable form or quality, and if the magnitude *is* 'points or contacts thus
5 qualified': it is paradoxical that a magnitude should consist of elements which are not magnitudes. Moreover, *where* will the points be? And are they motionless or moving? And every contact is always a contact of two somethings, i.e. there is always something besides the contact or the division or the point.

---

[1] i.e. 'through and through' division.
[2] i.e. the sum of the now separated parts.
[3] i.e. all the points into which the body has been dissolved by the 'through and through' division.
[4] Cf. above, 316^a 2 =5.

These, then, are the difficulties resulting from the supposition that any and every body, whatever its size, is divisible through and through. There is, besides, this further consideration. If, having divided a piece of wood 10 or anything else, I put it together, it is again equal to what it was, and is one. Clearly this is so, whatever the point at which I cut the wood. The wood, therefore, has been divided *potentially* through and through. What, then, is there in the wood besides the division? For even if we suppose there is some quality, yet how is the wood dissolved into such constituents [1] and how does it come-to-be out of them? Or how are such constituents separated so as to exist apart from one another?

Since, therefore, it is impossible for magnitudes to 15 consist of contacts or points, there must be indivisible bodies and magnitudes. Yet, if we *do* postulate the latter, we are confronted with equally impossible consequences, which we have examined in other works.[2] But we must try to disentangle these perplexities, and must therefore formulate the whole problem over again.

On the one hand, then, it is in no way paradoxical that 20 every perceptible body should be indivisible as well as divisible at any and every point. For the second predicate will attach to it *potentially*, but the first *actually*. On the other hand, it would seem to be impossible for a body to be, even potentially, divisible at all points simultaneously. For if it were possible, then it might actually occur, with the result, not that the body would simultaneously be actually *both* (indivisible and divided), but that it would be simultaneously divided at any and every point. Con- 25 sequently, nothing will remain and the body will have passed-away into what is incorporeal: and so it might come-to-be again either out of points or absolutely out of nothing. And how is that possible?

But now it is obvious that a body is in fact divided into separable magnitudes which are smaller at each division— into magnitudes which fall apart from one another and are

---

[1] i. e. points-of-division and quality.
[2] Cf. *Physics* 231^a 21 ff.; *de Caelo* 303^a 3 ff.; *de Lin. Insec.* 969^b 29 ff.

actually separated. Hence (it is urged) the process of
30 dividing a body part by part is not a 'breaking up' which
could continue *ad infinitum*; nor can a body be simultaneously divided at every point, for that is not possible;
but there is a limit, beyond which the 'breaking up' cannot proceed. The necessary consequence—especially if
coming-to-be and passing-away are to take place by
'association' and 'dissociation' respectively—is that a
body [1] must contain atomic magnitudes which are invisible.

317^a Such is the argument which is believed to establish the
necessity of atomic magnitudes: we must now show that it
conceals a faulty inference, and exactly where it conceals it.

For, since point is not 'immediately-next' to point,
magnitudes are 'divisible through and through' in one
sense, and yet not in another. When, however, it is ad-
5 mitted that a magnitude is 'divisible through and through',
it is thought there is a point not only anywhere, but also
everywhere, in it: hence it is supposed to follow, from the
admission, that the magnitude must be divided away into
nothing. For—it is supposed—there is a point everywhere
within it, so that it consists either of contacts or of points.
But it is only *in one sense* that the magnitude is 'divisible
through and through', viz. in so far as there is one point
anywhere within it and all its points are *everywhere* within it
if you take them singly one by one. But there are not
more points than one *anywhere* within it, for the points are
not 'consecutive': hence it is not simultaneously 'divisible
10 through and through'. For if it were, then, if it be
divisible at its centre, it will be divisible also at a point
'immediately-next' to its centre. But it is not so divisible:
for position is not 'immediately-next' to position, nor point
to point—in other words, division is not 'immediately-
next' to division, nor composition to composition.

Hence there are both 'association' and 'dissociation',
though neither (*a*) into, and out of, atomic magnitudes (for
15 that involves many impossibilities), nor (*b*) so that division
takes place through and through—for this would have
resulted only if point had been 'immediately-next' to

---

[1] i.e. every perceptible body: cf. above, 316^b 21.

point: but 'dissociation' takes place into small (i.e. relatively small) parts, and 'association' takes place out of
relatively small parts.

It is wrong, however, to suppose, as some assert, that
coming-to-be and passing-away in the unqualified and
complete sense are distinctively defined by 'association'
and 'dissociation', while the change that takes place in
what is continuous is 'alteration'. On the contrary, this is
where the whole error lies. For unqualified coming-to-be 20
and passing-away are not effected by 'association' and
'dissociation'. They take place when a thing changes,
from *this* to *that*, as a whole. But the philosophers we
are criticizing suppose that all such change[1] is 'alteration':
whereas in fact there is a difference. For in that which
underlies the change there is a factor corresponding to the
definition[2] and there is a material factor. When, then, the 25
change is in these constitutive factors, there will be coming-
to-be or passing-away: but when it is in the thing's
qualities, i.e. a change of the thing *per accidens*, there will
be 'alteration'.

'Dissociation' and 'association' affect the thing's susceptibility to passing-away. For if water has first been
'dissociated' into smallish drops, air comes-to-be out of it
more quickly: while, if drops of water have first been
'associated', air comes-to-be more slowly. Our doctrine
will become clearer in the sequel.[3] Meantime, so much 30
may be taken as established—viz. that coming-to-be
cannot be 'association', at least not the kind of 'association' some philosophers assert it to be.

3 Now that we have established the preceding distinctions,
we must first[4] consider whether there is anything which
comes-to-be and passes-away in the unqualified sense: or
whether nothing comes-to-be in this strict sense, but
everything always comes-to-be *something* and *out of something*—I mean, e.g., comes-to-be-healthy out of being-ill 35

[1] i.e. all change 'in what is continuous'.
[2] i.e. a 'formal' factor.
[3] Cf. 328ª 23 ff.
[4] The second main topic of investigation is formulated below,
317ᵇ 34-5.

and ill out of being-healthy, comes-to-be-small out of being-
317^b big and big out of being-small, and so on in every other
instance. For if there is to be coming-to-be without
qualification, 'something' must—without qualification—
'come-to-be out of not-being', so that it would be true to
say that 'not-being is an attribute of some things'. For
qualified coming-to-be is a process out of *qualified* not-being
5 (e. g. out of not-white or not-beautiful),· but *unqualified*
coming-to-be is a process out of *unqualified* not-being.

Now 'unqualified' means either (i) the primary predication within each Category, or (ii) the universal, i. e. the all-
comprehensive, predication. Hence, if 'unqualified not-
being' means the negation of 'being' in the sense of the
primary term of the Category in question, we shall have, in
'unqualified coming-to-be', a coming-to-be of a substance
out of not-substance. But that which is not a substance or
a 'this' clearly cannot possess predicates drawn from any
10 of the other Categories either—e.g. we cannot attribute to
it any quality, quantity, or position. Otherwise, properties
would admit of existence in separation from substances.
If, on the other hand, 'unqualified not-being' means 'what
is not in any sense at all', it will be a universal negation of
all forms of being, so that what comes-to-be will have to
come-to-be out of nothing.

Although we have dealt with these problems at greater
length in another work,[1] where we have set forth the
difficulties and established the distinguishing definitions, the
15 following concise restatement of our results must here be
offered :—

In one sense things come-to-be out of that which has no
'being' without qualification: yet in another sense they
come-to-be always out of 'what is'. For coming-to-be
necessarily implies the pre-existence of something which
potentially 'is', but *actually* 'is not'; and this something is
spoken of both as 'being' and as 'not-being'.

These distinctions may be taken as established : but even
then it is extraordinarily difficult to see how there can be
'unqualified coming-to-be' (whether we suppose it to occur

[1] *Physics* A. 6–9.

out of what potentially 'is', or in some other way), and we 20
must recall this problem for further examination. For the
question might be raised whether substance (i. e. the 'this')
comes-to-be at all. Is it not rather the 'such', the 'so great',
or the 'somewhere', which comes-to-be? And the same
question might be raised about 'passing-away' also. For
if a substantial thing comes-to-be, it is clear that there will
'be' (not actually, but potentially) a substance, out of
which its coming-to-be will proceed and into which the
thing that is passing-away will necessarily change. Then will 25
any predicate belonging to the remaining Categories attach
actually to this presupposed substance? In other words,
will that which is only potentially a 'this' (which only
potentially *is*), while without the qualification 'potentially'
it is not a 'this' (i. e. *is not*), possess, e. g., any determinate
size or quality or position? For (i) if it possesses none of
these determinations actually, but all of them only
potentially, the result is *first* that a being, which is not
a determinate being, is capable of separate existence; and
in addition that coming-to-be proceeds out of nothing pre-
existing—a thesis which, more than any other, preoccupied 30
and alarmed the earliest philosophers. On the other
hand (ii) if, although it is not a 'this somewhat' or a substance, it is to possess some of the remaining determinations
quoted above, then (as we said)[1] properties will be
separable from substances.

We must therefore concentrate all our powers on the
discussion of these difficulties and on the solution of a
further question—viz. What is the cause of the perpetuity 35
of coming-to-be? Why is there always unqualified,[2] as
well as *partial*,[3] coming-to-be?

'Cause' in this connexion has two senses. It means 318^a
(i) the source from which, as we say, the process 'originates',
and (ii) the matter. It is the material cause that we have
here to state. For, as to the other cause, we have already

---

[1] Cf. above, 317^b 10–11.
[2] 'Unqualified coming-to-be' = substantial change.
[3] 'Partial' = 'qualified' coming-to-be, i. e. change of quality,
quantity, or place.

explained (in our treatise on Motion[1]) that it involves
(a) something immovable through all time and (b) some-
5 thing always being moved.   And the accurate treatment of
the first of these—of the immovable 'originative source'—
belongs to the province of the other, or 'prior', philosophy:[2] while as regards 'that which sets everything else
in motion by being itself continuously moved', we shall
have to explain later[3] which amongst the so-called 'specific'
causes exhibits this character.   But at present we are to
state the material cause—the cause classed under the head
10 of matter—to which it is due that passing-away and coming-to-be never fail to occur in Nature.   For perhaps, if we
succeed in clearing up this question, it will simultaneously
become clear what account we ought to give of that which
perplexed us just now, i. e. of *unqualified* passing-away and
coming-to-be.

Our new question too—viz. 'what is the cause of the
unbroken continuity of coming-to-be?'—is sufficiently perplexing, if in fact what passes-away vanishes into 'what is
15 not' and 'what is not' is nothing (since 'what is not' is
neither a thing, nor possessed of a quality or quantity, nor
in any place).   If, then, some one of the things 'which are'
is constantly disappearing, why has not the whole of 'what
is' been used up long ago and vanished away—assuming of
course that the material of all the several comings-to-be
was finite?   For, presumably, the unfailing continuity of
coming-to-be cannot be attributed to the infinity of the
20 material.   That is impossible, for nothing is actually infinite.
A thing is infinite only potentially, i. e. the dividing of it
can continue indefinitely: so that we should have to suppose there is only one kind of coming-to-be in the world—
viz. one which never fails, because it is such that what
comes-to-be is on each successive occasion smaller than
before.   But in fact this is not what we see occurring.
25   Why, then, is this form of change necessarily ceaseless?
Is it because the passing-away of *this* is a coming-to-be of

something else, and the coming-to-be of *this* a passing-away
of *something else*?

The cause implied in this solution[1] must no doubt
be considered adequate to account for coming-to-be and
passing-away in their general character as they occur in all
existing things alike. Yet, if the same process is a coming- 30
to-be of *this* but a passing-away of *that*, and a passing-away
of *this* but a coming-to-be of *that*, why are some things said
to come-to-be and pass-away without qualification, but
others only with a qualification?

This distinction must be investigated once more,[2] for it
demands some explanation. ⟨It is applied in a twofold
manner.⟩[3] For (i) we say 'it is now passing-away' without
qualification, and not merely '*this* is passing-away': [4] and
we call *this* change 'coming-to-be', and *that* 'passing-
away', without qualification. And (ii) so-and-so 'comes-to-
be-something', but does not 'come-to-be' without qualification; for we say that the student 'comes-to-be-learned', 35
not 'comes-to-be' without qualification.

(i) Now we often divide terms into those which signify **318ᵇ**
a 'this somewhat' and those which do not. And ⟨the first
form of⟩[5] the distinction, which we are investigating, results
from a similar division of terms: for it makes a difference
into what the changing thing changes. Perhaps, e. g., the
passage into Fire is 'coming-to-be' *unqualified*, but 'passing-
away-of-something' (e. g. of Earth): whilst the coming-to-
be of Earth is *qualified* (not *unqualified*) 'coming-to-be', 5
though *unqualified* 'passing-away' (e. g. of Fire). This
would be the case on the theory set forth in Parmenides: [6]
for he says that the things into which change takes place
are two, and he asserts that these two, viz. *what is* and
what is not, are Fire and Earth. Whether we postulate

---

[1] i. e. the material cause, in the sense of πρώτη ὕλη: cf. 319ᵃ 18–22.
[2] 'Once more': for it was from this same peculiarity of linguistic
usage that Aristotle started (317ᵃ 32 ff.) to establish the being of ἁπλῆ
γένεσις.
[3] I have inserted this sentence in view of what follows: cf. 319ᵃ 3–11.
[4] i. e. not merely '*this* is passing-away and *that* is coming-to-be'.
[5] See note 3.
[6] The theory is put forward by Parmenides (fr. 8, ll. 51 ff.; Diels,
pp. 121–2) as the prevalent, but erroneous, view. See Burnet,
§§ 90, 91.

these,[1] or other things of a similar kind, makes no difference. For we are trying to discover not what undergoes these changes, but what is their characteristic manner. The passage, then, into what 'is' not except with a qualification is unqualified passing-away, while the passage into what 'is' without qualification is unqualified coming-to-be. Hence whatever the contrasted 'poles' of the changes may be—whether Fire and Earth, or some other couple—the one of them will be 'a being' and the other 'a not-being'.[2]

We have thus stated one characteristic manner in which *unqualified* will be distinguished from *qualified* coming-to-be and passing-away: but they are also distinguished according to the special nature of the material of the changing thing. For a material, whose constitutive differences signify more a 'this somewhat', is itself more 'substantial' or 'real': while a material, whose constitutive differences signify privation, is 'not real'. (Suppose, e. g., that 'the hot' is a positive predication, i.e. a 'form', whereas 'cold' is a privation, and that Earth and Fire differ from one another by these constitutive differences.)

The opinion, however, which most people are inclined to prefer, is that the distinction[3] depends upon the difference between 'the perceptible' and 'the imperceptible'. Thus, when there is a change into perceptible material, people say there is 'coming-to-be'; but when there is a change into invisible material, they call it 'passing-away'. For they distinguish 'what is' and 'what is not' by their perceiving and not-perceiving, just as what is knowable 'is' and what is unknowable 'is not'—perception on their view having the force of knowledge. Hence, just as they deem themselves to live and to 'be' in virtue of their perceiving or their capacity to perceive, so too they deem the things to be' *qua* perceived or perceptible--and in this they are in a sense on the track of the truth, though what they actually say is not true.

---

[1] *sc.* as the things into which the unqualified changes take place as the contrasted 'poles' of unqualified γένεσις and φθορά.

[2] i. e. one will be 'a positive real' and the other 'a negative something'.

[3] *sc.* between the *unqualified* and the *qualified* changes.

Thus unqualified coming-to-be and passing-away turn out to be different according to common opinion from what they are in truth.[1] For Wind and Air are in truth more real—more a 'this somewhat' or a 'form'—than Earth. But they are less real to perception—which explains why things are commonly said to 'pass-away' without qualifica- 30 tion when they change into Wind and Air, and to 'come-to-be'[2] when they change into what is tangible, i.e. into Earth.

We have now explained why there is 'unqualified coming-to-be' (though it is a passing-away-of-something) and 'unqualified passing-away' (though it is a coming-to-be-of-something). For this distinction of appellation depends upon 35 a difference in the material out of which, and into which, the changes are effected. It depends *either* upon whether the material is or is not 'substantial', *or* upon whether it is **319**^a more or less 'substantial', *or* upon whether it is more or less perceptible.

(ii) But why are some things said to 'come-to-be' without qualification, and others only to 'come-to-be-so-and-so', in cases different from the one we have been considering where two things come-to-be reciprocally out of one another? For at present we have explained no more than this:—why, 5 when two things change reciprocally into one another, we do not attribute coming-to-be and passing-away *uniformly* to them both, although every coming-to-be is a passing-away of something else and every passing-away some other thing's coming-to-be. But the question subsequently formulated involves a different problem—viz. why, although the learning thing is said to 'come-to-be-learned' but not to 10 'come-to-be' without qualification, yet the growing thing *is* said to 'come-to-be'.

The distinction here turns upon the difference of the Categories. For some things signify a *this somewhat*, others a *such*, and others a *so-much*. Those things, then, which do not signify substance, are not said to 'come-to-be' without qualification, but only to 'come-to-be-so-and-so'.

---

[1] 'In truth', i.e. according to Aristotle's own view which he has just stated (above, 318^b 14-18).
[2] *sc.* without qualification.

Nevertheless, in all changing things alike, we speak of
15 'coming-to-be'[1] when the thing comes-to-be something in
one[2] of the two Columns—e.g. in Substance, if it comes-to-
be Fire but not if it comes-to-be Earth; and in Quality, if
it comes-to-be learned but not when it comes-to-be ignorant.

We have explained why some things come-to-be without
qualification, but not others—both in general, and also
when the changing things are substances and nothing else;
and we have stated that the *substratum* is the material cause
of the continuous occurrence of coming-to-be, because it is
20 such as to change from contrary to contrary and because,
in substances, the coming-to-be of one thing is always
a passing-away of another, and the passing-away of one
thing is always another's coming-to-be. But there is no
need even to discuss the other question we raised—viz.
why coming-to-be continues though things are constantly
being destroyed.[3] For just as people speak of 'a passing-
away' without qualification when a thing has passed into
what is imperceptible and what in that sense 'is not', so
25 also they speak of 'a coming-to-be out of a not-being' when
a thing emerges from an imperceptible. Whether, therefore, the *substratum* is or is not something, what comes-to-
be emerges out of a 'not-being':[4] so that a thing 'comes-
to-be out of a not-being' just as much as it 'passes-away
into what is not'. Hence it is reasonable enough that
coming-to-be should never fail. For coming-to-be is a
passing-away of 'what is not' and passing-away is a coming-
to-be of 'what is not'.[5]

But what about that which 'is' not except with a quali-
30 fication?[6] Is it one of the two contrary poles of the change
—e. g. is Earth (i. e. the heavy) a 'not-being', but Fire (i. e.

---

[1] i.e. without qualification.

[2] i.e. in the Column containing the positive terms: cf. above;
318^b 14–18.

[3] Cf. above, 318^a 13–23.

[4] A 'not-being' in the popular sense of the term, i. e. an 'imperceptible'. The imperceptibility of the material is irrelevant to the
question of its reality.

[5] 'what is not' = what is imperceptible.

[6] The matter of substantial change, according to Aristotle's own
theory, is μὴ ὂν ἁπλῶς—i. e. it *is* not, unless you qualify 'is' and say it
'is-potentially'. Cf. above, 317^b 15–18.

the light) a 'being'?   Or, on the contrary, does 'what is'
include Earth as well as Fire, whereas 'what is not' is matter
—the matter of Earth and Fire alike?   And again, is the
matter of each different?   Or is it the same, since otherwise
they would not come-to-be reciprocally out of one another, 319ᵇ
i. e. contraries out of contraries?   For these things—Fire,
Earth, Water, Air—are characterized by 'the contraries'.[1]

Perhaps the solution is that their matter is in one sense
the same, but in another sense different.   For that which
underlies them, whatever its nature may be *qua* underlying
them, is the same: but its actual being is not the same.   So
4 much, then, on these topics.   Next we must state what the 5
difference is between coming-to-be and 'alteration'—for
we maintain that these changes are distinct from one
another.

Since, then, we must distinguish (*a*) the *substratum*,
and (*b*) the property whose nature it is to be predicated of the *substratum*; and since change of each of 10
these occurs; there is 'alteration' when the *substratum* is
perceptible and persists, but changes in its own properties,
the properties in question being opposed to one another
either as contraries or as intermediates.   The body, e. g.,
although persisting as the same body, is now healthy and
now ill; and the bronze is now spherical and at another
time angular, and yet remains the same bronze.   But
when nothing perceptible persists in its identity as a *sub-* 15
stratum, and the thing changes as a whole (when e.g. the
seed as a whole is converted into blood, or water into air,
or air as a whole into water), such an occurrence is no longer
'alteration'.   It is a coming-to-be of one substance and
a passing-away of the other—especially if the change proceeds from an imperceptible something to something
perceptible (either to touch or to all the senses), as when
water comes-to-be out of, or passes-away into, air: for air 20
is pretty well imperceptible.   If, however, in such cases, any
property (being one of a pair of contraries) persists, in the
thing that has come-to-be, the same as it was in the thing

---

[1] Cf. below, II. 1–3.

which has passed-away—if, e.g., when water comes-to-be
out of air, both are transparent or cold[1]—the *second* thing,
into which the *first* changes, must not be a property of this
persistent identical something.   Otherwise the change will
be 'alteration'.

25   Suppose, e.g., that *the musical man* passed-away and *an
unmusical man* came-to-be, and that *the man* persists as
something identical.   Now, if 'musicalness and unmusicalness' had not been a property essentially inhering in man,
these changes would have been a coming-to-be of unmusicalness and a passing-away of musicalness : but in fact
'musicalness and unmusicalness' are a property of the
persistent identity, viz. man.[2]   (Hence, as regards *man*,
these changes are 'modifications'; though, as regards
30 *musical man* and *unmusical man*, they are a passing-away
and a coming-to-be.)   Consequently such changes are
'alteration'.[3]

When the change from contrary to contrary is *in quantity*,
it is 'growth and diminution'; when it is *in place*, it is
'motion'; when it is in property, i.e. *in quality*, it is
320^{a} 'alteration': but when nothing persists, of which the resultant is a property (or an 'accident' in any sense of the
term), it is 'coming-to-be', and the converse change is
passing-away'.

'Matter', in the most proper sense of the term, is to be
identified with the *substratum* which is receptive of coming-
to-be and passing-away : but the *substratum* of the remaining kinds of change is also, in a certain sense, 'matter',
5 because all these *substrata* are receptive of 'contrarieties'
of some kind.   So much, then, as an answer to the ques-

---

[1] Aristotle is not saying that water and air are in fact 'cold', but is
only quoting a common view in illustration.

[2] I follow Philoponos in transposing νῦν . . . ὑπομένοντος (which the
manuscripts read after φθορά in l. 30) to l. 28 after τοῦ δὲ φθορά.

[3] Aristotle's doctrine is: (i) If 'musicalness and unmusicalness'
were not a property of man, the change in which 'a musical man
becomes unmusical' would be a φθορά of *musicalness* and a γένεσις
of *unmusicalness*.   But (ii) since 'musicalness and unmusicalness' are
a property of man, the change is in fact an 'alteration' of man from
a state of musicalness to a state of unmusicalness.   At the same time,
(iii) the change is a φθορά of *musical man* and a γένεσις of *unmusical
man*.

tions (i) whether coming-to-be 'is' or 'is not'—i. e. what
are the precise conditions of its occurrence—and (ii) what
5 'alteration' is: but we have still to treat of growth.[1] We
must explain (i) wherein growth differs from coming-to-be
and from 'alteration', and (ii) what is the process of growing and the process of diminishing in each and all of the 10
things that grow and diminish.

Hence our first question is this: Do these changes differ
from one another solely because of a difference in their
respective 'spheres'? In other words, do they differ
because, while a change from *this* to *that* (viz. from potential to actual *substance*) is coming-to-be, a change in the
sphere of *magnitude* is growth and one in the sphere of
quality is 'alteration'—both growth and 'alteration' being 15
changes from what is-potentially to what is-actually
magnitude and quality respectively? Or is there also
a difference in the manner of the change, since it is evident
that, whereas neither what is 'altering' nor what is coming-
to-be necessarily changes its place, what is growing or
diminishing changes its spatial position of necessity, though
in a different manner from that in which the moving thing
does so? For that which is being moved changes its place 20
as a whole: but the growing thing changes its place like
a metal that is being beaten, retaining its position as a whole
while its parts change their places. They change their
places, but not in the same way as the parts of a revolving
globe. For the parts of the globe change their places
while the whole continues to occupy an equal place: but
the parts of the growing thing expand over an ever-increas-
ing place and the parts of the diminishing thing contract 25
within an ever-diminishing area.

It is clear, then, that these changes—the changes of that
which is coming-to-be, of that which is 'altering', and of
that which is growing—differ *in manner* as well as *in sphere*.
But how are we to conceive the 'sphere' of the change
which is growth and diminution? The 'sphere' of growing
and diminishing is believed to be magnitude. Are we to

---

[1] Cf. above, 315^a 26–28.

suppose that body and magnitude come-to-be out of some-
30 thing which, though potentially magnitude and body, is
actually incorporeal and devoid of magnitude? And since
this description may be understood in two different ways,
in which of these two ways are we to apply it to the process
of growth? Is the matter,[1] out of which growth takes
place, (i) 'separate' and existing alone by itself, or (ii)
'separate' but contained in another body?[2]

Perhaps it is impossible for growth to take place in either
320ᵇ of these ways. For since the matter[3] is 'separate', either
(*a*) it will occupy no place (as if it were a point), or (*b*) it
will be a 'void', i.e. a non-perceptible body. But the first
of these alternatives is impossible. For since what comes-
to-be out of this incorporeal and sizeless something will
always be 'somewhere', it too must be 'somewhere'—
5 either intrinsically or indirectly.[4] And the second alternative necessarily implies that the matter is contained in some
other body. But if it is to be 'in' another body and yet
remains 'separate' in such a way that it is in no sense
a part of that body (neither a part of its substantial being
nor an 'accident' of it), many impossibilities will result.
It is as if we were to suppose that when, e.g., air comes-to-
be out of water the process were due not to a change of the
10 water, but to the matter of the air being 'contained in' the
water as in a vessel. This is impossible. For (i) there is
nothing to prevent an indeterminate number of matters
being thus 'contained in' the water, so that they might
come-to-be actually an indeterminate quantity of air;[5] and
(ii) we do not in fact see air coming-to-be out of water in
this fashion, viz. withdrawing out of it and leaving it
unchanged.

It is therefore better to suppose that in all instances of

---

[1] i.e. the supposed incorporeal and sizeless matter.

[2] It is clear from what follows that the incorporeal and sizeless
matter is assumed to be 'separate'—to be real independently of body—
under both alternatives.

[3] i.e. the supposed incorporeal and sizeless matter.

[4] i.e. either as itself occupying a place, or as contained within
a body which itself occupies a place.

[5] The original is obscure owing to its extreme compression: I have
expanded it in accordance with Zabarella's interpretation.

coming-to-be the matter is inseparable,[1] being numerically identical and one with the 'containing' body, though isolable from it by definition. But the same reasons also forbid us to regard the matter, out of which the body comes-to-be, 15 as points or lines. The matter is that of which points and lines are limits, and it is something that can never exist without quality and without form.

Now it is no doubt true, as we have also established elsewhere,[2] that one thing 'comes-to-be' (in the unqualified sense) out of another thing: and further it is true that the efficient cause of its coming-to-be is either (i) an actual thing (which is the same as the effect either *generically* —for the efficient cause of the coming-to-be of a hard thing is not a hard thing[3]—or *specifically*, as e.g. fire is the 20 efficient cause of the coming-to-be of fire or one man of the birth of another), or (ii) an actuality.[4] Nevertheless, since there is also a matter out of which corporeal substance itself comes-to-be (corporeal substance, however, already characterized as such-and-such a determinate body, for there is no such thing as body in general), this same matter is also the matter of magnitude and quality—being separable from these matters by definition, but not separable in place unless Qualities are, in their turn, separable.[5] 25

It is evident, from the preceding[6] development and discussion of difficulties, that growth is not a change out of something which, though potentially a magnitude, actually possesses no magnitude. For, if it were, 'the void' would exist in separation; but we have explained in a former work[7] that this is impossible. Moreover, a change of that kind is not peculiarly distinctive of growth, but characterizes

---

[1] 'inseparable' from the actual body in which it is contained.

[2] Cf. *Physics* A. 7; *Metaph.* 1032ª 12 ff.

[3] The efficient cause of the coming-to-be of a hard thing (e. g. of ice or terra-cotta) is something cold or hot (a freezing wind or a baking fire); cf. *Meteor.* 382ª 22 ff. Such efficient causes are only generically, not specifically, identical with their effects. I have transposed the words σκληρὸν γὰρ οὐχ ὑπὸ σκληροῦ γίνεται so as to read them as a parenthesis after ὁμογενοῦς in 320^b 19.

[4] An 'actuality' or 'form': cf. *Metaph.* 1032ª 25 ff.

[5] i.e. unless Qualities or Adjectivals are separable from Substances.

[6] Cf. above, 320ª 27–^b 12.

[7] Cf. *Physics* Δ. 6–9.

30 coming-to-be as such or in general. For growth is an increase, and diminution is a lessening, of the magnitude which
is there already—that, indeed, is why the growing thing
must possess some magnitude. Hence growth must not
be regarded as a process from a matter without magnitude
to an actuality of magnitude: for this would be a body's
coming-to-be rather than its growth.

We must therefore come to closer quarters with the
321^a subject of our inquiry. We must 'grapple' with it (as it
were) from its beginning, and determine the precise character
of the growing and diminishing whose causes we are investigating.

It is evident (i) that any and every part of the growing
thing has increased, and that similarly in diminution every
part has become smaller: also (ii) that a thing grows by
5 the accession, and diminishes by the departure, of something. Hence it must grow by the accession either
(*a*) of something incorporeal or (*b*) of a body. Now, if
(*a*) it grows by the accession of something incorporeal,
there will exist *separate* a void: but (as we have stated
before) [1] it is impossible for *a matter of magnitude* to exist
'separate'. If, on the other hand, (*b*) it grows by the
accession of a body, there will be two bodies—that which
grows and that which increases it—in the same place:
and this too is impossible.

10 But neither is it open to us to say that growth or
diminution occurs in the way in which e. g. air is generated
from water. For, although the volume has then become
greater, the change will not be growth, but a coming-to-be
of the one—viz. of that into which the change is taking
place—and a passing-away of the contrasted body. It is
not a *growth* of either. Nothing grows in the process;
unless indeed there be something common to both things·
15 (to that which is coming-to-be and to that which passed-
away), e. g. 'body', and this grows. The water has not
grown, nor has the air: but the former has passed-
away and the latter has come-to-be, and—if anything has
grown—there has been a growth of 'body'. Yet this too

---

[1] Cf. above, 320^a 27 – ^{b} 25.

is impossible. For our account of growth must preserve the characteristics of that which is growing and diminishing. And these characteristics are three: (i) any and every part of the growing magnitude is made bigger (e. g. if flesh 20 grows, every particle of the flesh gets bigger), (ii) by the accession of something, and (iii) in such a way that the growing thing is preserved and persists. . For whereas a thing does not persist in the processes of unqualified coming-to-be or passing-away, that which grows or 'alters' persists in its identity through the 'altering' and through the growing or diminishing, though the quality (in 'altera- 25 tion') and the size (in growth) do not remain the same. Now if the generation of air from water is to be regarded as growth, a thing might grow without the accession (and without the persistence) of anything, and diminish without the departure of anything—and that which grows need not persist. But this characteristic[1] must be preserved: for the growth we are discussing has been assumed to be thus characterized.

One might raise a further difficulty. What is 'that which 30 grows'? Is it that to which something is added? If, e. g., a man grows in his shin, is it the shin which is greater[2]— but not that 'whereby' he grows, viz. not the food? Then why have not both 'grown'? For when A is added to B, both A and B are greater, as when you mix wine with water; for each ingredient is alike increased in volume. Perhaps the explanation is that the substance of the one[3] remains unchanged, but the substance of the other (viz. of 35 the food) does not. For indeed, even in the mixture of wine 321[b] and water, it is the prevailing ingredient which is said to have increased in volume. We say, e. g., that the wine has increased, because the whole mixture acts as wine but not as water. A similar principle applies also to 'alteration'. Flesh is said to have been 'altered' if, while its character and substance remain, some one of its essential properties, which was not there before, now qualifies it: on the other 5

---

[1] viz. the third characteristic—that the growing thing 'persists'.
[2] i. e. has 'grown'.
[3] i. e. the substance of the shin.

hand, that 'whereby' it has been 'altered' may have undergone no change, though sometimes it too has been affected.
The altering agent, however, and the originative source of
the process are in the growing thing and in that which is
being 'altered': for the efficient cause is in these.[1] No doubt
the food, which has come in, may sometimes expand as well
as the body that has consumed it (that is so, e.g., if, after
having come in, a food is converted into wind[2]), but when
10 it has undergone this change it has passed-away: and the
efficient cause is not in the food.

We have now developed the difficulties sufficiently and
must therefore try to find a solution of the problem. Our
solution must preserve intact the three characteristics of
growth—that the growing thing persists, that it grows by
the accession (and diminishes by the departure) of something, and further that every perceptible particle of it has
15 become either larger or smaller. We must recognize also
(a) that the growing body is not 'void' and that yet there
are not two magnitudes in the same place, and (b) that it
does not grow by the accession of something incorporeal.

Two preliminary distinctions will prepare us to grasp
the cause of growth. We must note (i) that the organic
parts[3] grow by the growth of the tissues[4] (for every organ
is composed of these as its constituents); and (ii) that flesh,
20 bone, and every such part[5]—like every other thing which
has its form immersed in matter—has a twofold nature: for
the form as well as the matter is called 'flesh' or 'bone'.

Now, that any and every part of the tissue *qua* form
should grow—and grow by the accession of something—is
possible, but not that any and every part of the tissue *qua*
matter should do so. For we must think of the tissue after

---

[1] And therefore it is these which are said to grow or to be 'altered'.
[2] Aristotle may be thinking of the conversion of a flatulent food into
wind. But more probably he has in mind the maintenance and growth
of the ἔμφυτον (or σύμφυτον) πνεῦμα: cf. *de Spiritu* 481ᵃ 1 ff.
[3] The Greek is τὰ ἀνομοιομερῆ, i.e. those parts (of the living thing)
whose texture is not uniform throughout.
[4] The Greek is τὰ ὁμοιομερῆ, i.e. those parts whose texture is uniform
throughout: cf. above, 314ᵃ 19-20. In living things such parts correspond roughly to 'the tissues'.
[5] i.e. every 'homoeomerous' part (or every 'tissue').

the image of flowing water that is measured by one and 25
the same measure: particle after particle comes-to-be, and
each successive particle is different.[1] And it is in this
sense that the matter of the flesh grows, some flowing
out and some flowing in fresh; not in the sense that fresh
matter accedes to every particle of it. There is, however,
an accession to every part of its figure or 'form'.

That growth has taken place proportionally,[2] is more
manifest in the organic parts—e.g. in the hand. For *there*
the fact that the matter is distinct from the form is 30
more manifest than in flesh, i. e. than in the tissues. That
is why there is a greater tendency to suppose that a
corpse still possesses flesh and bone than that it still has
a hand or an arm.

Hence in one sense it is true that any and every part
of the flesh has grown; but in another sense it is false.
For there has been an accession to every part of the flesh
in respect to its form, but not in respect to its matter.
The whole, however, has become larger. And this increase 35
is due (*a*) on the one hand to the accession of something,
which is called 'food' and is said to be 'contrary' to flesh, 322^a
but (*b*) on the other hand to the transformation of this food
into the same form as that of flesh—as if, e.g., 'moist'
were to accede to 'dry' and, having acceded, were to be
transformed and to become 'dry'. For in one sense 'Like
grows by Like', but in another sense 'Unlike grows by
Unlike'

One might discuss what must be the character of that
'whereby' a thing grows. Clearly it must be potentially 5
that which is growing—potentially flesh, e.g., if it is flesh
that is growing. Actually, therefore, it must be 'other'
than the growing thing. This 'actual other', then, has
passed-away and come-to-be flesh. But it has not been
transformed into flesh alone by itself (for that would have

---

[1] I think this clause refers to the matter of the tissue, not to the
water. In Aristotle's simile, the 'measure' corresponds to the tissue's
form, and the 'water' to its matter. The matter is a flux of different
particles always coming-to-be and passing-away, always 'flowing in
and out' of the structural plan which is the 'form'.
[2] i. e. by an expansion of all parts of the 'form'.

been a coming-to-be, not a growth): on the contrary, it
is the growing thing which has come-to-be flesh ⟨and grown⟩[1]
by the food. In what way, then, has the food been modified by the growing thing?[2] Perhaps we should say that
it has been 'mixed' with it, as if one were to pour water
10 into wine and the wine were able to convert the new
ingredient into wine. And as fire lays hold of the in-
flammable,[3] so the active principle of growth, dwelling
in the growing thing (i. e. in that which is actually flesh),
lays hold of an acceding food which is potentially flesh and
converts it into actual flesh. The acceding food, therefore,
must be *together with* the growing thing:[4] for if it were
apart from it, the change would be a coming-to-be.[5] For
15 it is possible to produce fire by piling logs on to the already
burning fire. That is 'growth'. But when the logs themselves are set on fire, that is 'coming-to-be'.

'Quantum-in-general' does not come-to-be any more
than 'animal' which is neither man nor any other of the
specific forms of animal: what 'animal-in-general' is in
coming-to-be, that 'quantum-in-general' is in growth.
But what does come-to-be in growth is flesh or bone—
or a hand or arm (i. e. the tissues of these organic parts).[6]
20 Such things come-to-be, then, by the accession not of
quantified-flesh but of a quantified-something. In so far
as this acceding food is potentially the double result—
e. g. is potentially so-much-flesh—it produces growth: for
it is bound to become actually both *so-much* and *flesh*.
But in so far as it is potentially flesh only, it nourishes:
for it is thus that 'nutrition' and 'growth' differ by their
definition. That is why a body's 'nutrition' continues so

---

[1] All the manuscripts read ηὐξήθη after τούτου in 322[a] 9. We must
either delete it, or correct it into ηὔξησεν (cf. Philoponos, ed. Vitelli,
p. 117, l. 12), or transpose it so as to read it after τούτῳ in [a] 8. I have
adopted the last alternative in my translation.

[2] i. e. 'been modified' so as to be transformed into flesh.

[3] i. e. 'lays hold' of it and converts it into fire.

[4] i. e. 'must be together with' it when this conversion takes place.

[5] i. e. an independent coming-to-be of flesh, not a growth of the
already existing tissue.

[6] i. e. what comes-to-be in growth is so-much flesh or bone, or
a hand or arm of such and such a size: not 'quantum-in-general',
but a 'quantified-something'.

long as it is kept alive (even when it is diminishing), though
not its 'growth'; and why nutrition, though 'the same' ₂₅
as growth, is yet different from it in its actual being. For in
so far as that which accedes is potentially 'so-much-flesh' it
tends to increase flesh : whereas, in so far as it is potentially
'flesh' only, it is nourishment.

The form of which we have spoken[1] is a kind of power
immersed in matter—a duct, as it were. If, then, a matter
accedes—a matter, which is potentially a duct and also ₃₀
potentially possesses determinate quantity—the · ducts to
which it accedes will become bigger. But if it[2] is no
longer able to act—if it has been weakened by the continued influx of matter, just as water, continually mixed
in greater and greater quantity with wine, in the end makes
the wine watery and converts it into water—then it will cause
a diminution of the *quantum* ;[3] though still the form persists.[4]

6 ⟨In discussing the causes of coming-to-be⟩[5] we must first **322ᵇ**
investigate the *matter*, i. e. the so-called 'elements'. We
must ask whether they really are elements or not, i.e. whether
each of them is eternal or whether there is a sense in which
they come-to-be : and, if they do come-to-be, whether all
of them come-to-be in the same manner, reciprocally out
of one another, or whether one amongst them is something

---

[1] i.e. the form which grows in every part of itself: cf. above,
321ᵇ 22-34.
[2] i.e. this form or power immersed in matter.
[3] i. e. a diminution of the size of the tissue whose form it is.
[4] For the reading and interpretation of 322ᵃ 28-33 see my text
and commentary.
[5] I have added these words to explain 'first': cf. Zabarella, whose
interpretation I have followed.

5 primary. Hence we must begin by explaining certain preliminary matters, about which the statements now current are vague.

For all ⟨the pluralist philosophers⟩—those who generate the 'elements' as well as those who generate the bodies that are compounded of the elements—make use of 'dissociation' and 'association', and of 'action' and 'passion'. Now 'association' is 'combination'; but the precise meaning of the process we call 'combining' has not been explained. Again, ⟨all the monists make use of 'alteration':
10 but⟩ without an agent and a patient there cannot be 'altering' any more than there can be 'dissociating' and 'associating'. For not only those who postulate a plurality of elements employ their reciprocal action and passion to generate the compounds: those who derive things from a single element are equally compelled to introduce 'acting'.[1] And in this respect Diogenes is right when he argues that
15 'unless all things were derived from one, reciprocal action and passion could not have occurred'.[2] The hot thing, e. g., would not be cooled and the cold thing in turn be warmed: for heat and cold do not change reciprocally into one another, but what changes (it is clear) is the *substratum*. Hence, whenever there is action and passion between two things, that which underlies them must be a single something. No doubt, it is not true to say that *all* things are of
20 this character:[3] but it is true of all things between which there is reciprocal action and passion.

But if we must investigate 'action-passion' and 'combination', we must also investigate 'contact'. For action and passion (in the proper sense of the terms) can only occur between things which are such as to touch one
25 another; nor can things enter into combination at all unless they have come into a certain kind of contact. Hence

---

[1] I have added the explicit reference to 'the pluralists' at ^b6 and to 'the monists' at ^b9, because Aristotle's argument in the present passage presupposes this classification and the consequences that were drawn from it in the first chapter.

[2] Cf. Diogenes, fr. 2 (Diels, p. 334).

[3] i. e. are transformations of a single *substratum*, or 'derived from one thing', as Diogenes maintained.

we must give a definite account of these three things—of 'contact', 'combination', and 'acting'.

Let us start as follows. All things which admit of 'combination' must be capable of reciprocal contact: and the same is true of any two things, of which one 'acts' and the other 'suffers action' in the proper sense of the terms. For this reason we must treat of 'contact' first.

Now every term which possesses a variety of meanings 30 includes those various meanings *either* owing to a mere coincidence of language, *or* owing to a real order of derivation in the different things to which it is applied: but, though this may be taken to hold of 'contact' as of all such terms, it is nevertheless true that 'contact' *in the proper sense* applies only to things which have 'position'. And 'position' belongs only to those things which also have a 'place': for in so far as we attribute 'contact' to the **323^a** mathematical things, we must also attribute 'place' to them, whether they exist in separation or in some other fashion.[1] Assuming, therefore, that 'to touch' is—as we have defined it in a previous work [2]—'to have the extremes together' only those things will touch one another which, being 5 separate magnitudes and possessing position, have their extremes 'together'. And since position belongs only to those things which also have a 'place', while the primary differentiation of 'place' is 'the above' and 'the below' (and the similar pairs of opposites), all things which touch one another will have 'weight' or 'lightness'—*either* both these qualities *or* one or the other of them.[3] But bodies which are heavy or light are such as to 'act' and 'suffer 10 action'. Hence it is clear that those things are by nature such as to touch one another, which (being separate magnitudes) have their extremes 'together' and are able to move, and be moved by, one another.

The manner in which the 'mover' moves the 'moved' is

---

[1] i.e. whether they exist in separation from the perceptible things, or whether they 'are' e.g. as inseparable adjectives of the φυσικὰ σώματα or as abstracted objects of thought.

[2] Cf. *Physics* 226^b 21-23.

[3] i.e. if A and B are in reciprocal contact, *either* A must be heavy and B light, or A light and B heavy: *or* A and B must both be heavy, or both be light.

not always the same : on the contrary, whereas one kind of 'mover' can only impart motion by being itself moved, another kind can do so though remaining itself unmoved.

15 Clearly therefore we must recognize a corresponding variety in speaking of the 'acting' thing too : for the 'mover' is said to 'act' (in a sense) and the 'acting' thing to 'impart motion'. Nevertheless there is a difference and we must draw a distinction. For not every 'mover' can 'act', if (a) the term 'agent' is to be used in contrast to 'patient' and (b) 'patient' is to be applied only to those things whose motion is a 'quali-

20 tative affection'—i.e. a quality, like 'white' or 'hot', in respect to which they are 'moved' only in the sense that they are 'altered' : on the contrary, to 'impart motion' is a wider term than to 'act'[1] Still, so much, at any rate, is clear : the things which are 'such as to impart motion', if that description be interpreted in one sense, will touch the things which are 'such as to be moved by them'—while they will not touch them, if the description be interpreted in a different sense. But the disjunctive definition of 'touching' must include and distinguish (a) 'contact in general' as the relation between two things which, having position, are such that one is able to impart motion and the other to be moved, and (b) 'reciprocal contact' as the relation between two things, one able to impart motion and the other able to be moved in such a way that 'action and

25 passion' are predicable of them.

As a rule, no doubt, if A touches B, B touches A. For indeed practically all the 'movers' within our ordinary experience impart motion by being moved : in their case, what touches inevitably must, and also evidently does, touch something which reciprocally touches it. Yet, if A moves B, it is possible—as we sometimes express it—for A 'merely to touch' B, and that which touches need not

30 touch a something which touches it. Nevertheless it is commonly supposed that 'touching' must be reciprocal. The reason of this belief is that 'movers' which belong to the same kind as the 'moved' impart motion by being moved. Hence if anything imparts motion without itself

---

[1] i.e. if to 'act' be understood in the narrow sense just explained.

being moved, it may touch the 'moved' and yet itself be touched by nothing—for we say sometimes that the man who grieves us 'touches' us, but not that we 'touch' him.

The account just given may serve to distinguish and define the 'contact' which occurs in the things of Nature. 7 Next in order we must discuss 'action' and 'passion'. 323^b The traditional theories on the subject are conflicting. For (i) most thinkers are unanimous in maintaining (a) that 'like' is always unaffected by 'like', because (as they argue) neither of two 'likes' is more apt than the other either to 5 act or to suffer action, since all the properties which belong to the one belong identically and in the same degree to the other; and (b) that 'unlikes', i.e. 'differents', are by nature such as to act and suffer action reciprocally. For even when the smaller fire is destroyed by the greater, it suffers this effect (they say) owing to its 'contrariety'—since the great is contrary to the small. But (ii) Demokritos dis- 10 sented from all the other thinkers and maintained a theory peculiar to himself. He asserts that agent and patient are identical, i.e. 'like'. It is not possible (he says) that 'others', i.e. 'differents', should suffer action from one another : on the contrary, even if two things, being 'others', do act in some way on one another, this happens to them 15 not *qua* 'others' but *qua* possessing an identical property.

Such, then, are the traditional theories, and it looks as if the statements of their advocates were in manifest conflict. But the reason of this conflict is that each group is in fact stating *a part*, whereas they ought to have taken a comprehensive view of the subject *as a whole*. For (i) if A and B are 'like'—absolutely and in all respects without difference from one another—it is reasonable to infer that neither is 20 in any way affected by the other. Why, indeed, should either of them tend to act any more than the other? Moreover, if 'like' can be affected by 'like', a thing can also be affected by itself: and yet if that were so—if 'like' tended in fact to act *qua* 'like'—there would be nothing indestructible or immovable, for everything would move itself. And (ii) the same consequence follows if A and B are absolutely 25 'other', i.e. in no respect identical. *Whiteness* could not be affected in any way by *line* nor *line* by *whiteness*—

except perhaps 'coincidentally', viz. if the line happened
to be white or black: for unless two things either are, or are
composed of, 'contraries', neither drives the other out of
30 its natural condition. But (iii) since only those things
which either involve a 'contrariety' or are 'contraries'—
and not any things selected at random—are such as to
suffer action and to act, agent and patient must be 'like'
(i.e. identical) in kind and yet 'unlike' (i.e. contrary) in
species. (For it is a law of nature that body is affected by
body, flavour by flavour, colour by colour, and so in
324^a general what belongs to any kind by a member of the same
kind—the reason being that 'contraries' are in every case
within a single identical kind, and it is 'contraries' which
reciprocally act and suffer action.) Hence agent and patient
must be in one sense identical, but in another sense other
5 than (i.e. 'unlike') one another. And since (a) patient and
agent are generically identical (i.e. 'like') but specifically
'unlike', while (b) it is 'contraries' that exhibit this character: it is clear that 'contraries' and their 'intermediates'
are such as to suffer action and to act reciprocally—for indeed
it is these that constitute the entire sphere of passing-away
and coming-to-be.

10 We can now understand why fire heats and the cold thing
cools, and in general why the active thing assimilates to
itself the patient. For agent and patient are contrary to
one another, and coming-to-be is a process into the contrary: hence the patient *must* change into the agent, since
it is only thus that coming-to-be will be a process into the
contrary. And, again, it is intelligible that the advocates
of both views, although their theories are not the same, are
15 yet in contact with the nature of the facts. For sometimes
we speak of the *substratum* as suffering action (e. g. of 'the
man' as being healed, being warmed and chilled, and similarly in all the other cases), but at other times we say 'what is
cold is being warmed', 'what is sick is being healed': and
in both these ways of speaking we express the truth, since
in one sense it is the 'matter', while in another sense it is
the 'contrary', which suffers action. (We make the same
20 distinction in speaking of the agent: for sometimes we say
that 'the man', but at other times that 'what is hot', pro-

duces heat.)   Now the one group of thinkers supposed that
agent and patient must possess something identical, because
they fastened their attention on the *substratum* : while the
other group maintained the opposite because their attention
was concentrated on the 'contraries'.

We must conceive the same account to hold of action 25
and passion as that which is true of 'being moved' and
'imparting motion'.   For the 'mover', like the 'agent', has
two meanings.   Both (*a*) that which contains the originative source of the motion is thought to 'impart motion' (for
the originative source is first amongst the causes), and also
(*b*) that which is last, i. e. immediately next to the moved
thing and to the coming-to-be.[1]   A similar distinction holds
also of the agent : for we speak not only (*a*) of the doctor, 30
but also (*b*) of the wine, as healing.   Now, in motion, there
is nothing to prevent *the first mover* being unmoved (indeed,
as regards some 'first movers' this is actually necessary) although *the last mover* always imparts motion by being itself
moved : and, in action, there is nothing to prevent *the first
agent* being unaffected, while *the last agent* only acts by
suffering action itself.   For (*a*) if agent and patient have not
the same matter, agent acts without being affected : thus 35
the art of healing produces health without itself being acted
upon in any way by that which is being healed.   But **324**^b
(*b*) the food, in acting, is itself in some way acted upon :
for, in acting, it is simultaneously heated or cooled or
otherwise affected.   Now the art of healing corresponds
to an 'originative source', while the food corresponds to
'the last' (i. e. 'contiguous') mover.[2]

Those active powers, then, whose forms are not embodied 5
in matter, are unaffected : but those whose forms are in
matter are such as to be affected in acting.   For we maintain that one and the same 'matter' is *equally*, so to say,
the basis of either of the two opposed things—being as it
were a 'kind';[3] and that *that which can be hot* must be
made hot, provided the heating agent is there, i. e. comes
near.   Hence (as we have said) some of the active powers 10

---

[1] By 'the coming-to-be' (τὴν γένεσιν) we must apparently understand
'that which is coming-to-be' (τὸ γινόμενον).

[2] Cf. above, 324^a 26–9.

[3] i. e. a kind, of which the two opposed things are contrasted species.

are unaffected while others are such as to be affected; and what holds of motion is true also of the active powers. For as in motion 'the first mover' is unmoved, so among the active powers 'the first agent' is unaffected.

The active power is a 'cause' in the sense of that from which the process originates: but the end, for the sake of 15 which it takes place, is not 'active'. (That is why *health* is not 'active', except metaphorically.) For when the agent is there, the patient *becomes* something: but when 'states'[1] are there, the patient no longer *becomes* but already *is*—and 'forms' (i.e. 'ends') are a kind of 'state'. As to the 'matter', it (*qua* matter) is passive. Now fire contains 'the hot' embodied in matter: but a 'hot' separate from 20 matter (if such a thing existed) could not suffer any action. Perhaps, indeed, it is impossible that 'the hot' should exist in separation from matter: but if there are any entities thus separable, what we are saying would be true of them.

We have thus explained what action and passion are, what things exhibit them, why they do so, and in what 25 manner. We must go on[2] to discuss how it is possible for **8** action and passion to take place.

Some philosophers think that the 'last' agent—the 'agent' in the strictest sense—enters in through certain pores, and so the patient suffers action. It is in this way, they assert, that we see and hear and exercise all our other senses. Moreover, according to them, things are seen through air 30 and water and other transparent bodies, because such bodies possess pores, invisible indeed owing to their minuteness, but close-set and arranged in rows: and the more transparent the body, the more frequent and serial they suppose its pores to be.

Such was the theory which some philosophers (including Empedokles) advanced in regard to the structure of certain bodies. They do not restrict it to the bodies which act and suffer action: but 'combination' too, they say, takes 35 place 'only between bodies whose pores are in reciprocal symmetry'. The most systematic and consistent theory, 325ᵃ however, and one that applied to all bodies, was advanced

---

[1] i.e. like 'health'

[2] For this sense of πάλιν see Bonitz, *Index* 559ᵇ 13 ff. Perhaps, however, Aristotle means 'We must go back and discuss'.

by Leukippos and Demokritos : and, in maintaining it, they took as their starting-point what naturally comes first.[1]

For some of the older philosophers[2] thought that 'what is' must of necessity be 'one' and immovable. The void, they argue, 'is not': but unless there is a void with a separate being of its own, 'what is' cannot be moved—nor again can it be 'many', since there is nothing to keep things apart. And in *this* respect,[3] they insist, the view that the universe is not 'continuous' but 'discretes-in-contact'[4] is no better than the view that there are 'many' (and not 'one') and a void.[5] For ⟨suppose that the universe is discretes-in-contact. Then⟩,[6] if it is divisible through and through, there is no 'one', and therefore no 'many' either, but the Whole is void; while to maintain that it is divisible at some points, but not at others, looks like an arbitrary fiction. For up to what limit is it divisible? And for what reason is part of the Whole indivisible, i.e. a *plenum*, and part divided? Further, they maintain, it is equally[7] necessary to deny the existence of motion.

Reasoning in this way, therefore, they were led to transcend sense-perception, and to disregard it on the ground that 'one ought to follow the argument': and so they assert that the universe is 'one' and immovable. Some of them add that it is 'infinite', since the limit (if it had one) would be a limit against the void.[8]

There were, then, certain thinkers who, for the reasons we have stated, enunciated views of this kind as their theory of 'The Truth'.[9] . Moreover,[10] although these

---

[1] Perhaps we should read κατὰ φύσιν, ᾗπερ ἔστιν and understand the words as a reference to Parmenides (cf. e.g. fr. 8, l. 1; Diels, p. 118).

[2] The reference is to Parmenides, Melissos, and (probably) Zeno.

[3] i.e. for rendering intelligible the being of a 'many'.

[4] This appears to be the view of Empedokles, as Aristotle here expresses it : cf. below, 325^b 5–10.

[5] This appears to be the view of the Pythagoreans : cf. *Physics* 213^b 22–7.

[6] I have added these words to bring out the connexion of thought, which is clear enough in the original without any addition.

[7] i.e. the existence of motion is just as impossible on the hypothesis of Empedokles as on that of the Pythagoreans.

[8] Cf. Melissos, e. g. fr. 3, 5, 7 (Diels, pp. 144, 145).

[9] These words (περὶ τῆς ἀληθείας) seem to be intended to suggest The Way of Truth' in the poem of Parmenides.

[10] One or more arguments against the Eleatic theory appear to have dropped out before ἔτι in ^a 17.

opinions appear to follow logically in a dialectical discussion, yet to believe them seems next door to madness
20 when one considers the facts.   For indeed no lunatic seems
to be so far out of his senses as to suppose that fire and ice
are ' one': it is only between what *is* right, and what *seems*
right from habit, that some people are mad enough to see
no difference.

Leukippos, however, thought he had a theory which
harmonized with sense-perception and would not abolish
25 either coming-to-be and passing-away or motion and the
multiplicity of things. He made these concessions to the facts
of perception: on the other hand, he conceded to the Monists
that there could be no motion without a void.   The result
is a theory which he states as follows: 'The void is a "not-
'being", and no part of " what is " is a " not-being "; for
' what " is " in the strict sense of the term is an absolute
'*plenum*. This *plenum*, however, is not " one ": on the
30 'contrary, it is a " many " infinite in number and invisible
' owing to the minuteness of their bulk.   The " many "
' move in the void (for there is a void)¹: and by coming
' together they produce " coming-to-be ", while by separating
' they produce " passing-away ".² Moreover, they act and
' suffer action wherever they chance to be in contact (for
' *there* they are not " one "), and they generate by being put
' together and becoming intertwined.   From the genuinely-
35 ' one, on the other hand, there never could have come-to-be
' a multiplicity, nor from the genuinely-many a " one ":
325^b ' that is impossible. But ' (just as Empedokles and some of
the other philosophers say that things suffer action through
their pores,³ ¡so) 'all " alteration " and all " passion " take
' place in the way that has been explained: breaking-up (i.e.
' passing-away) is effected by means of the void, and so too
5 ' is growth—solids creeping in to fill the void places.'

Empedokles too is practically bound to adopt the same

---

¹ i.e. there is a void, though it is a 'not-being' or 'unreal'.
² I am greatly indebted to the translation given by Burnet (§ 173)
of 324^b 35—325^a 32, though I have not been able to accept his version
in all its details.
³ The comparison with 'Empedokles and some of the other philosophers' is of course not part of the argument which Aristotle is here
reproducing from Leukippos.

theory as Leukippos. For he must say that there are
certain solids which, however, are indivisible—unless there
are continuous pores all through the body. But this last
alternative is impossible: for *then* there will be nothing
solid in the body (nothing beside the pores) but all of it
will be void. It is necessary, therefore, for his 'contiguous
discretes' to be indivisible, while the intervals between 10
them—which he calls 'pores'—must be void. But this is
precisely Leukippos's theory of action and passion.

Such, approximately, are the current explanations of the
manner in which some things 'act' while others 'suffer
action'. And as regards the Atomists, it is not only clear
what their explanation is: it is also obvious that it follows
with tolerable consistency from the assumptions they employ. 15
But there is less obvious consistency in the explanation
offered by the other thinkers. It is not clear, for instance,
how, on the theory of Empedokles, there is to be 'passing-
away' as well as 'alteration'. For the primary bodies of
the Atomists—the primary constituents of which bodies are
composed, and the ultimate elements into which they are
dissolved—are indivisible, differing from one another only in
figure. In the philosophy of Empedokles, on the other
hand, it is evident that all the other bodies down to the 20
'elements' have their coming-to-be and their passing-
away: but it is not clear how the 'elements' themselves,
severally in their aggregated masses, come-to-be and pass-
away. Nor is it possible for Empedokles to explain how
they do so, since he does not assert that Fire too[1] (and
similarly every one of his other 'elements') possesses 'elementary constituents' of itself.

Such an assertion would commit him to doctrines like
those which Plato has set forth in the *Timaeus*.[2] For 25
although both Plato and Leukippos postulate elementary
constituents that are indivisible and distinctively characterized by figures, there is this great difference between the
two theories: the 'indivisibles' of Leukippos (i) are solids,
while those of Plato are planes, and (ii) are characterized
by an infinite variety of figures, while the characterizing

---

[1] i. e. as well as the composite bodies.
[2] Cf. *Timaeus* 53 c ff.

figures employed by Plato are limited in number.   Thus
30 the 'comings-to-be' and the 'dissociations' result from the
'indivisibles' (a) *according to Leukippos* through the void and
through contact (for it is at the point of contact that each of
the composite bodies is divisible[1]), but (b) *according to Plato*
in virtue of contact alone, since he denies there is a void.

Now we have discussed 'indivisible planes' in the preceding treatise.[2]   But with regard to the assumption of
35 'indivisible solids', although we must not now enter upon
a detailed study of its consequences, the following criticisms
fall within the compass of a short digression :—

326^a   (I) The Atomists are committed to the view that every 'indivisible' is incapable alike of receiving a sensible property
(for nothing can 'suffer action' except through the void) and
of producing one—no 'indivisible' can be, e.g., either hard
or cold.[3]   Yet it is surely a paradox that an exception is
5 made of 'the hot'—'the hot' being assigned as peculiar to
the spherical figure : for, that being so, its 'contrary' also
('the cold') is bound to belong to another of the figures.
If, however, these properties (heat and cold) do belong to
the 'indivisibles', it is a further paradox that they should
not possess heaviness and lightness, and hardness and
10 softness.   And yet Demokritos says 'the more any indivisible exceeds, the heavier it is'—to which we must
clearly add 'and the hotter it is'.   But if *that* is their
character, it is impossible they should not be affected
by one another : the 'slightly-hot indivisible', e.g., will
inevitably suffer action from one which far exceeds it in
heat.[4]   Again, if any 'indivisible' is 'hard', there must
also be one which is 'soft' : but 'the soft' derives its very
name from the fact that it suffers a certain action—for
'soft' is that which yields to pressure.   (II) But further,

---

[1] Cf. above, 325^a 32-4.

[2] Cf. *de Caelo* Γ. 1, especially 298^b 33 ff., Γ. 7 and Δ. 2.

[3] Or perhaps this clause is a quotation : 'since "no indivisible can
be either hard or cold".'

[4] If, as Demokritos asserts, the 'indivisibles' differ in weight, being
heavy in direct proportion to their mass, his 'spherical indivisibles'
(Aristotle argues) must differ in the degree of their heat on the same
principle.   But if A is hotter than B, B is susceptible to the action of
A.   Hence Demokritos has violated a fundamental thesis of his own
theory (cf. 326^a 1-2), viz. that every 'indivisible' must be ἀπαθές.

not only is it paradoxical (i) that no property except figure 15
should belong to the 'indivisibles': it is also paradoxical
(ii) that, if other properties do belong to them, one only of
these additional properties should attach to each—e.g. that
this 'indivisible' should be cold and *that* 'indivisible' hot.
For, on that supposition, their substance would not even be
uniform.[1] And it is equally impossible (iii) that more than
one of these additional properties should belong to the
single 'indivisible'. For, being *indivisible*, it will possess
these properties in the same point[2]—so that, if it ' suffers
action' by being chilled, it will also, *qua* chilled, ' act' or 20
'suffer action' in some other way. And the same line of
argument applies to all the other properties too: for the
difficulty we have just raised confronts, as a necessary consequence, all who advocate ' indivisibles' (whether solids or
planes), since their 'indivisibles' cannot become either
'rarer' or 'denser' inasmuch as there is no void in them.
(III) It is a further paradox that there should be small 25
'indivisibles', but not large ones. For it is natural enough,
from the ordinary point of view, that the larger bodies
should be more liable to fracture than the small ones, since
they (viz. the large bodies) are easily broken up because
they collide with many other bodies. But why should
indivisibility *as such* be the property of small, rather than
of large, bodies? (IV) Again, is the substance of all those 30
solids uniform, or do they fall into sets which differ from
one another—as if, e. g., some of them, in their aggregated
bulk,[3] were ' fiery ', others ' earthy '? For (i) if all of them
are uniform in substance, what is it that separated one from
another ? Or why, when they come into contact, do they
not coalesce into one, as drops of water run together when
drop touches drop (for the two cases are precisely parallel)?
On the other hand (ii) if they fall into differing sets, how
are these characterized ? It is clear, too, that *these*,[4] rather 35
than the ' figures ', ought to be postulated as ' original reals ', 326ᵇ

[1] The uniformity of the substance or 'stuff' of the atoms was
a fundamental doctrine in the theory. Cf. *Physics* 203ᵃ 34 – ᵇ 2,
de Caelo 275ᵇ 31-2 ; Burnet, p. 336₃.
[2] i.e. in its single, indivisible, undifferentiated identity.
[3] Cf. above, 325ᵇ 22.
[4] i.e. these qualitatively-distinct sets of atoms.

i. e. causes from which the phenomena result. Moreover, if they differed in substance, they would both act and suffer action on coming into reciprocal contact. (V) Again, what is it which sets them moving? For if their 'mover' is other than themselves, they are such as to 'suffer action'. If, on the other hand, each of them sets itself in motion, either (a) it will be divisible ('imparting motion' *qua this,*
5 'being moved' *qua that*), or (b) contrary properties will attach to it in the same respect—i. e. 'matter' will be identical-in-potentiality as well as numerically-identical.[1]

As to the thinkers who explain modification of property through the movement facilitated by the pores, if this is supposed to occur notwithstanding the fact that the pores are filled, their postulate of pores is superfluous. For if the whole body suffers action under these conditions, it would
10 suffer action in the same way even if it had no pores but were just its own continuous self. Moreover, how can their account of 'vision through a *medium*' be correct? It is impossible for ⟨the visual ray⟩[2] to penetrate the transparent bodies at their 'contacts'; and impossible for it to pass through their pores if every pore be full. For how will that[3] differ from having no pores at all? The body will be
15 uniformly 'full' throughout. But, further, even if these passages, though they must *contain* bodies, are 'void', the same consequence will follow once more.[4] And if they are 'too minute to admit any body', it is absurd to suppose there is a 'minute' void and yet to deny the existence of a 'big' one (no matter how small the 'big' may be[5]), or to imagine 'the void' means anything else than a body's place
20 —whence it clearly follows that to every body there will correspond a void of equal cubic capacity.

---

[1] For the doctrine implied in this argument, cf. *Physics* 190^a 24, 192^a 1 ff.

[2] I have added these words because Aristotle is referring to Empedokles's theory of vision. Cf. Empedokles, fr. 84 (Diels, pp. 196-7); Plato, *Timaeus* 45 B ff.

[3] *sc.* having pores, all of which are 'full'.

[4] i. e. the body will still be impenetrable, even if the pores as such (as channels) are distinguished in thought from what fills them. For *in fact* the pores are always 'full' and the body is a *plenum* throughout—though perhaps not a 'uniform' *plenum*.

[5] 'Big' is a relative term and may include a void in any degree bigger than the infinitesimal.

As a general criticism we must urge that to postulate pores is superfluous. For if the agent produces no effect by touching the patient, neither will it produce any by passing through its pores. On the other hand, if it acts by contact, then—even without pores—some things will 'suffer action' and others will 'act', provided they are by nature adapted for reciprocal action and passion. Our arguments have shown that it is either false or futile to 25 advocate pores in the sense in which some thinkers conceive them. But since bodies are divisible through and through, the postulate of pores is ridiculous: for, *qua* divisible, a body can fall into separate parts.[1]

9 Let us explain the way in which things in fact possess the power of generating, and of acting and suffering action: 30 and let us start from the principle we have often enunciated. For, assuming the distinction between (*a*) that which is *potentially* and (*b*) that which is *actually* such-and-such, it is the nature of the first, precisely in so far as it is what it is, to suffer action *through and through*, not merely to be susceptible in some parts while insusceptible in others. But its susceptibility varies in degree, according as it is more or less such-and-such, and one would be more justified in speaking of 'pores' in this connexion[2]: for instance, in the metals there are veins of 'the susceptible' stretching con- 35 tinuously through the substance. 327^a

So long, indeed, as any body is naturally coherent and one, it is insusceptible. So, too, bodies are insusceptible so long as they are not in contact either with one another or with other bodies which are by nature such as to act and suffer action. (To illustrate my meaning: Fire heats not only when in contact, but also from a distance. For the fire heats the air, and the air—being by nature such as both 5 to act and suffer action—heats the body.) But the supposition that a body is 'susceptible in some parts, but insusceptible in others' ⟨is only possible for those who hold an erroneous view concerning the divisibility of magnitudes.

---

[1] Cf. above, 316^b 28-9. Division *eo ipso* opens a channel in the body.

[2] viz. to express such lines of greater susceptibility.

For us)[1] the following account results from the distinctions we established at the beginning.[2] For (i) if magnitudes are not divisible through and through—if, on the contrary, there are indivisible solids or planes—then indeed no body would be susceptible through and through: but neither
10 would any be continuous. Since, however, (ii) this is false, i. e. since every body is divisible, there is no difference between 'having been divided into parts which remain in contact' and 'being divisible'. For if a body '*can* be separated at the contacts' (as some thinkers express it), then, even though it has not yet been divided, it will be in a state of dividedness—since, as it *can* be divided, nothing inconceivable results.[3] And (iii) the supposition is open to
15 this general objection—it is a paradox that 'passion' should occur in this manner *only*, viz. by the bodies being split. For this theory abolishes 'alteration': but we see the same body *liquid* at one time and *solid* at another, without losing its continuity. It has suffered this change not by 'division' and 'composition', nor yet by 'turning' and 'intercontact'
20 as Demokritos asserts; for it has passed from the liquid to the solid state without any change of 'grouping' or 'position' in the constituents of its substance.[4] Nor are there contained within it those 'hard' (i. e. congealed) particles 'indivisible in their bulk': on the contrary, it is liquid—and again, solid and congealed—uniformly all through. This theory, it must be added, makes growth and diminution impossible also. For if there is to be *apposition* (instead of the growing thing having changed as
25 a whole, either by the admixture of something or by its own transformation), increase of size will not have resulted in any and every part.[5]

So much, then, to establish that things generate and are generated, act and suffer action, reciprocally; and to distinguish the way in which these processes *can* occur from the (impossible) way in which some thinkers say they occur.

---

[1] A clause to this effect appears to have dropped out before διορί-
σαντας in ᵃ6.
[2] Cf. above, 316ᵃ 14—317ᵃ 17.
[3] i. e. if this potentiality be realized: cf. 316ᵃ 19. The argument turns on Aristotle's conception of τὸ δυνατόν: cf. *Metaph.* 1047ᵃ 24–6.
[4] Cf. above, 315ᵇ 33—316ᵃ 1.   [5] Cf. above, 321ᵃ 2–26.

10 But we have still to explain 'combination', for that was the 30
third of the subjects we originally[1] proposed to discuss.
Our explanation will proceed on the same method as before.
We must inquire: What is 'combination', and what is that
which can 'combine'? Of what things, and under what
conditions, is 'combination' a property? And, further,
does 'combination' exist in fact, or is it false to assert its
existence?

For, according to some thinkers, it is impossible for one 35
thing to be combined with another. They argue that (i) if
both the 'combined' constituents persist unaltered, they are 327ᵇ
no more 'combined' now than they were before, but are in
the same condition: while (ii) if *one* has been destroyed,
the constituents have not been 'combined'—on the contrary,
one constituent *is* and the other *is not*, whereas 'combination' demands uniformity of condition in them both:
and on the same principle (iii) even if *both* the combining 5
constituents have been destroyed as the result of their
coalescence, *they* cannot 'have been combined' since *they*
have no being at all.

What we have in this argument is, it would seem,
a demand for the precise distinction of 'combination' from
coming-to-be and passing-away (for it is obvious that 'combination', if it exists, must differ from these processes) and
for the precise distinction of the 'combinable' from that
which is such as to come-to-be and pass-away. As soon,
therefore, as these distinctions are clear, the difficulties 10
raised by the argument would be solved.

Now (i) we do not speak of the wood as 'combined' with
the fire, nor of its burning as a 'combining' either of its
particles with one another or of itself with the fire: what
we say is that 'the fire is coming-to-be, but the wood is
passing-away'. Similarly, we speak neither (ii) of the food
as 'combining' with the body, nor (iii) of the shape as 'com- 15
bining' with the wax and thus fashioning the lump. Nor
can body 'combine' with white, nor (to generalize) 'properties' and 'states' with 'things': for we *see* them persisting unaltered.[2] But again (iv) white and knowledge cannot

---

[1] Cf. above, 322ᵇ 5 ff.
[2] *sc.* in the resulting complex (e. g. 'white-body' or 'learned-man ').

be 'combined' either, nor any other of the 'adjectivals'.
20 (Indeed, this is a blemish in the theory of those[1] who assert
that 'once upon a time all things were together and combined'. For not everything can 'combine' with everything.
On the contrary, both of the constituents that are combined
in the compound must originally have existed in separation:
but no property can have separate existence.)

Since, however, some things *are-potentially* while others
are-actually, the constituents combined in a compound can
'be' in a sense and yet 'not-be'. The compound may
25 *be-actually* other than the constituents from which it has
resulted; nevertheless each of them may still *be-potentially*
what it was before they were combined, and both of them
may survive undestroyed. (For this was the difficulty that
emerged in the previous argument: and it is evident that the
combining constituents not only coalesce, having formerly
existed in separation, but also can again be separated
out from the compound.) The constituents, therefore,
30 neither (a) *persist actually*, as 'body' and 'white' persist:
nor (b) are they *destroyed* (either one of them or both), for
their 'power of action'[2] is preserved. Hence these difficulties may be dismissed: but the problem immediately
connected with them—'whether combination is something
relative to perception'—must be set out and discussed.

When the combining constituents have been divided into
parts so small, and have been juxtaposed in such a manner,
35 that perception fails to discriminate them one from another,
328ᵃ have they then 'been combined'? Or ought we to say
'No, not until any and every part of one constituent is
juxtaposed to a part of the other'?[3] The term, no doubt,
is applied in the former sense: we speak, e.g., of wheat
having been 'combined' with barley when each *grain* of
the one is juxtaposed to a *grain* of the other. But every
body is divisible and therefore, since body 'combined'[4]

---

[1] Aristotle is perhaps thinking of the 'Sphere' of Empedokles, as
well as of the μῖγμα of Anaxagoras.

[2] Cf. below, 328ᵃ 28-31 and 334ᵇ 8-30.

[3] The difference between these two views—both of which Aristotle
rejects—is one of degree. According to the first view, the constituents
are divided into parts too small for the normal vision to discriminate,
and then shuffled. According to the second, the constituents are
divided into 'least' parts, i.e. into atoms: and these are shuffled.

[4] For μικτόν = μιχθέν cf. e.g. below, 334ᵇ 31.

with body is uniform in texture throughout, *any and every part* of each constituent ought to be juxtaposed to a part of 5 the other.

No body, however, can be divided into its 'least' parts: and 'composition' is not identical with 'combination', but other than it. From these premises it clearly follows (i) that so long as the constituents are preserved in small particles, we must not speak of them as 'combined'. (For this will be a 'composition' instead of a 'blending' or 'combination': nor will every portion of the resultant exhibit the same ratio between its constituents as the whole. But 10 we maintain that, if 'combination' has taken place, the compound *must* be uniform in texture throughout—any part of such a compound being the same as the whole, just as any part of water is water: whereas, if 'combination' is 'composition of the small particles', nothing of the kind will happen. On the contrary, the constituents will only be 'combined' relatively to perception: and the same thing will be 'combined' to one percipient, if his sight is not sharp, ⟨but not to another,⟩[1] while to the eye of Lynkeus 15 nothing will be 'combined'.) It clearly follows (ii) that we must not speak of the constituents as 'combined' in virtue of a division such that *any and every part* of each is juxtaposed to a part of the other: for it is impossible for them to be thus divided. Either, then, there is no 'combination', or we have still to explain the manner in which it can take place.

Now, as we maintain,[2] some things are such as to act and others such as to suffer action from them. Moreover, some things—viz. those which have the same matter— 20 'reciprocate', i. e. are such as to act upon one another and to suffer action from one another ; while other things, viz. agents which have not the same matter as their patients, act without themselves suffering action. Such agents cannot 'combine'—that is why neither the art of healing nor health produces health by 'combining' with the bodies of the patients. Amongst those things, however, which are reci-

---

[1] The words I have added represent the antithesis implied by the beginning of the sentence : but Aristotle prefers to clinch his argument by the reference to Lynkeus, at the cost of a slight anacoluthon.

[2] Cf. above, I. 7.

procally active and passive, some are easily-divisible. Now
(i) if a great quantity (or a large bulk) of one of these easily-
25 divisible 'reciprocating' materials be brought together with
a little (or with a small piece) of another, the effect produced
is not 'combination', but increase of the dominant: for the
other material is transformed into the dominant. (That is
why a drop of wine does not 'combine' with ten thousand
gallons of water: for its form is dissolved, and it[1] is changed
so as to merge in the total volume of water.) On the other
hand (ii) when there is a certain equilibrium between their
30 'powers of action', then each of them changes out of its own
nature towards the dominant: yet neither becomes the other,
but both become an intermediate with properties common
to both.[2]

Thus it is clear that only those agents are 'combinable'
which involve a contrariety—for these are such as to suffer
action reciprocally. And, further, they combine more
freely if small pieces of each of them are juxtaposed.
For in that condition they change one another more easily
35 and more quickly; whereas this effect takes a long time
when agent and patient are present in bulk.

328^b   Hence, amongst the divisible susceptible materials, those
whose shape is readily adaptable have a tendency to com-
bine: for they are easily divided into small particles, since
that is precisely what 'being readily adaptable in shape'
implies. For instance, liquids are the most 'combinable'
of all bodies—because, of all divisible materials, the liquid
is most readily adaptable in shape, unless it be viscous.
5 Viscous liquids, it is true, produce no effect except to
increase the volume and bulk. But when one of the constituents is alone susceptible—or superlatively susceptible,
the other being susceptible in a very slight degree—the
compound resulting from their combination is either no
greater in volume or only a little greater. This is what
happens when tin is combined with bronze. For some
things display a hesitating and ambiguous attitude towards

---

[1] *sc.* the drop of wine.
[2] Each of the constituents, *qua* acting on the other, is *relatively*
'dominant'. Neither of them is *absolutely* 'dominant', for each
'suffers action' from the other. Hence each meets the other half-
wa and the resultant is a com romise between them.

one another—showing a slight tendency to combine and 10
also an inclination to behave as 'receptive matter' and
'form' respectively. The behaviour of these metals is
a case in point. For the tin almost vanishes, behaving
as if it were an immaterial property of the bronze: having
been combined, it disappears, leaving no trace except the
colour it has imparted to the bronze. The same phenomenon
occurs in other instances too.

It is clear, then, from the foregoing account, that 'com- 15
bination' occurs, what it is, to what it is due, and what
kind of thing is 'combinable'. The phenomenon depends
upon the fact that some things are such as to be (*a*) reciprocally susceptible and (*b*) readily adaptable in shape,
i. e. easily divisible. For such things can be 'combined'
without its being necessary *either* that they should have
been destroyed *or* that they should survive absolutely unaltered: and their 'combination' need not be a 'composition',
nor merely 'relative to perception'. On the contrary: any- 20
thing is 'combinable' which, being readily adaptable in
shape, is such as to suffer action and to act; and it is
'combinable with' another thing similarly characterized
(for the 'combinable' is relative to the 'combinable'); and
'combination' is unification of the 'combinables', resulting
from their 'alteration'

BOOK II

I   We have explained under what conditions 'combination',
'contact', and 'action-passion' are attributable to the things
which undergo natural change. Further, we have discussed
'unqualified' coming-to-be and passing-away, and explained
under what conditions they are predicable, of what subject,
and owing to what cause. Similarly, we have also discussed 30
'alteration', and explained what 'altering' is and how it

differs from coming-to-be and passing-away. But we have still to investigate the so-called 'elements' of bodies

For the complex substances whose formation and maintenance are due to natural processes all presuppose the perceptible bodies as the condition of their coming-to-be and passing-away: but philosophers disagree in regard to the matter which underlies these perceptible bodies. Some maintain it is single, supposing it to be, e. g., Air or Fire, 35 or an 'intermediate' between these two (but still a body 329ᵃ with a separate existence). Others, on the contrary, postulate two or more materials—ascribing to their 'association' and 'dissociation', or to their 'alteration', the coming-to-be and passing-away of things. (Some, for instance, postulate Fire and Earth: some add Air, making three: and some, like Empedokles, reckon Water as well, thus postulating four.)

5 Now we may agree that the primary materials, whose change (whether it be 'association and dissociation' or a process of another kind) results in coming-to-be and passing-away, are rightly described as 'originative sources, i. e. elements'. But (i) those thinkers are in error who postulate, beside the bodies we have mentioned, a single 10 matter—and that a corporeal and separable matter. For this 'body' of theirs cannot possibly exist without a 'perceptible contrariety': this 'Boundless', which some thinkers identify with the 'original real', must be either light or heavy, either cold or hot.[1] And (ii) what Plato has written in the *Timaeus* is not based on any precisely-articulated conception. For he has not stated clearly 15 whether his 'Omnirecipient'[2] exists in separation from the 'elements'; nor does he make any use of it. He says, indeed, that it is a *substratum* prior to the so-called 'elements'—underlying them, as gold underlies the things that are fashioned of gold. (And yet this comparison, if thus expressed, is itself open to criticism. Things 20 which come-to-be and pass-away cannot be called by the name of the material out of which they have come-to-be: it is only the results of 'alteration' which retain the name of the *substratum* whose 'alterations' they

---

[1] Cf. below, 332ᵃ 20-6.   [2] Cf. *Timaeus* 51 a.

are. However, he actually says[1] that 'far the truest account is to affirm that each of them[2] is "gold"'.) Nevertheless he carries his analysis of the 'elements'—solids though they are—back to 'planes',[3] and it is impossible for 'the Nurse'[4] (i.e. the primary matter) to be identical with 'the planes'.

Our own doctrine is that although there is a matter of the perceptible bodies (a matter out of which the so-called 25 'elements' come-to-be), it has no separate existence, but is always bound up with a contrariety. A more precise account of these presuppositions has been given in another work[5]: we must, however, give a detailed explanation of the primary bodies as well, since they too are similarly derived from the matter.[6] We must reckon as an 'origina- 30 tive source' and as 'primary' the matter which underlies, though it is inseparable from, the contrary qualities: for 'the hot' is not matter for 'the cold' nor 'the cold' for 'the hot', but the *substratum* is matter for them both. We therefore have to recognize three 'originative sources': *firstly* that which is potentially perceptible body, *secondly* the contrarieties (I mean, e.g., heat and cold), and *thirdly* Fire, 35 Water, and the like. *Only* 'thirdly', however: for these bodies change into one another (they are not immutable 329 as Empedokles and other thinkers assert, since 'alteration' would then have been impossible), whereas the contrarieties do not change.

Nevertheless, even so[7] the question remains: What sorts of contrarieties, and how many of them, are to be accounted 'originative sources' of body? For all the other thinkers assume and use them without explaining why they are 5 *these* or why they are just *so many*.

2   Since, then, we are looking for 'originative sources' of

---

[1] Cf. *Timaeus* 49 d–50 c.
[2] i.e. each of the things that are 'fashioned of gold'.
[3] Cf. *Timaeus* 53 c ff.   [4] Cf. *Timaeus*, e.g. 49 a, 52 d.
[5] Cf. *Physics* A. 6–9, where πρώτη ὕλη and 'the contrariety' (εἶδος and στέρησις) are accurately defined and distinguished as presuppositions of γένεσις.
[6] The account in the *Physics* applied generally to the γένεσις of any and every perceptible body. Aristotle now proposes to apply it to the γένεσις of the *primary* perceptible bodies in particular.
[7] i.e. notwithstanding the sketch Aristotle has just given.

perceptible body; and since 'perceptible' is equivalent[1]
to 'tangible', and 'tangible' is that of which the perception
is touch; it is clear that not all the contrarieties constitute
10 'forms' and 'originative sources' of body, but only those which
correspond to touch. For it is in accordance with a contrariety—a contrariety, moreover, of *tangible* qualities—that
the primary bodies are differentiated. That is why neither
whiteness (and blackness), nor sweetness (and bitterness),
nor (similarly) any quality belonging to the other[2] perceptible contrarieties either, constitutes an 'element'. And
yet vision is prior to touch, so that its object also is prior
15 to the object of touch. The object of vision, however, is
a quality of tangible body not *qua* tangible, but *qua* something else—*qua* something which may well be naturally
prior to the object of touch.

Accordingly, we must segregate the tangible differences
and contrarieties, and distinguish which amongst them are
primary. Contrarieties correlative to touch are the following:
20 hot-cold, dry-moist, heavy-light, hard-soft, viscous-brittle,
rough-smooth, coarse-fine. Of these (i) heavy and light
are neither active nor susceptible. Things are not called
'heavy' and 'light' because they act upon, or suffer action
from, other things. But the 'elements' must be reciprocally
active and susceptible, since they 'combine' and are transformed into one another. On the other hand (ii) hot and
25 cold, and dry and moist, are terms, of which the first pair
implies *power to act* and the second pair *susceptibility*.
'Hot' is that which 'associates' things of the same kind
(for 'dissociating', which people attribute to Fire as its
function, *is* 'associating' things of the same class, since
its effect is to eliminate what is foreign), while 'cold' is
30 that which brings together, i.e. 'associates', homogeneous
and heterogeneous things alike. And 'moist' is that which,
being readily adaptable in shape, is not determinable by
any limit of its own: while 'dry' is that which is readily
determinable by its own limit, but not readily adaptable in
shape.

---

[1] *sc.* in this connexion: the tangible qualities are the only qualities
which characterize *all* perceptible bodies.
[2] *sc.* the other *non-tangible* perceptible contrarieties.

From moist and dry are derived (iii) the fine and coarse, viscous and brittle, hard and soft, and the remaining tangible differences. For (a) since the moist has no determinate 35 shape, but is readily adaptable and follows the outline of that which is in contact with it, it is characteristic of it 330^a to be 'such as to fill up'. Now 'the fine' is 'such as to fill up'. For 'the fine' consists of subtle particles; but that which consists of small particles is 'such as to fill up', inasmuch as it is in contact[1] whole with whole—and 'the fine' exhibits this character[2] in a superlative degree. Hence it is evident that the fine derives from the moist, while the coarse derives from the dry. Again (b) 'the viscous' derives 5 from the moist: for 'the viscous' (e. g. oil) is a 'moist' modified in a certain way. 'The brittle', on the other hand, derives from the dry: for 'brittle' is that which is *completely* dry—so completely, that its solidification has actually been due to failure of moisture. Further (c) 'the soft' derives from the moist. For 'soft' is that which yields to pressure by retiring into itself, though it does not yield by total displacement as the moist does—which explains why the moist 10 is not 'soft', although 'the soft' derives from the moist. 'The hard', on the other hand, derives from the dry: for 'hard' is that which is solidified, and the solidified is dry.

The terms 'dry' and 'moist' have more senses than one. For 'the damp', as well as the moist, is opposed to the dry: and again 'the solidified', as well as the dry, is opposed to the moist. But all these qualities derive from the dry and 15 moist we mentioned first.[3] For (i) the dry is opposed to the damp: i. e. 'damp' is that which has foreign moisture on its surface ('sodden' being that which is penetrated to its core[4]), while 'dry'[5] is that which has lost foreign moisture. Hence it is evident that the damp will derive from the moist, and 'the dry' which is opposed to it will derive from the primary dry. Again (ii) the 'moist' and the 20 solidified derive in the same way from the primary pair.

---

[1] 'in contact' with the vessel which contains it.
[2] The fine, owing to the subtlety (= the smallness) of its particles, leaves no corner of its containing receptacle unfilled.
[3] Cf. above, 329^b 30-2.
[4] *sc.* by foreign moisture: cf. below, ^a 22.
[5] i. e. the 'dry' which is contrasted with the damp: the 'dried'

For 'moist'[1] is that which contains moisture *of its own*
deep within it ('sodden' being that which is deeply
penetrated by *foreign* moisture), whereas 'solidified' is that
which has lost this inner moisture. Hence these too
derive from the primary pair, the ' solidified' from the dry
and the 'liquefiable' from the moist.

25 It is clear, then, that all the other differences reduce to
the first four, but that these admit of no further reduction.
For the hot is not *essentially* moist or dry, nor the moist
essentially hot or cold: nor are the cold and the dry deriva-
tive forms, either of one another or of the hot and the
moist. Hence these must be four.

30 The elementary qualities are four, and any four terms 3
can be combined in six couples. Contraries, however, refuse
to be coupled : for it is impossible for the same thing to
be hot and cold, or moist and dry. Hence it is evident that
the 'couplings' of the elementary qualities will be four :
330^b hot with dry and moist with hot, and again cold with dry
and cold with moist. And these four couples have attached
themselves to the *apparently* 'simple' bodies (Fire, Air,
Water, and Earth) in a manner consonant with theory.
For Fire is hot and dry, whereas Air is hot and moist
5 (Air being a sort of aqueous vapour); and Water is
cold and moist, while Earth is cold and dry. Thus the
differences are reasonably distributed among the primary
bodies, and the number of the latter is consonant with
theory. For all who make the simple bodies ' elements '
postulate either one, or two, or three, or four. Now (i) those
10 who assert there is *one* only, and then generate everything
else by condensation and rarefaction, are in effect making
their ' originative sources ' two, viz. the rare and the dense,
or rather the hot and the cold : for it is these which are the
moulding forces, while the 'one'[2] underlies them as a
'matter'. But (ii) those who postulate *two* from the
start—as Parmenides postulated Fire and Earth—make
15 the intermediates (e. g. Air and Water) blends of these.

---

[1] i.e. the 'moist' which is contrasted with the solidified : the
'liquefiable'.
[2] i.e. the single element of which these monistic theories postulate.

The same course is followed (iii) by those who advocate
three.[1] (We may compare what Plato does in 'The
Divisions': for he makes 'the middle' a blend.[2]) Indeed,
there is practically no difference between those who postulate *two* and those who postulate *three*, except that the former
split the middle 'element' into two, while the latter treat it
as only one. But (iv) some advocate *four* from the start, 20
e. g. Empedokles: yet he too draws them together so as to
reduce them to *the two*, for he opposes all the others to
Fire.

In fact, however, fire and air, and each of the bodies we
have mentioned, are not simple, but blended. The 'simple'
bodies are indeed similar in nature to them, but not
identical with them. Thus the 'simple' body corresponding
to fire is 'such-as-fire', not fire: that which corresponds to
air is 'such-as-air': and so on with the rest of them. But 25
fire is an excess of heat, just as ice is an excess of cold.
For freezing and boiling are excesses of heat and cold
respectively. Assuming, therefore, that ice is a freezing of
moist and cold, fire analogously will be a boiling of dry and
hot: a fact, by the way, which explains why nothing
comes-to-be either out of ice or out of fire.   30

The 'simple' bodies, since they are four, fall into two
pairs which belong to the two regions, each to each: for
Fire and Air are forms of the body moving towards the
'limit', while Earth and Water are forms of the body which
moves towards the 'centre'.[3] Fire and Earth, moreover,
are extremes and purest: Water and Air, on the contrary, 331[a]
are intermediates and more like blends. And, further, the
members of either pair are contrary to those of the other,
Water being contrary to Fire and Earth to Air; for the
qualities constituting Water and Earth are contrary to
those that constitute Fire and Air. Nevertheless, since
they are four, each of them is characterized *par excellence*

[1] Cf. above, 329[a] 2. Philoponos attributes this trialistic theory to
Ion of Chios.
[2] I take 'The Divisions' to mean that section of the *Timaeus*
(35 a ff.) in which Plato describes the making of the Soul. Aristotle's
point is merely that Plato makes 'the middle' of his three kinds of
'substance' a 'blend' of the other two.
[3] Cf. *de Caelo*, e. g. 269[b] 20-9, 308[a] 14-33, 311[a] 15 ff.

by a single quality: Earth by dry rather than by cold,
5 Water by cold rather than by moist, Air by ~moist rather
than by hot, and Fire by hot rather than by dry.

It has been established before [1] that the coming-to-be of **4**
the 'simple' bodies is reciprocal. At the same time, it is
manifest, even on the evidence of perception, that they *do*
come-to-be: for otherwise there would not have been 'altera-
10 tion', since 'alteration' is change in respect to the qualities
of the objects of touch. Consequently, we must explain
(i) what is the manner of their reciprocal transformation,
and (ii) whether every one of them can come-to-be out of
every one—or whether some can do so, but not others.
Now it is evident that all of them are by nature such as
to change into one another: for coming-to-be is a change
15 into contraries and out of contraries, and the 'elements' all
involve a contrariety in their mutual relations because their
distinctive qualities are contrary. For in some of them
both qualities are contrary—e. g. in Fire and Water, the first
of these being dry and hot, and the second moist and cold:
while in others *one* of the qualities (though only one) is
contrary—e. g. in Air and Water, the first being moist and
20 hot, and the second moist and cold. It is evident, therefore,
if we consider them in general, that every one is by nature
such as to come-to-be out of every one: and when we come
to consider them severally, it is not difficult to see the
manner in which their transformation is effected. For,
though all will result from all, both the speed and the
facility of their conversion will differ in degree.
25 Thus (i) the process of conversion will be quick between
those which have interchangeable 'complementary factors',
but slow between those which have none. The reason is
that it is easier for a single thing to change than for many.
Air, e.g., will result from Fire if a single quality changes:
for Fire, as we saw, is hot and dry while Air is hot and
moist, so that there will be Air if the dry be overcome by
30 the moist. Again, Water will result from Air if the hot be
overcome by the cold: for Air, as we saw, is hot and moist

---

[1] The reference is probably neither to 314^b 15–26 nor to 329^a 35, but
to *de Caelo* 304^b 23 ff.

while Water is cold and moist, so that, if the hot changes, there will be Water. So too, in the same manner, Earth will result from Water and Fire from, Earth, since the two 'elements' in both these couples have interchangeable 'complementary factors'. For Water is moist and cold while Earth is cold and dry—so that, if the moist be over- 35 come, there will be Earth: and again, since Fire is dry and hot while Earth is cold and dry, Fire will result from Earth 331[b] if the cold pass-away.

It is evident, therefore, that the coming-to-be of the 'simple' bodies will be cyclical; and that this cyclical method of transformation is the easiest, because the *consecutive* 'elements' contain interchangeable 'complementary factors'.[1] On the other hand (ii) the transformation of Fire into Water and of Air into Earth, and again of Water 5 and Earth into Fire and Air respectively, though possible, is more difficult because it involves the change of more qualities. For if Fire is to result from Water, both the cold and the moist must pass-away: and again, both the cold and the dry must pass-away if Air is to result from Earth. So, too, if Water and Earth are to result from 10 Fire and Air respectively—both qualities must change.

This second method of coming-to-be, then, takes a longer time. But (iii) if one quality in each of two 'elements' pass-away, the transformation, though easier, is not reciprocal. Still, from Fire *plus* Water there will result Earth and[2] Air, and from Air *plus* Earth Fire and[3] Water. For there will be Air, when the cold of the Water and the 15 dry of the Fire have passed-away (since the hot of the latter and the moist of the former are left): whereas, when the hot of the Fire and the moist of the Water have passed-away, there will be Earth, owing to the survival of the dry of the Fire and the cold of the Water. So, too, in the same way, Fire and Water will result from Air *plus* Earth. For there will be Water, when the hot of the Air and the dry 20

---

[1] Aristotle has shown that, by the conversion of a single quality in each case, Fire is transformed into Air, Air into Water, Water into Earth, and Earth into Fire. This is a *cycle* of transformations. Moreover, the 'elements' have been taken in their natural consecutive series, according to their order in the Cosmos.

[2] *sc.* alternatively.   [3] *sc.* alternatively.

of the Earth have passed-away (since the moist of the
former and the cold of the latter are left): whereas, when
the moist of the Air and the cold of the Earth have passed-
away, there will be Fire, owing to the survival of the hot of
the Air and the dry of the Earth—qualities essentially
constitutive of Fire. Moreover, this mode of Fire's coming-
25 to-be is confirmed by perception. For flame is *par excellence* Fire: but flame is burning smoke, and smoke consists of Air and Earth.

No transformation, however, into any of the 'simple'
bodies can result from the passing-away of one elementary
quality in each of two 'elements' when they are taken in
their consecutive order,[1] because either *identical* or *contrary*
30 qualities are left in the pair: but no 'simple' body can be
formed either out of identical, or out of contrary, qualities.
Thus no 'simple' body would result, if the dry of Fire and
the moist of Air were to pass-away: for the hot is left in
both. On the other hand, if the hot pass-away out of both,
the contraries—dry and moist—are left. A similar result
will occur in all the others too: for all the *consecutive*
'elements' contain one identical, and one contrary, quality.[2]
35 Hence, too, it clearly follows that, when one of the *consecutive* 'elements' is transformed into one, the coming-to-
be is effected by the passing-away of a single quality:
whereas, when two of them are transformed into a third,
more than one quality must have passed-away.[3]

332^a   We have stated that all the 'elements' come-to-be out
of any one of them; and we have explained the manner in
which their mutual conversion takes place. Let us never- 5
theless supplement our theory by the following speculations
concerning them.

---

[1] Cf. above, note on 331^b 4.

[2] If the 'elements' are taken in their natural order, Water (e. g.) is
'consecutive' to Earth, and Air to Water. Water is moist and cold.
It shares its 'cold' with Earth and its 'moist' with Air: its 'moist' is
contrary to Earth's 'dry', and its 'cold' is contrary to Air's 'hot'

[3] If, e. g., Fire *plus* Air are to be transformed into Water or into
Earth, it is not enough that a single quality should be eliminated from
each of the generating pair: for this would leave either two 'hots' or
a 'dry' and a 'moist' (cf. 331^b 26–33). Either Fire's 'dry' or Air's
'moist' must be eliminated: and, *in addition*, the 'hot' of one must
be eliminated and the 'hot' of the other be converted into 'cold'.

If Water, Air, and the like are a 'matter' of which the 5
natural bodies consist, as some thinkers in fact believe,
these 'elements' must be either one, or two, or more. Now
they cannot all of them be *one*—they cannot, e. g., all be
Air or Water or Fire or Earth—because 'Change is into
contraries'.[1] For if they all were Air, then (assuming Air
to persist) there will be 'alteration' instead of coming-to-be.
Besides, nobody supposes a single 'element' to persist, as
the basis of all, in such a way that it is Water as well as Air 10
(or any other 'element') *at the same time*. So there will be
a certain contrariety, i. e. a differentiating quality:[2] and
the other member of this contrariety, e. g. heat, will belong
to some other 'element', e. g. to Fire. But Fire will
certainly not be 'hot Air'. For a change of that kind[3]
(*a*) is 'alteration', and (*b*) is not what is observed. Moreover (*c*) if Air is again to result out of the Fire, it will do
so by the conversion of the hot into its contrary: this 15
contrary, therefore, will belong to Air, and Air will be
a cold something: hence it is impossible for Fire to be 'hot
Air', since in that case the same thing will be simultaneously
hot and cold. Both Fire and Air, therefore, will be something else which is the same; i.e. there will be some
'matter', other than either, common to both.

The same argument applies to all the 'elements', proving
that there is no single one of them out of which they all 20
originate. But neither is there, beside these four, some
other body from which they originate—a something intermediate, e. g., between Air and Water (coarser than Air,
but finer than Water), or between Air and Fire (coarser
than Fire, but finer than Air). For the supposed 'intermediate' will be Air and Fire when a pair of contrasted
qualities is added to it: but, since one of every two contrary qualities is a 'privation', the 'intermediate' never
can exist—as some thinkers assert the 'Boundless' or the 25
'Environing' exists—in isolation.[4] It is, therefore, equally

---

[1] For this 'law of nature', cf. *Physics* 224^a 21—226^b 17.
[2] If Air is to 'alter' into (e. g.) Fire, we must assume a pair of
contrasted differentiating qualities, and assign one to Fire and the
other to Air.
[3] i. e. Air becoming Fire by being heated.
[4] i. e. bare of all qualities. The 'Boundless' was criticized above,

and indifferently any one of the 'elements', or else it is nothing.

Since, then, there is nothing—at least, nothing *perceptible* —prior to these,[1] they must be all.[2] That being so, either they must always persist and not be transformable into one another: or they must undergo transformation—either all
30 of them, or some only (as Plato wrote in the *Timaeus*).[3] Now it has been proved before[4] that they must undergo reciprocal transformation. It has also been proved[5] that the speed with which they come-to-be, one out of another, is not uniform—since the process of reciprocal transformation is relatively *quick* between the 'elements' with a 'complementary factor', but relatively *slow* between those which possess no such factor. Assuming, then, that the contrariety, in respect to which they are transformed, is
35 *one*, the 'elements' will inevitably be two: for it is 'matter' that is the 'mean' between the two contraries, and matter
332ᵇ is imperceptible and inseparable from them.[6] Since, however, the 'elements' are seen to be more than two, the contrarieties must at the least be two. But the contrarieties being two, the 'elements' must be four (as they evidently are) and cannot be three: for the 'couplings' are four, since, though six are possible,[7] the two in which the
5 qualities are contrary to one another cannot occur.

These subjects have been discussed before[8]: but the following arguments will make it clear that, since the 'elements' are transformed into one another, it is impossible for any one of them—whether it be at the end or in the middle[9]—to be an 'originative source' of the rest. There

329ᵃ8-13: there too Aristotle attributes the conception to 'some people', without mentioning Anaximander by name.

[1] *sc.* Earth, Air, Fire, and Water.
[2] i. e. all the 'simple' bodies there are. [3] Cf. *Timaeus* 54 b-d.
[4] Cf. above, 331ᵃ12-20. [5] Cf. above, 331ᵃ22 ff.
[6] One contrariety produces two 'elements' only: for πρώτη ὕλη has no separate subsistence and does not constitute a *third* 'element' alongside of its two contrary informations. Perhaps, however, we ought to translate: 'for the supposed "intermediate" is nothing but "matter", and that is imperceptible and incapable of separate existence.'
[7] i. e. *mathematically* 'possible'.
[8] Cf. above, II. 2 and 3.
[9] i. e. at either end, or in the middle, of the 'natural series' of the 'elements'.

can be no such 'originative element' at the ends: for all of
them would then be Fire or Earth, and this theory amounts
to the assertion that all things[1] are made of Fire or Earth.
Nor can a 'middle-element' be such an 'originative source' 10
—as some thinkers suppose that Air is transformed both
into Fire and into Water, and Water both into Air and into
Earth, while the 'end-elements' are not further transformed
into one another. For the process must come to a stop,
and cannot continue *ad infinitum* in a straight line in either
direction, since otherwise an infinite number of contrarieties
would attach to the single 'element'. Let E stand for 15
Earth, W for Water, A for Air, and F for Fire. Then
(i) since A is transformed into F and W, there will be a
contrariety belonging to A F. Let these contraries be whiteness and blackness. Again (ii) since A is transformed into
W, there will be another contrariety[2]: for W is not the
same as F. Let this second contrariety be dryness and
moistness, D being dryness and M moistness. Now if, 20
when A is transformed into W, the 'white' persists, Water
will be moist and white: but if it does not persist, Water
will be black since change is into contraries. Water, therefore, must be either white or black. Let it then be the
first. On similar grounds, therefore, D (dryness) will also
belong to F. Consequently F (Fire) as well as Air will be
able to be transformed into Water: for it has qualities 25
contrary to those of Water, since Fire was *first* taken to be
black and *then* to be dry, while Water was moist and *then*
showed itself white. Thus it is evident that all the 'elements'
will be able to be transformed out of one another; and that,
in the instances we have taken, E (Earth) also will contain
the remaining two 'complementary factors', viz. the black 30
and the moist (for these have not yet been coupled).

We have dealt with this last topic before the thesis we
set out to prove.[3] That thesis—viz. that the process cannot
continue *ad infinitum*—will be clear from the following
considerations. If Fire (which is represented by F) is not

---

[1] Or perhaps 'that all the "elements" result from Fire or Earth by
"alteration"'—a view which Aristotle has already refuted (cf. 332^a
6-20).
  [2] *sc.* belonging to A W.   [3] Cf. above, 332^b 12-13.

to revert, but is to be transformed in turn into some other
'element' (e. g. into Q), a new contrariety, other than those
35 mentioned, will belong to Fire and Q: for it has been
333ª assumed that Q is not the same as any of the four, E W
A and F. Let K, then, belong to F and Y to Q. Then K
will belong to all four, E W A and F: for they are transformed into one another. This last point, however, we may
admit, has not yet been proved: but at any rate it is clear
that if Q is to be transformed in turn into yet another
5 'element', yet another contrariety will belong not only to
Q but also to F (Fire). And, similarly, every addition of
a new 'element' will carry with it the attachment of a new
contrariety to the preceding 'elements'. Consequently, if
the 'elements' are infinitely many, there will also belong *to
the single 'element'* an infinite number of contrarieties. But
if that be so, it will be impossible to define any 'element'·
impossible also for any to come-to-be. For if one is to
result from another, it will have to pass through such a vast
10 number of contrarieties—and indeed even more than any
determinate number. Consequently (i) into some 'elements' transformation will never be effected—viz. if the
intermediates are infinite in number, as they must be if the
'elements' are infinitely many: further (ii) there will not even
be a transformation of Air into Fire, if the contrarieties are
infinitely many: moreover (iii) all the 'elements' become one.
For all the contrarieties of the 'elements' above F must belong
15 to those below F, and *vice versa*: hence they will all be one.

As for those who agree with Empedokles that the **6**
'elements' of body are more than one, so that they are not
transformed into one another[1]—one may well wonder in
what sense it is open to them to maintain that the 'elements' are comparable. Yet Empedokles says 'For these
20 are all not only equal . . .'[2]
   If (i) it is meant that they are comparable in their amount,
all the 'comparables' must possess an identical something
whereby they are measured. If, e. g., one pint of Water

---

[1] i. e. so that the 'elements' are genuinely or irreducibly 'many'.
The theory of Empedokles is directly opposed to the theory Aristotle
has been maintaining.
[2] Empedokles, fr. 17, l. 27 (Diels, p. 179).

yields ten of Air, both are measured by the same unit; and therefore both were from the first an identical something. On the other hand, suppose (ii) they are not 'comparable in their amount' in the sense that so-much of the one yields so-much of the other, but comparable in 'power of action'[1] (a pint of Water, e.g., having a power of cooling 25 equal to that of ten pints of Air); even so, they *are* 'comparable in their amount', though not *qua* 'amount' but *qua* 'so-much power'.[2] There is also (iii) a third possibility. Instead of comparing their powers by the measure of their amount, they might be compared as terms in a 'correspondence': e.g., 'as *x* is hot, so correspondingly *y* is white'. But 'correspondence', though it means equality in the 30 *quantum*, means similarity[3] in a *quale*. Thus it is manifestly absurd that the 'simple' bodies, though they are not transformable, are comparable not merely as 'corresponding', but by a measure of their powers; i.e. that so-much Fire is comparable with many-times-that-amount of Air, as being 'equally' or 'similarly' hot. For the same thing, if it be greater in amount, will, since it belongs to the same kind,[4] have its *ratio* correspondingly increased.

A further objection to the theory of Empedokles is that 35 it makes even *growth* impossible, unless it be increase by addition. For his Fire increases by Fire: 'And Earth **333ᵇ** increases its own frame and Ether increases Ether.'[5] These, however, are cases of addition: but it is not by addition that growing things are believed to increase. And it is far more difficult for him to account for the *coming-to-be* which occurs in nature. For the things which come-to- 5 be by natural process all exhibit, in their coming-to-be, a uniformity either absolute or highly regular: while any

---

[1] Cf. above, 327ᵇ 31, 328ᵃ 28-31; below, 334ᵇ 8-30.

[2] i.e. we are comparing the *amounts of cooling energy* possessed by one pint of Water and ten pints of Air respectively.

[3] i.e. *only* 'similarity'. Empedokles might have said the 'elements' were all *analogous* or *similar* without inconsistency: but he asserts that they are *equal*, i.e. quantitatively comparable (and therefore, ultimately, transformable).

[4] *sc.* as the thing of less amount with which it is being compared.

[5] Cf. Empedokles, fr. 37 (Diels, p. 186). By αἰθήρ Empedokles means Air (not Fire) as Aristotle recognizes elsewhere: perhaps, therefore, the words 'Fire increases by Fire' are a paraphrase of a verse now lost.

exceptions—any results which are in accordance neither with the invariable nor with the general rule—are products of chance and luck. Then what is the cause determining that man comes-to-be from man, that wheat (instead of an olive) comes-to-be from wheat, either invariably or gener-ally? Are we to say 'Bone comes-to-be if the "elements" be put together in such-and-such a manner'? For, accord-
10 ing to his own statements, nothing comes-to-be from their 'fortuitous consilience', but only from their 'consilience' in a certain proportion. What, then, is the cause of this proportional consilience? Presumably not Fire or Earth. But neither is it Love and Strife: for the former is a cause of 'association' only, and the latter only of 'dissociation'. No: the cause in question is the essential nature of each thing—not merely (to quote his words) 'a mingling and
15 a divorce of what has been mingled'[1] And *chance*, not *proportion*, 'is the name given to these occurrences':[2] for things can be 'mingled' fortuitously.

The cause, therefore, of the coming-to-be of the things which owe their existence to nature is that they are ın such-and-such a determinate condition:[3] and it is *this* which con stitutes the 'nature' of each thing—a 'nature' about which he says nothing. What he says, therefore, is no explanation of 'nature'.[4] Moreover, it is *this* which is both 'the excel-lence' of each thing and its 'good': whereas he assigns the
20 whole credit to the 'mingling'.[5] (And yet *the 'elements'* at all events are 'dissociated' not by Strife, but by Love: since the 'elements' are by nature prior to the Deity, and they too are Deities.)[6]

Again, his account of motion is vague. For it is not an adequate explanation to say that 'Love and Strife set things

---

[1] Cf. Empedokles, fr. 8 (Diels, p. 175). The same fragment is quoted above, 314ᵇ 7–8.

[2] Aristotle appears to be parodying the last line of Empedokles, fr. 8.

[3] i.e. that they are compounds produced by the consilience of their constituents in a certain proportion.

[4] i.e. Empedokles' poem, in spite of its title (Περὶ φύσεως), tells us nothing about nature.

[5] Cf. *Metaph.* 984ᵇ 32—985ᵃ 10.

[6] This sentence is a belated criticism of the functions Empedokles attributed to Love and Strife: perhaps we ought to read it after αἴτιον (above, ᵇ 13). The 'Deity' is the 'Sphere': cf. Empedokles, fr. 27, 28, 29 (Diels, pp. 183–184).

moving', unless the very nature of Love is a movement of *this* kind and the very nature of Strife a movement of *that* kind. He ought, then, either to have defined or to have [25] postulated these characteristic movements, or to have demonstrated them—whether strictly or laxly or in some other fashion. Moreover, since (*a*) the 'simple' bodies *appear* to move 'naturally' as well as by compulsion, i. e. in a manner contrary to nature (fire, e. g., appears to move upwards without compulsion, though it appears to move by compulsion downwards); and since (*b*) what is 'natural' is contrary to that which is due to compulsion, and movement by compulsion actually occurs;[1] it follows that 'natural movement' can also occur in fact. Is *this*, then, the move- [30] ment that Love sets going? No: for, on the contrary, the 'natural movement' moves Earth downwards and resembles 'dissociation', and Strife rather than Love is its cause—so that in general, too. Love rather than Strife would seem to be contrary to nature. And unless Love or Strife is actually setting them in motion, the 'simple' bodies themselves have absolutely no movement or rest. But this is [35] paradoxical: and what is more, they do in fact obviously move.[2] For though Strife 'dissociated',[3] it was not by 334[a] Strife that the 'Ether' was borne upwards. On the contrary, sometimes he attributes its movement to something like *chance* ('For *thus*, as it ran, it *happened* to meet them then, though often otherwise'[4]), while at other times he says it is the *nature* of Fire to be borne upwards, but 'the Ether' (to quote his words) 'sank down upon the Earth [5] with long roots'.[5] With such statements, too, he combines the assertion that the Order of the World is the same *now*, in the reign of Strife, as it was *formerly* in the reign of Love. What, then, is the 'first mover' of the 'elements'? What causes their motion? Presumably not Love and Strife : on the contrary, these are causes of a *particular* motion, if at least we assume that 'first mover' to be an 'originative source'.[6]

---

[1] i. e. according to Empedokles himself.
[2] i. e. according to Empedokles' own statements.
[3] i. e. though Strife initiated the disintegration of the Sphere.
[4] Cf. Empedokles, fr. 53 (Diels, p. 189).
[5] Cf. fr. 54, *ibid.*   [6] *sc.* a first cause of motion in general.

10 An additional paradox is that the soul should consist of the 'elements', or that it should be one of them. How are the soul's 'alterations' to take place? How, e. g., is the change from being musical to being unmusical, or how is memory or forgetting, to occur? For clearly, if the soul be Fire, only such modifications will happen to it as characterize Fire *qua* Fire : while if it be compounded out of the 'elements', only the corporeal modifications will occur in it. But the changes we have mentioned are none 15 of them corporeal.

The discussion of these difficulties, however, is a task **7** appropriate to a different investigation:[1] let us return to the 'elements' of which bodies are composed. The theories that 'there is something common to all the "elements"', and that 'they are reciprocally transformed', are so related that those who accept *either* are bound to accept *the other* as well. Those, on the other hand, who do not make their coming-to-be reciprocal—who refuse to suppose that any one of the 'elements' comes-to-be out of any other *taken* 20 *singly*, except in the sense in which bricks come-to-be out of a wall—are faced with a paradox. How, on their theory, are flesh and bones or any of the other compounds to result from the 'elements' *taken together*?

Indeed, the point we have raised constitutes a problem even for those who generate the 'elements' out of one another. In what manner does anything other than, and beside, the 'elements' come-to-be out of them? Let me illustrate my meaning. Water can come-to-be out of Fire and Fire out of Water ; for their *substratum* is something 25 common to them both. But flesh too, presumably, and marrow come-to-be out of them. How, then, do such things come-to-be? For (*a*) how is the manner of their coming-to-be to be conceived by those who maintain a theory like that of Empedokles? They must conceive it as *com-position*—just as a wall comes-to-be out of bricks and stones : and the 'Mixture', of which they speak, will be composed of the 'elements', these being preserved in it

---

[1] Cf. *de Anima*, A. 4 and 5, especially 408ª 18–23 and 409ᵇ 23 ff., where Aristotle exposes the failure of Empedokles to account for the soul.

unaltered but with their small particles juxtaposed each to 30
each. That will be the manner, presumably, in which flesh
and every other compound results from the 'elements'
Consequently, it follows that Fire and Water do not come-
to-be 'out of any and every part of flesh'. For instance,
although a sphere might come-to-be out of *this* part of
a lump of wax and a pyramid out of *some other* part, it was
nevertheless possible for either figure to have come-to-be
out of either part indifferently : *that* is the manner of 35
coming-to-be when 'both Fire and Water come-to-be out
of any and every part of flesh'. Those, however, who maintain the theory in question, are not at liberty to conceive **334**^{b}
that 'both come-to-be out of flesh' in that manner, but only
as a stone and a brick 'both come-to-be out of a wall'—
viz. each out of a different place or part. Similarly (*b*)
even for those who postulate a single matter of their
'elements' there is a certain difficulty in explaining how
anything is to result from two of them taken together—e.g.
from 'cold' and 'hot', or from Fire and Earth. For if flesh 5
consists of both and is neither of them, nor again is a 'composition' of them in which they are preserved unaltered,
what alternative is left except to identify the resultant of
the two 'elements ' with their matter ? For the passing-
away of either 'element' produces *either* the other *or* the
matter.

Perhaps we may suggest the following solution. (i) There
are differences of degree in hot and cold. Although, therefore, when either is fully real without qualification, the other
will exist potentially ; yet, when neither exists in the full 10
completeness of its being, but both by combining destroy
one another's excesses so that there exist instead a hot
which (for a 'hot') is cold and a cold which (for a 'cold') is
hot ; then what results from these two contraries will be
neither their matter, nor either of them existing in its full
reality without qualification. There will result instead an
'intermediate': and this 'intermediate', according as it is
potentially more hot than cold or *vice versa*, will possess 15
a power-of-heating that is double or triple its power-of-
cooling, or otherwise related thereto in some similar ratio.

Thus all the other bodies will result from the contraries, or rather from the 'elements', in so far as these have been 'combined': while the 'elements' will result from the contraries, in so far as these 'exist potentially' in a special sense—not as matter 'exists potentially', but in the sense explained above. And when a thing comes-to-be in *this*
20 manner, the process is 'combination'; whereas what comes-to-be in the other manner[1] is matter. Moreover (ii) contraries also 'suffer action', in accordance with the disjunctively-articulated definition established in the early part of this work.[2] For the actually-hot is potentially-cold and the actually-cold potentially-hot; so that hot and cold, unless they are equally balanced, are transformed into one another (and all the other contraries behave in a similar
25 way). It is thus, then, that *in the first place* the 'elements' are transformed; and that ⟨*in the second place*⟩ [3] out of the 'elements' there come-to-be flesh and bones and the like—the hot becoming cold and the cold becoming hot when they[4] have been brought to the 'mean'. For at the 'mean' is neither hot nor cold. The 'mean', however, is of considerable extent and not indivisible.[5] Similarly, it is *qua* reduced to a 'mean' condition that the dry and the moist, as well as the contraries we have used as examples,
30 produce flesh and bone and the remaining compounds.

All the compound bodies—all of which exist in the 8 region belonging to the central body [6]—are composed of all the 'simple' bodies. For they all contain Earth because every 'simple' body is to be found specially and most abundantly in its own place. And they all contain Water
35 because (*a*) the compound must possess a definite outline

---

[1] *sc.* in the only manner which was taken into account in the formulation of the problem at 334ᵇ 6-7.

[2] Cf. above, I. 7, where Aristotle explains the precise sense in which action-passion is between contraries, and under what conditions contraries in 'acting' are themselves 'acted upon' by their patients.

[3] There is no expressed εἶτα (answering to πρῶτον in ᵇ 24) but it is implied.

[4] *sc.* these extremes, the completely-hot and the completely-cold.

[5] i.e. the 'mean' is a *stretch*, not a *point*.

[6] Or perhaps 'in the region about the centre'.

and Water, alone of the 'simple' bodies, is readily adapt- 335ᵃ
able in shape: moreover (b) Earth has no power of cohesion
without the moist. On the contrary, the moist is what
holds it together; for it would fall to pieces if the moist
were eliminated from it completely.

They contain Earth and Water, then, for the reasons we
have given: and they contain Air and Fire, because these are
contrary to Earth and Water (Earth being contrary to Air 5
and Water to Fire, in so far as one Substance can be
'contrary' to another). Now all compounds presuppose
in their coming-to-be constituents which are contrary to
one another: and in all compounds there is contained one
set of the contrasted extremes.[1] Hence the other set[2]
must be contained in them also, so that every compound
will include all the 'simple' bodies.

Additional evidence seems to be furnished by the food 10
each compound takes. For all of them are fed by substances which are the same as their constituents, and all
of them are fed by more substances than one. Indeed,
even the plants, though it might be thought they are
fed by one substance only, viz. by Water, are fed by
more than one: for Earth has been mixed with the
Water. That is why farmers too endeavour to mix before
watering.[3]

Although food is akin to the matter, that which is fed 15
is the 'figure'—i.e. the 'form'—taken along with the
matter.[4] This fact enables us to understand why, whereas
all the 'simple' bodies come-to-be out of one another, Fire
is the only one of them which (as our predecessors also
assert) 'is fed'.[5] For Fire alone—or more than all the
rest—is akin to the 'form' because it tends by nature
to be borne towards the limit. Now each of them naturally 20
tends to be borne towards its own place: but the 'figure'
—i.e. the 'form'—of them all is at the limits.

[1] i.e. cold-dry (Earth) and cold-moist (Water).
[2] i.e. hot-moist (Air) and hot-dry (Fire).
[3] Plants are nourished *naturally* by water impregnated with earth
and *artificially* by water mixed with manure, which is a kind of earth.
    Cf. above, 321ᵇ 16—322ᵃ 33.
[5] Cf. *de Vita et Morte* 469ᵇ 21 ff., *Meteor.* 354ᵇ 33 ff.; Theophrastos,
fr. iii. 1, § 4 (Wimmer, iii, p. 51).

Thus we have explained that all the compound bodies are composed of all the 'simple' bodies.

Since some things are such as to come-to-be and pass- **9**
25 away, and since coming-to-be in fact occurs in the region about the centre, we must explain the *number* and the *nature* of the 'originative sources' of all coming-to-be alike:[1] for a grasp of the true theory of any universal facilitates the understanding of its specific forms.

The 'originative sources', then, of the things which come-to-be are equal in number to, and identical in kind with, those in the sphere of the eternal and primary things.
30 For there is *one* in the sense of 'matter', and a *second* in the sense of 'form': and, in addition, the *third* 'originative source' must be present as well. For the two first are not sufficient to bring things into being, any more than they are adequate to account for the primary things.

Now cause, in the sense of material origin, for the things which are such as to come-to-be is 'that which can be-and-not-be': and this is identical with 'that which can come-to-be-and-pass-away', since the latter, while it *is* at one time, at another time *is not*. (For whereas some things *are* of necessity, viz. the eternal things, others of necessity
35 *are not*. And of these two sets of things, since they cannot
335ᵇ diverge from the necessity of their nature, it is impossible for the first *not to be* and impossible for the second *to be*. Other things, however, can both *be* and *not be*.) Hence coming-to-be and passing-away must occur within the field
5 of 'that which can be-and-not-be'. This, therefore, is cause in the sense of material origin for the things which are such as to come-to-be; while cause, in the sense of their 'end', is their 'figure' or 'form'—and that is the formula expressing the essential nature of each of them.

But the third 'originative source' must be present as well—the cause vaguely dreamed of by all our predecessors,

---

[1] Cf. above, 314ᵃ 2 and 318ᵃ 25–27.

definitely stated by none of them. On the contrary (*a*) some amongst them thought the nature of 'the Forms' was 10 adequate to account for coming-to-be. Thus Sokrates in the *Phaedo* first blames everybody else for having given no explanation;[1] and then lays it down that 'some things are Forms, others Participants in the Forms', and that 'while a thing is said to "be" in virtue of the Form, it is said to "come-to-be" *qua* "sharing in", to "pass-away" *qua* "losing", the Form'. Hence he thinks that 'assuming 15 the truth of these theses, the Forms *must* be causes both of coming-to-be and of passing-away'.[2] On the other hand (*b*) there were others who thought 'the matter' was adequate by itself to account for coming-to-be, since 'the movement originates from the matter'.

Neither of these theories, however, is sound. For (*a*) if the Forms are causes, why is their generating activity intermittent instead of perpetual and continuous—since there always *are* Participants as well as Forms? Besides, in 20 some instances we *see* that the cause is other than the Form. For it is the doctor who implants health and the man of science who implants science, although 'Health itself' and 'Science itself' *are* as well as the Participants: and the same principle applies to everything else that is produced in accordance with an art. On the other hand (*b*) to say that 'matter generates owing to its movement' 25 would be, no doubt, more scientific than to make such statements as are made by the thinkers we have been criticizing. For what 'alters' and transfigures plays a greater part[3] in bringing things into being; and we are everywhere accustomed, in the products of nature and of art alike, to look upon that which can initiate movement as the producing cause. Nevertheless this second theory is not right either.

For, to begin with, it is characteristic of matter to suffer 30 action, i. e. to be moved: but to move, i. e. to act, belongs to a different 'power'.[4] This is obvious both in the things

---

[1] Cf. Plato, *Phaedo* 96 a–99 c.   [2] Cf. Plato, *Phaedo* 100 b–101 e.
[3] *sc.* than the Forms.
[4] Matter is a δύναμις in the passive sense: that which initiates movement is a δύναμις in the sense of an active force. Cf. e.g. *Metaph.* 1046ᵃ 9–29, 1048ᵃ 25–ᵇ 9.

that come-to-be by art and in those that come-to-be by
nature. Water does not of itself produce ᷉out of itself
an animal: and it is the art, not the wood, that makes
a bed. Nor is this their only error. They make a second
35 mistake in omitting the more controlling cause: for they
336^a eliminate the essential nature, i. e. the 'form'. And what
is more, since they remove the formal cause, they invest
the forces they assign to the 'simple' bodies—the forces
which enable these bodies to bring things into being—with
too instrumental a character. For 'since' (as they say)
'it is the nature of the hot to dissociate, of the cold to
5 bring together, and of each remaining contrary either to act
or to suffer action', it is out of such materials and by their
agency (so they maintain) that everything else comes-to-be
and passes-away. Yet (*a*) it is evident that even Fire is
itself moved, i. e. suffers action. Moreover (*b*) their procedure is virtually the same as if one were to treat the
saw (and the various instruments of carpentry) as 'the cause'
10 of the things that come-to-be: for the wood *must* be divided
if a man saws, *must* become smooth if he planes, and so on
with the remaining tools. Hence, however true it may be
that Fire is active, i. e. sets things moving, there is a further
point they fail to observe—viz. that Fire is inferior to the
tools or instruments in the manner in which it sets things
moving.

As to our own theory—we have given a general account
of the causes in an earlier work,[1] and we have now explained
and distinguished the 'matter' and the 'form'.[2] Further, **10**
15 since the change which is motion has been proved[3] to be
eternal, the continuity of the occurrence of coming-to-be
follows necessarily from what we have established: for the
eternal motion, by causing 'the generator'[4] to approach
and retire, will produce coming-to-be uninterruptedly. At
the same time it is clear that we were also right when,
20 in an earlier work,[5] we called motion (not coming-to-be)
'the primary form of change'. For it is far more reason-

---

[1] Cf. *Physics* B. 3–9.   [2] Cf. above, 335ᵃ 32–ᵇ 7.
[3] Cf. *Physics* Θ. 7–9.
[4] i. e. the sun, as will appear presently.
[5] Cf. *Physics* 260ᵃ26–261ᵃ26.

able that *what is* should cause the coming-to-be of *what is
not*, than that *what is not* should cause the being of *what is*.
Now that which is being moved *is*, but that which is coming-
to-be *is not*: hence, also, motion is prior to coming-to-be.

We have assumed, and have proved,[1] that coming-to-be
and passing-away happen to things continuously; and we 25
assert that motion causes coming-to-be. That being so, it
is evident that, if the motion be single, *both* processes cannot
occur since they are contrary to one another : for it is a law
of nature that the same cause, provided it remain in the
same condition, always produces the same effect, so that,
from a single motion, either coming-to-be or passing-away
will always result. The movements must, on the contrary,
be more than one, and they must be contrasted with one 30
another either by the sense of their motion[2] or by its
irregularity :[3] for contrary effects demand contraries as
their causes.

This explains why it is not the primary motion[4] that
causes coming-to-be and passing-away, but the motion
along the inclined circle :[5] for this motion not only possesses
the necessary continuity, but includes a duality of movements as well. For if coming-to-be and passing-away are 336ᵇ
always to be continuous, there must be some body always
being moved (in order that these changes may not fail) and
moved with a duality of movements (in order that both
changes, not one only, may result). Now the continuity of
this movement is caused by the motion of the whole :[6] but
the approaching and retreating of the moving body are
caused by the inclination.[7] For the consequence of the
inclination is that the body becomes alternately remote 5
and near ; and since its distance is thus unequal, its movement will be irregular. Therefore, if it generates by approaching and by its proximity, it—this very same body—

---

[1] Cf. above, 317ᵇ 33 ff.   [2] Cf. *de Caelo* 270ᵇ 32—271ᵃ 33.
[3] Cf. *de Caelo* 288ᵃ 13-27 ; *Physics* 228ᵇ 15—229ᵃ 6.
[4] i.e. the revolution of the πρῶτος οὐρανός.
[5] i.e. the annual movement of the sun in the ecliptic or zodiac circle.
[6] i.e. the revolution of the πρῶτος οὐρανός (the outermost sphere)
which carries along with it all the concentric spheres.
[7] i.e. the inclination of the ecliptic to the equator of the outermost
sphere, which (on Aristotle's theory) is the equator of the universe and
is in the same plane as the terrestrial equator.

destroys by retreating and becoming remote: and if it generates by many successive approaches, it also destroys by many
successive retirements. For contrary effects demand contraries
10 as their causes; and the natural processes of passing-away
and coming-to-be occupy equal periods of time. Hence,
too, the times—i. e. the lives—of the several kinds of living
things have a number by which they are distinguished: for
there is an Order controlling all things, and every time
(i. e. every life) is measured by a period. Not all of them,
however, are measured by the same period, but some by
a smaller and others by a greater one: for to some of them
15 the period, which is their measure, is a year, while to some
it is longer and to others shorter.

And there are facts of observation in manifest agreement
with our theories. Thus we see that coming-to-be occurs
as the sun approaches and decay as it retreats; and we see
that the two processes occupy equal times. For the dura-
tions of the natural processes of passing-away and coming-
20 to-be are equal. Nevertheless it often happens that things
pass-away in too short a time. This is due to the 'inter-
mingling' by which the things that come-to-be and pass-
away are implicated with one another. For their matter is
'irregular', i. e. is not everywhere the same: hence the
processes by which they come-to-be must be 'irregular' too,
i. e. some too quick and others too slow. Consequently the
phenomenon in question occurs, because the 'irregular'
coming-to-be of these things is the passing-away of other
things.[1]

25 Coming-to-be and passing-away will, as we have said,
always be continuous, and will never fail owing to the cause
we stated.[2] And this continuity has a sufficient reason on
our theory. For in all things, as we affirm, Nature always
strives after 'the better'. Now 'being' (we have explained
elsewhere[3] the exact variety of meanings we recognize in
30 this term) is better than 'not-being': but not all things can
possess 'being', since they are too far removed from the
'originative source'. God therefore adopted the remaining

---

[1] For the reading and interpretation of 336^b 20–24 see my text and
commentary.
[2] Cf. above, 318^a 9 ff.
[3] Cf. e.g. *Metaph.* 1017^a 7 ff.

alternative, and fulfilled the perfection of the universe by making coming-to-be uninterrupted: for the greatest possible coherence would thus be secured to existence, because that 'coming-to-be should itself come-to-be perpetually' is the closest approximation to eternal being.

The cause of this perpetuity of coming-to-be, as we have often said, is circular motion: for that is the only motion **337^a** which is continuous. That, too, is why all the other things —the things, I mean, which are reciprocally transformed in virtue of their 'passions' and their 'powers of action', e.g. the 'simple' bodies—imitate circular motion. For when Water is transformed into Air, Air into Fire, and the Fire 5 back into Water, we say the coming-to-be 'has completed the circle', because it reverts again to the beginning. Hence it is by imitating circular motion that rectilinear motion too is continuous.

These considerations serve at the same time to explain what is to some people a baffling problem—viz. why the 'simple' bodies, since each of them is travelling towards its own place, have not become dissevered from one another in 10 the infinite lapse of time. The reason is their reciprocal transformation. For, had each of them persisted in its own place instead of being transformed by its neighbour, they would have got dissevered long ago. They are transformed, however, owing to the motion with its dual character:[1] and because they are transformed, none of them is able to persist in any place allotted to it by the Order.[2]   15

It is clear from what has been said (i) that coming-to-be and passing-away actually occur, (ii) what causes them, and (iii) what subject undergoes them. But (a) if there is to be movement (as we have explained elsewhere, in an earlier work[3]) there must be something which initiates it; if there is to be movement always, there must always be something which initiates it; if the movement is to be continuous, what initiates it must be single, unmoved, ungenerated, and 20

---

[1] The sun's annual movement, by which it alternately approaches and retreats, causes the alternate ascent and descent of Water, Air, and Fire. They are thus brought into contact, with the result that their constitutive contrary qualities act and suffer action reciprocally, and the 'simple' bodies themselves are transformed.

[2] Cf. above, 336^b 12.

[3] *Physics* 255^b 31—260^a 10. Cf. also *Metaph.* 1072^a 19—1074^b 14.

incapable of 'alteration'; and if the circular[1] movements
are more than one, their initiating causes[2] must all of them,
in spite of their plurality, be in some way subordinated
to a single 'originative source'. Further (b) since time is
continuous, movement must be continuous, inasmuch as
there can be no time without movement. Time, therefore,
is a 'number'[3] of some continuous movement—a 'number',
25 therefore, of the circular movement, as was established in
the discussions at the beginning.[4] But (c) is movement[5]
continuous because of the continuity of that which is moved,
or because that in which the movement occurs (I mean, e. g.,
the place or the quality) is continuous? The answer
must clearly be 'because that which is moved is continuous'.
(For how can the quality be continuous except in virtue of
the continuity of the thing to which it belongs? But if the
continuity of 'that in which' contributes to make the move-
30 ment continuous, this is true only of 'the place in which';
for that has 'magnitude' in a sense.) But (d) amongst
continuous bodies which are moved, only that which is
moved in a circle is 'continuous' in such a way that it
preserves its continuity with itself throughout the movement.
The conclusion therefore is that *this* is what produces
continuous movement, viz. the body which is being moved
in a circle; and its movement makes time continuous.

Wherever there is continuity in any process (coming-to- II
35 be or 'alteration' or any kind of change whatever) we
337ᵇ observe 'consecutiveness', i. e. *this* coming-to-be after *that*
without any interval. Hence we must investigate whether,
amongst the consecutive members, there is any whose future
being is necessary; or whether, on the contrary, every one

---

[1] i. e. the supposed continuous movements which, *qua* continuous,
must be circular.

[2] I follow Philoponos and Pacius in referring ταύτας (ª21) to the
ἀρχαί which the circular movements imply.

[3] i. e. time is that which is *numerable* (ἀριθμός = τὸ ἀριθμούμενον or
τὸ ἀριθμητόν, not ᾧ ἀριθμοῦμεν) in continuous movement: cf. *Physics*
219ᵇ 1–8.

[4] *sc.* at the beginning of Aristotle's 'Philosophy of Nature' ·
cf. *Physics* 217ᵇ 29–224ª 17.

[5] Aristotle uses κίνησις in its general sense, in which it includes
ἀλλοίωσις and αὔξησις as well as φορά, but he is thinking primarily
of φορά.

of them may fail to come-to-be. For that some of them may fail to occur, is clear. (*a*) We need only appeal to the distinction between the statements '*x* will be' and '*x* is about to .', which depends upon this fact. For if it be true to say of *x* that it 'will be', it must at some time be true to say of it that 'it is': whereas, though it be true to say of *x* *now* that 'it is about to occur', it is quite possible for it not to come-to-be—thus a man might not walk, though he is now 'about to' walk. And (*b*) since (to appeal to a general principle) amongst the things which 'are' some are capable also of 'not-being', it is clear that the same ambiguous character will attach to them no less when they are coming-to-be: in other words, their coming-to-be will not be necessary.

Then are all the things that come-to-be of this contingent character? Or, on the contrary, is it absolutely necessary for some of them to come-to-be? Is there, in fact, a distinction in the field of ' coming-to-be ' corresponding to the distinction, within the field of ' being ', between things that cannot possibly 'not-be' and things that can ' not-be'? For instance, is it necessary that solstices shall come-to-be, i. e. impossible that they should fail to be able to occur?

Assuming that the antecedent must have come-to-be if the consequent is to be (e. g. that foundations must have come-to-be if there is to be a house: clay, if there are to be foundations), is the converse also true? If foundations have come-to-be, must a house come-to-be? The answer seems to be that the necessary *nexus* no longer holds, unless it is ' necessary' for the consequent (as well as for the antecedent)[1] to come-to-be—' necessary' *absolutely*. If that be the case, however, 'a house must come-to-be if foundations have come-to-be ', as well as *vice versa*. For the antecedent was assumed to be so related to the consequent that, if the latter is to be, the antecedent must have come-to-be before it. If, therefore, it is necessary that the consequent should come-to-be, the antecedent also must have come-to-be: and if the antecedent has come-to-be, then the conse-

---

[1] Cf. above, ^b14-15: the coming-to-be of the antecedent was *conditionally* necessary, i.e. necessarily presupposed in the being of the consequent.

quent also must come-to-be—not, however, because of the antecedent, but because the future being of the consequent was assumed as necessary. Hence, in any sequence, when the being of the consequent is necessary, the *nexus* is reciprocal—in other words, when the antecedent has come-25 to-be the consequent must always come-to-be too.

Now (i) if the sequence of occurrences is to proceed *ad infinitum* 'downwards',[1] the coming-to-be of any determinate 'this' amongst the later members of the sequence will not be *absolutely*, but only *conditionally*, necessary. For it will always be necessary that some other[2] member shall have come-to-be before 'this' as the presupposed condition of the necessity that 'this' should come-to-be: consequently, since what is 'infinite' has no 'originative source', neither will there be in the infinite sequence any 'primary' member which will make it 'necessary' for the remaining members to come-to-be.[3]

30 Nor again (ii) will it be possible to say with truth, even in regard to the members of a limited sequence, that it is 'absolutely necessary' for any one of them to come-to-be. We cannot truly say, e. g., that 'it is absolutely necessary for a house to come-to-be when foundations have been laid': for (unless it is *always* necessary for a house to be coming-to-be) we should be faced with the consequence that, when foundations have been laid, a thing, which need not always be, must always be. No: if its coming-to-be is to be 35 'necessary', it must be 'always' in its coming-to-be. For what is 'of necessity' coincides with what is 'always', **338^a** since that which 'must be' cannot possibly 'not-be'. Hence a thing is eternal if its 'being' is necessary: and if it is eternal, its 'being' is necessary. And if, therefore, the 'coming-to-be' of a thing is necessary, its 'coming-to-be' is eternal; and if eternal, necessary.

It follows that the coming-to-be of anything, if it is 5 absolutely necessary, must be cyclical—i. e. must return

---

[1] i. e. so that effect *will* succeed effect endlessly.

[2] i. e. some other *still later* member of the sequence.

[3] i. e. the infinite sequence will not contain any absolutely necessary member which will serve as the ground of the conditional necessity of the other members. The 'primary' member or ἀρχή, in the sequence proceeding *ad infinitum* 'downwards', would have to be a τέλος — i. e. an absolutely necessary 'end-event'.

upon itself. For coming-to-be must either be limited or not limited: and if not limited, it must be either rectilinear or cyclical. But the first of these last two alternatives is impossible if coming-to-be is to be eternal, because there could not be any 'originative source' whatever in an infinite rectilinear sequence, whether its members be taken 'downwards' (as future events) or 'upwards' (as past events). Yet coming-to-be must have an 'originative source' ⟨if it is to be necessary and therefore eternal⟩,[1] nor can it be eternal 10 if it is limited.[2] Consequently it must be cyclical. Hence the *nexus* must be reciprocal. By this I mean that the necessary occurrence of 'this' involves the necessary occurrence of its antecedent: and conversely that, given the antecedent, it is also necessary for the consequent to come-to-be. And this reciprocal *nexus* will hold continuously throughout the sequence: for it makes no difference whether the reciprocal *nexus*, of which we are speaking, is mediated by two, or by many, members.

It is in circular movement, therefore, and in cyclical 15 coming-to-be that the 'absolutely necessary' is to be found. In other words, if the coming-to-be of any things is cyclical, it is 'necessary' that each of them is coming-to-be and has come-to-be: and if the coming-to-be of any things is 'necessary', their coming-to-be is cyclical.

The result we have reached is logically concordant with the eternity of circular motion, i.e. the eternity of the revolution of the heavens (a fact which approved itself on other and independent evidence),[3] since precisely those movements which belong to, and depend upon, this eternal **338^b** revolution 'come-to-be' of necessity, and of necessity 'will be'. For since the revolving body is always setting something else in motion, the movement of the things it moves must also be circular. Thus, from the being of the 'upper revolution' it follows that the sun revolves in this determinate manner; and since the sun revolves *thus*, the seasons in consequence come-to-be in a cycle, i.e. return upon themselves; and since they come-to-be cyclically, so in 5

[1] A clause to this effect seems to have dropped out after ἀρχήν in ^{a} 10.

[2] On the reading and interpretation see my text and commentary.

[3] Cf. *Physics* Θ. 7-9.

their turn do the things whose coming-to-be the seasons initiate.

Then why do some things manifestly come-to-be in this cyclical fashion (as, e. g., showers and air, so that it must rain if there is to be a cloud and, conversely, there must be a cloud if it is to rain), while men and animals do not 'return upon themselves' so that the same individual
10 comes-to-be a second time (for though your coming-to-be presupposes your father's, his coming-to-be does not pre-suppose yours)? Why, on the contrary, does this coming-to-be seem to constitute a rectilinear sequence?

In discussing this new problem, we must begin by inquiring whether all things 'return upon themselves' in a uniform manner; or whether, on the contrary, though in some sequences what recurs is *numerically* the same, in other sequences it is the same *only in species*.[1] In consequence of this distinction, it is evident that those things, whose 'substance'—that which is undergoing the process—
15 is imperishable, will be numerically, as well as specifically, the same in their recurrence: for the character of the process is determined by the character of that which undergoes it. Those things, on the other hand, whose 'substance' is perishable (not imperishable) must 'return upon themselves' in the sense that what recurs, though specifically the same, is not the same numerically. That is why, when Water comes-to-be from Air and Air from Water, the Air is the same 'specifically', not 'numerically': and if these too recur numerically the same,[2] at any rate this does not happen with things whose 'substance' comes-to-be—whose 'substance' is such that it is essentially capable of not-being.

---

[1] i. e. in some cycles the same individual eternally recurs: in others the same *species* or *specific form* is eternally represented in the succession of its perishing individual embodiments.

[2] As, e. g., a follower of Empedokles would maintain.

Printed in England at the Oxford University Press